CONTEXTUAL LEADERSHIP™

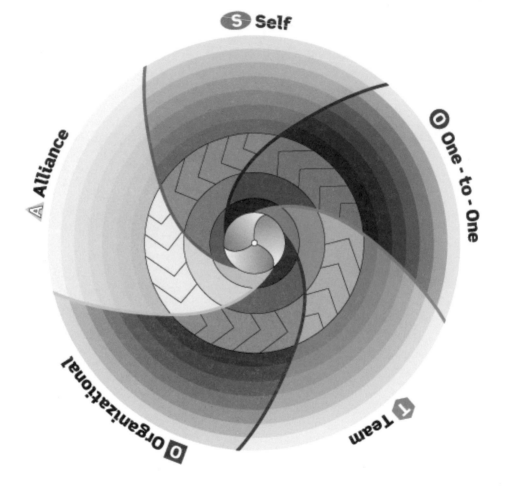

PRAISE FOR *ACHIEVE LEADERSHIP GENIUS*

"As a student of leadership, who has seen most corporate and academic leadership approaches being taught today, I feel this book represents the most comprehensive, well-researched, integrated practical paradigm for personal and organizational leadership in today's market. *Achieve Leadership Genius* sets a new standard that will stand for decades to come."

> —Matthew F. Manion, President and CEO, Catholic Leadership Institute, Malvern, PA

"Corporations are more complicated than ever before. The challenges leaders face are correspondingly complex. *Achieve Leadership Genius* provides a framework for succeeding in this environment that is both compelling and comprehensive."

> —Douglas G. Myers, CEO and Executive Director, Zoological Society of San Diego

"Instead of a book on general leadership with a 'one shoe fits all' approach, at last we have a leadership book with a 'closet full of shoes' that not only recognizes the different contexts in which we wear them, but also identifies how to receive the most benefit while they are worn. The authors present this material in an organized and understandable format that allows the reader to quickly find the help needed for the specific leadership challenge at hand."

> —Donovan Oberholtzer, Chairman of the Board, Stauffers of Kissel Hill

"*Achieve Leadership Genius* recognizes the true complexity of leadership and provides leaders and aspiring leaders with the tools and understanding to navigate today's complex and ever-changing environment. A required read for anyone leading an organization today or who wants to lead one in the future."

> —Jeffrey C. Wiemann, CEO, American Red Cross, San Diego/Imperial Counties Chapter

"As the CEO of a global concern, I need a leadership approach that transcends cultures. With their Contextual Leadership Model, the authors have created a language of leadership that can be adapted, embraced, and practiced by our managers from London to Los Angeles, Sydney to Shanghai."

> —Garry Ridge, CEO, WD-40 Company

"My colleagues, Drea, Susan, and Dick, have continually enriched the management and leadership literature over the years and now with *Achieve Leadership Genius* they have moved the goal posts once again. An important read."

> —Ken Blanchard, co-author, *The One Minute Manager* and *Leading At A Higher Level*

"Leadership study and guidance is at risk of becoming another frivolous commodity. This book elevates it to a serious platform. No glib formulas here, but a wise approach to identifying and nourishing your individual and particular skills for leadership."

> —Dr. Sidney Harman, Executive Chairman, Harman International

"*Achieve Leadership Genius* is a landmark book because it introduces a whole new way to think about leadership. This book has identified and then addressed the complexities that are a part of leadership in business. For more than 30 years other authors have been attempting to make what we do appear simple. How refreshing to find a book that represents real innovation in leadership theory which will provide solid benefits for every reader."

 —James C. Estill, President and CEO, Calloway's Nursery, Inc.

"Often authors trivialize the complexities of leadership by producing quick fix, glib publications assuring the reader that if the few steps expounded are followed, their troubles will be over. This publication is different. It is written in a simple and easy-to-understand style, but it does not avoid dealing with the complexities of leadership responsibility. The authors have done an outstanding job in combining their wisdom to produce a publication which really does hold the key to any who wish to achieve leadership genius."

 —Reg Garters, Chief Executive, New Zealand Institute of Management,
  Canterbury, New Zealand

"Values-driven leaders consciously and conscientiously choose the values they apply; they realize that every act of leadership either demonstrates or rejects their values. Part of the genius in *Achieve Leadership Genius* is how the authors integrate values into the very lifeblood of their comprehensive approach to leadership."

 —Morris Massey, creator/presenter of the "What You Are..."
  video training series

"This book is an incredibly comprehensive roadmap to becoming a highly skilled and successful leader. The alignment to individual-, team-, and organizational-based contexts with the five leadership practices provides a very innovative knowledge-building approach."

 —Steve Walling, Chairman/CEO, Plasticolors, Inc.

"*Achieve Leadership Genius* is exactly that...pure genius. The authors have not only synthesized 100 years of accumulated leadership knowledge into an accessible framework, the SOTOA framework offers both a strategic approach and tactical methods for developing leadership at every level."

 —Kurt Gering, Director, Master of Science in Executive Leadership,
  University of San Diego

"Seldom do books on leadership offer such a coherent, holistic, and integrated approach to developing the inherent leadership capacity that we all possess. The Contextual Leadership framework offered by the authors provides both an understanding of the rich complexity of leading across multiple contexts and a practical set of tools any leader can apply to refine and hone their skill and achieve immediate impact."

 —Robert J. Spitzer, S.J., Ph.D., President, Gonzaga University, author of *The
  Spirit of Leadership: Optimizing Creativity and Change in Organizations*

ACHIEVE LEADERSHIP GENIUS

FT Press

FINANCIAL TIMES

In an increasingly competitive world, it is quality
of thinking that gives an edge—an idea that opens new
doors, a technique that solves a problem, or an insight
that simply helps make sense of it all.

We work with leading authors in the various arenas
of business and finance to bring cutting-edge thinking
and best-learning practices to a global market.

It is our goal to create world-class print publications
and electronic products that give readers
knowledge and understanding that can then be
applied, whether studying or at work.

To find out more about our business
products, you can visit us at www.ftpress.com.

ACHIEVE LEADERSHIP GENIUS

HOW YOU LEAD DEPENDS ON WHO, WHAT, WHERE, AND WHEN YOU LEAD

DREA ZIGARMI
SUSAN FOWLER
DICK LYLES

FT Press
FINANCIAL TIMES

Vice President, Publisher: Tim Moore
Editorial Assistant: Pamela Boland
Associate Editor-in-Chief and Director of Marketing: Amy Neidlinger
Cover Designer: Chuti Prasertsith
Managing Editor: Gina Kanouse
Project Editor: Michael Thurston
Copy Editor: Water Crest Publishing
Indexer: Lisa Stumpf
Compositor: Moore Media, Inc.
Manufacturing Buyer: Dan Uhrig

FT Press
FINANCIAL TIMES

© 2007 by Drea Zigarmi, Susan Fowler, Dick Lyles
Publishing as FT Press
Upper Saddle River, New Jersey 07458

FT Press offers excellent discounts on this book when ordered in quantity for bulk purchases or special sales. For more information, please contact U.S. Corporate and Government Sales, 1-800-382-3419, corpsales@pearsontechgroup.com. For sales outside the U.S., please contact International Sales at international@pearsoned.com.

Printed in the United States of America
First Printing May, 2007
ISBN 0-13-235376-8

Pearson Education LTD.
Pearson Education Australia PTY, Limited.
Pearson Education Singapore, Pte. Ltd.
Pearson Education North Asia, Ltd.
Pearson Education Canada, Ltd.
Pearson Educatión de Mexico, S.A. de C.V.
Pearson Education—Japan
Pearson Education Malaysia, Pte. Ltd.

Library of Congress Cataloging-in-Publication Data
Zigarmi, Drea.
  Achieve leadership genius : how you lead depends on who, what, where and when you lead / Drea Zigarmi, Susan Fowler, Dick Lyles.
      p. cm.
  Includes bibliographical references.
  ISBN 0-13-235376-8 (hardback : alk. paper) 1. Leadership. 2. Management. 3. Self-management (Psychology) 4. Teams in the workplace. 5. Interpersonal relations. I. Fowler, Susan, 1951- I. II. Lyles, Richard III. Title.
  HD57.7.Z54 2007
  658.4'092—dc22
                                            2006030408

*This book is dedicated to two groups of people,
with equal caring and devotion to both.*

*First, we dedicate it to that enlightened group of people who want to be
good leaders yet understand that good leadership is not simple. This group
knows that the key to long-term success in leadership lies in an ever-
expanding understanding of the intricacies of a host of issues, not the least
of which is the performance of those who follow.*

*Second, we dedicate this book to the huge segment of the population who
labor under poor leadership. We should never forget the cost and the consequences of poor leadership. Bad leaders not only deny their organization
the opportunity to realize its vision and fulfill its purpose, but they also
rob from their followers the opportunity to find fulfillment in their work,
to develop their potential, and to reap the rewards of top performance. Our
hearts go out to the victims of poor leadership with the earnest hope that
this book will somehow help to improve the plight of at least a few.*

CONTENTS

ACHIEVE LEADERSHIP GENIUS COMPANION WEB SITE

The following bonus chapters can be accessed from the book's companion Web site by registering your book at www.ftpress.com (see the last page of this book for more information).

RESPOND IN THE SELF CONTEXT

RESPOND IN THE ONE-TO-ONE CONTEXT

RESPOND IN THE TEAM CONTEXT

RESPOND IN THE ORGANIZATIONAL CONTEXT

RESPOND IN THE ALLIANCE CONTEXT

APPENDIX: BENEATH THE WATERLINE

FOREWORD

I've always held that genius was something you are born with; success is born of hard work. Ironically, when a person reaches a certain level of success by virtue of their hard work, people call that person a genius. As a result the term "genius" has become confusing and its true meaning lost in translation.

That's why, when asked to write the foreword to this book, I had more than a few reservations. I wondered if the authors wanted me to take the presumptuous stand that by endorsing their book I was being held up as an example—that I am, in fact, a leadership genius. There was a part of my ego that was flattered, but the better part of me was uncomfortable.

That was before I read the book. Now I'm intrigued with the way the authors define genius—the genesis of the word embodies what all leaders should be striving to do. But I'm even more intrigued with the idea that you can master the practice of leadership if you understand three things:

- Leadership is not easy.
- How you lead depends on the *context* in which you are leading.
- Because leadership is a practice, you need skill and skill requires practice.

This book will have you looking at leadership from a totally new perspective—actually, five perspectives that the authors call "contexts." There are two contexts where I have excelled in leading, two I have struggled in, and one context that will challenge me as long as I live.

I prefer to dwell on the successes, of course. If something works, I want to know why so I can replicate it. For me, it's leading in the Alliance Context. I think the strategic relationship we forged between Borghese Cosmetics and Costco is a wonderful example. We co-brand a line of Borghese cosmetics under the Kirkland brand with the moniker *Kirkland Signature by Borghese*. The alliance establishes a new paradigm in the world of beauty by introducing a prestigious brand into a high-volume retail environment. That's exciting!

My leadership in the Organizational Context is also a strength—as CEO and owner of LaPrairie, for example, we realized a 100% increase in sales and profits by developing innovative products, as well as sales and marketing programs in just three years before selling to an international skin- and beauty-care company.

But as you know we also learn from our areas of struggle and failures. I can't tell you how many times I've awakened in the middle of the night perplexed over how to deal with an employee's performance—or lack thereof. As the authors point out, it takes an entirely different set of skills to lead in the One-to-One Context. I know I can and need to improve my ability to develop, nurture, and sustain an employee's motivation and productivity if I'm going to develop the bench strength needed for my company to succeed beyond my grasp. The same is true for mastering the more complex leadership skills demanded in the Team Context.

Perhaps the most significant realization for me is that true leadership genius is having the skill to lead effectively across and within each of the five contexts—and that includes leading yourself in the Self Context. That means a lifetime of challenging assumptions, consciously choosing to be values-driven rather than giving into my sometimes inappropriate instinctive behavior, and creating harmony between my inner self and outer persona.

Whew! No one said leadership was easy. Well, actually plenty of people have trivialized leadership. This book is a breath of fresh air. It's honest about the complexities of leadership. It's also responsible. It doesn't set you up for failure. Indeed, it does just the opposite. Within these pages you will find the true meaning of leadership genius and how to achieve it.

by Georgette Mosbacher,
CEO and President, Borghese Inc.

ABOUT THE AUTHORS

Drea Zigarmi is a Founding Partner of Leadership Legacies, LLC, Founding Associate of The Ken Blanchard Companies®, and President of Zigarmi Associates, Inc. For the past 25 years, he has been head of research and development for The Ken Blanchard Companies. He has co-authored several best-selling books, including *Leadership and The One Minute Manager* and *The Leader Within*. He co-authored with Ken Blanchard the widely-used Leader Behavior Analysis II® instrument, the Development Task Analysis® form, and participant materials used in Situational Leadership® II seminars.

Drea is a highly respected and experienced management consultant, author, and powerful trainer and motivational speaker. His diverse client list includes Fortune 500 companies such as Pfizer, Eli Lilly, GM, Toyota, Honda, Lockheed, Gulf Oil, and Chevron; athletic teams such as the San Diego Padres, Baltimore Orioles, and Chicago Cubs; and government organizations and nonprofits such as the Department of Defense, the U.S. Post Office, the County of San Diego, and Denver Public Schools. All have benefited from his work in the areas of management and organizational development, performance appraisal, and productivity improvement.

Drea's consulting activities involve an emphasis on long-term organizational change through leadership skill building. During the past 25 years, he has taught seminars and given speeches in 25 countries. His publications include numerous training programs, book chapters, assessments, and *The Team Leader's Idea-A-Day Guide* (co-authored with Susan Fowler). He has taught at the University of Massachusetts, Miami University in Oxford, Ohio, and presently at the University of San Diego School of Business.

Drea received his BA in science from Norwich University, a Master's in philosophy and Doctoral in administration and organizational behavior from the University of Massachusetts in Amherst. He currently resides in San Diego, California.

Susan Fowler is a Founding Partner of Leadership Legacies, LLC, and a Senior Consulting Partner with The Ken Blanchard Companies. She is the co-author with Ken Blanchard of *Self Leadership and the One Minute Manager*, published in 2005.

Susan has established a solid and respected track record as a keynote speaker and as an innovative product designer and developer in the field of leadership training. She is the recipient of the lifetime achievement award for creative training designs from the North American Society for Games and Simulations. Susan has consulted with such clients as Harley Davidson, MasterCard, AMF Bowling, Dow Chemical, KPMG, Black & Decker, SC Johnson, TJX Retailers, The Catholic Leadership Institute, Pfizer, Kinko's, Apple Computers, The National Basketball Association, and dozens of others. She gained extensive, worldwide public seminar presentation experience with CareerTrack.

Susan's goal is to be a catalyst for personal change and the teacher of the skills necessary to sustain self-motivation. Susan brings a unique perspective to her programs because of her extensive professional experience in the field of advertising, her broadcast work in television and radio, and her undergraduate degree in marketing from the University of Colorado. As one of the world's foremost experts on personal empowerment, she has delivered training seminars, workshops, and keynote speeches to more than 50,000 people, in over 20 countries and in all 50 of the United States. Audiences applaud her high energy, sense of humor, insight, and pragmatic solutions to workplace issues.

With Ken Blanchard and Laurence Hawkins, she created—and is the lead developer of—Situational Self Leadership, a best-of-class self-leadership and personal empowerment program. Her publications include *Overcoming Procrastination*, *Mentoring*, *The Team Leader's Idea-A-Day Guide* (co-authored with Drea Zigarmi), and *Empowerment* (co-authored with Ken Blanchard). Susan is an adjunct professor for the University of San Diego's Master of Science in Executive Leadership program. She currently resides in San Diego, California.

Dick Lyles is a Founding Partner of Leadership Legacies, LLC. He has served as CEO of several companies, and has been a consultant to companies of all sizes in virtually every industry around the world for the past 30 years. A partial list of clients includes Exxon, Pfizer, The San Diego Zoo, Mobil Canada, Ericsson, The Kingdom of Saudi Arabia, The New Zealand

Dairy Board, Hughes Aircraft Company, Plasticolors, Stauffers of Kissel Hill, HealthCare Partners, Calloway's Nurseries, The Australian Institute of Management, Aspen Skiing Company, and the Association of Zoos and Aquariums.

Early in his career, Dick became known as a management problem solver and corporate troubleshooter. His first book was published in 1982, and his training program based on these concepts has been offered on six continents, in nine languages, and in seventeen countries. His expertise includes corporate strategy, structure, customer service, marketing, communication, change, and leadership.

In 1976, he and his wife, Martha, founded Maric College, a college for nurses and allied health professionals. Since then, he has launched several other successful companies.

He is the author or co-author of seven books, including a best-selling parable entitled *Winning Ways: Four Secrets for Getting Great Results by Working Well with People*. His books have been published in more than three dozen languages around the world.

Dick is also a renowned radio talk show host, having hosted "LifeWorks," a program helping listeners learn about career-, job-, work-, and business-related issues.

Lyles holds a Bachelor of Science degree in engineering from the U.S. Naval Academy at Annapolis, a Master's degree in human behavior, and a Doctorate in business administration. He currently resides in Poway, California.

ACKNOWLEDGMENTS

Writing a book is a humbling experience. On a less-grandiose scale, we can relate to Academy Award winners who receive the credit for performances or services in which they were just one of many who made the magic happen. But unlike the Oscar winners, we don't have to cram our "thank you's" into 30-second acceptance speeches and risk getting dragged off stage for droning on too long. We get a couple of pages to memorialize those for whom we act as the front guys.

It's politically correct to put Tim Moore, our Financial Times Press/Prentice Hall publisher, first on the list, but it's also the right thing to do. Tim is working proof that there are honorable, hardworking, and nurturing task masters who know how to bring a project to fruition and have fun doing it. It's been a "beautiful thing" that we hope continues into the future. Ba-da bing!

A book is the epitome of a team effort, and our high-impact team members deserve recognition: resourceful agent Ed Knappman; first editor Russ Hall, who kept our spirits up even as early manuscripts were turned down; personal editor Maril Blanchard, who toiled virtually with those painful first chapters; marketing queen Amy Neidlinger; empathetic project editor Michael Thurston; eagle-eyed copy editor Sarah Kearns of Water Crest Publishing; the dependable Pamela Boland; and of course, COE Martha Lyles, Chief of Everything we don't want to do and we love her for it.

We are especially grateful to have brilliant colleagues, who are also friends, as supporters of our work: magnificent Betsy Myers; COO, Barack Obama for president; remarkable Donna Kalikow, executive director, John F. Kennedy Center for Public Leadership at Harvard; exceptional Kurt Gering, Sorana Dobrota, and our students at the University of San Diego Masters in Executive Leadership program; the executive management team at Mammoth Mountain; Judd Hoekstra; Terre Thomas; Mark Paskowitz; Dave DeLambo; Sister Regina Kusnir; Dave Woods; Martha Lawrence;

Scott Blanchard; Vicki Essary; Poppy Miller of Wildflower Graphics; Skye Turner; creative Peter Turner of Magic Lantern Paper Products; nurturing Dominic Perri; the brilliant David Facer; talented and wise beyond her years Alexa Zigarmi; forever our friend Maril Adrian; and a special heartfelt shout out to Dick Tapply for his ongoing insight and encouragement.

We have heroes who have helped shape our thinking, such as the amazing Michael O'Connor, the loving and nurturing spirit that is Ken Blanchard, the indomitable Pat Zigarmi, the visionary Jesse Stoner, and the wise Warren Bennis—our man of many seasons.

We were more than fortunate to test some of the concepts in this book through an unconventional source—The Catholic Leadership Institute. It's difficult to overstate the contributions of Tim Flanagan, Matt Manion, Father Bill Dickinson, Dan Cellucci, and Kathy Lennon. Their intelligence and passion combined with their high standards for excellence positively challenged us at every juncture. We are sincerely and immeasurably grateful to them.

Saving the best for last, we need to recognize the woman whose loving and competent work is sprinkled throughout this entire effort, Marsha Wilson. Couldn't have done it without you!

INTRODUCTION

It takes guts—or enormous hubris—to title a book *Achieve Leadership Genius*. It's important for you to know that we don't glibly promote the concept of genius. For some, the concept will provoke criticism, maybe even cynicism. After all, the designation of genius is typically reserved for people such as Leonardo da Vinci and Newton, Einstein and Stephen Hawking, Benjamin Franklin and Mahatma Gandhi, Martha Graham and Stevie Wonder. But we'd like you to consider another aspect of genius. According to the ancient Romans who invented the concept of genius, every man had a genius (and every woman a juno) who guarded over them. Eventually the concept of genius came to be the attendant spirit of a place entrusted in its care or a personal guardian spirit who granted intellect and prowess to an individual (male or female).

We like the idea that as a leader you are responsible for those entrusted to your care. To us, striving to achieve leadership genius means learning to develop an individual, rally a team, guide an organization, run an alliance, and even manage yourself.

This book was written to help give you the requisite understanding and skill to achieve leadership genius—the ability to develop and sustain peak performance of those you lead. But you may wonder, *Is it reasonable to assume that I might possibly deserve to be considered a leadership genius?* We say *Yes*. That's why this book was written—to introduce a new model of leadership based on over a hundred years of leadership study and practice. We call it Contextual Leadership. And we hope that the more you understand what we mean by Contextual Leadership, the more you'll understand how to achieve leadership genius.

DILEMMAS

We have a dilemma. How do we convince you to not only embrace the concept of leadership genius, but to also tackle the study, focus, and practice to become one? How do we encourage you to help others develop their own leadership capacity? Imagine if organizations were filled with leadership geniuses—we would all experience exponential benefits.

Ample research validates that leaders are the differentiating factor for creating and sustaining high performance in individuals and for organizations.[1] Logic dictates that the more effective you are as a leader, the more your employees will be engaged and your customers satisfied. Engaged employees and satisfied customers result in organizational effectiveness.[2]

How can it be, then, that some organizations don't have formal leadership development programs? How can it be that individuals with leadership roles don't spend as much time working to become excellent leaders as they do developing their other job- or role-related competencies? Why is there no national or world-recognized leadership certification process? These are interesting questions that get at the unfortunate truth of things—leadership expertise has not been valued, promoted, or taken as seriously as it should be. Therefore it is up to you—the reader of this book—to engage in self-education and the development of your potential leadership genius.

The mere fact that you purchased this book (or that someone thought to give it to you) is a statement about your dedication to leadership. Now, *you* have a dilemma—to read it or not. Because most people only get through the first chapter of a book, publishers want authors to keep books short and sweet. Leaders such as you just don't have time to read, they figure, and especially not tomes on leadership—given all the other reading and busyness in your life. Sometimes you buy books with no intention of reading them, hoping that by osmosis the information will filter in as it sits on your bedside table. So here's our challenge to you: Just read Part One. If all we do is raise your awareness about Contextual Leadership, we think it will make a difference in the way you lead. But we also hope that if you read the rest of this introduction, you might see the value of reading past the first couple of chapters. So indulge us; let us tell you why we wrote this obviously not short book and why you should invest in reading it.

WHY SHOULD YOU READ THIS BOOK?

If you've read books on leadership or studied the topic in the past, most likely you found leadership advice falling into two categories. The first is a general normative approach to leadership that recommends what leaders should be and do: The Leadership Secrets of . . . (fill in the blank with ancient Chinese philosophers, retired corporate CEOs, or current-day athletic coaches). This one-size-fits-all approach can be inspiring and thought-provoking, as when Warren Bennis, the leadership guru who made leadership a legitimate academic topic, writes about managers doing things right and leaders doing the right thing.[3] Or, when Kouzes and Posner encourage you to lead from the heart.[4]

The intention of this generalized leadership perspective is to provide insight, provoke thought, and inspire you to lead. Its downfall is that often it becomes a cookie-cutter strategy that in reality is too broad, conceptual, or theoretical to apply in a given situation.

The second type of leadership approach takes a narrower, more subject-oriented approach: *The Five Dysfunctions of a Team, Self Leadership and the One Minute Manager*, or *Leading Change*.[5] This more prescriptive approach can be useful, as when it suggests specific techniques and skills for leading in a given situation.

The intention of this second more targeted leadership perspective it to provide tactical or prescriptive leadership behavior that can be applied to a particular situation. Its downfall is that it fails to connect the dots so you can see how your efforts are interrelated depending on who, what, where, when, and why you are leading. One of our pet peeves is the way organizations teach leadership skills in isolation without an organizing framework that integrates, leverages, and thereby sustains the leader's skill-building over time.

Now here comes *this* book introducing what we will call the Contextual Leadership approach. Why get excited? Because this is the first time a model of leadership has combined both generalized and prescriptive leadership approaches, integrated the scholarly work and research of the past 100 years of leadership study with the personal experiences of seasoned leaders and coaches, and organized it all into one overarching framework that helps you make sense of leadership. Contextual Leadership is a new approach to leadership that you can actually use.

To be forthcoming, it is important to also tell you what Contextual Leadership isn't. As you can tell from the size of the book, it isn't simple, simplistic, or even necessarily easy. There's a reason for that. No one said genius was easy.

THE ANTI-QUICK FIX APPROACH TO LEADERSHIP

You've been there—a day when one of your direct reports barges into your office to ask the same question for the umpteenth time. A day when you struggle through a meeting that's a total waste of time and energy. A day when people in the organization resist the move to a new software system. A day when you realize that one of your biggest clients is demanding quality control parameters that exceed your current capability. We figure there are three kinds of responses to these types of situations: One—you are oblivious to the fact that there are leadership skills to handle the situations more effectively, so you figure misery, confusion, and stress is just part of the job. Two—you just read one of those short, story-based books on leadership filled with novel and compelling ideas and are wondering at this moment how what you've read is relevant. Three—you think you should be able to handle the situation given your dedication to being a better leader and all the training you've received over the years and . . . it's just that you're still not sure what to do next.

At these moments where you sense that your leadership efforts are inadequate, you may also realize the inevitable: Leadership should be a joy; quick fixes don't permanently resolve the gritty issues and dilemmas you face daily, and all the training you've received wasn't presented in a useful framework that allows you to access what you learned and apply it in the moment you need it. Don't get us wrong. We love the short parable or fun-to-read leadership primers—among the three of us, we've published at least six of them.[6] They have their place. We appreciate training; among the three of us, we've personally put thousands of people through seminars and workshops. But— and this is a big *but*—we think it is time to admit that leadership is more complex than you've been led to believe. You need a comprehensive approach to leadership that addresses these complexities. Leaders, authors, and publishers seem scared to death to admit that the practice of leadership is both an art and a science that requires the same dedication and commitment to master as practicing accounting, law, medicine, or music.

We are firmly convinced that leadership is contextual, complex, conditional, and skill-based. Discount this, and your leadership efforts will be less effective.

GOOD THINKING

Backed by solid research (ours and others) and many years of experience working in organizations private and public, secular and non-secular, and large and small, Contextual Leadership does four things that will make a difference to you and the way you lead:

1. Identifies five contexts in which you lead—the Self, One-to-One, Team, Organizational, and Alliance Contexts.

2. Establishes five practices of leadership that you need to apply *across* contexts.

3. Describes the different possibilities you need to consider *within* each context.

4. Prescribes specific leadership skills that you need for responding to a particular situation within a particular context.

There is a difference between good thinking made simple and simplistic thinking. Our intention is to take good thinking and make it accessible—hopefully bringing order to the complexities. To that end, this book is divided into five parts, as described next.

PART ONE—THE FIVE CONTEXTS

This overview of Contextual Leadership presents the significance, challenge, and promise of leadership in each of the Self, One-to-One, Team, Organizational, and Alliance Contexts. A chapter is devoted to each context, as shown in Table I.1.

TABLE I.1

ORGANIZATION OF PART ONE—THE FIVE CONTEXTS

Self Context Context	One-to-One Context	Team Context	Organizational Context	Alliance Context
Chapter 1	Chapter 2	Chapter 3	Chapter 4	Chapter 5

PART TWO—THE FIVE LEADERSHIP PRACTICES

There are five generalized leadership practices—Prepare, Envision, Initiate, Assess, and Respond. While the practices are common to all five contexts, the skills required to apply them within each context vary in form and complexity. This meaty part of the book has a set of chapters devoted to each practice and how the practice may vary from context to context. Table I.2 shows how the chapters are organized.

TABLE I.2

ORGANIZATION OF PART TWO—THE FIVE LEADERSHIP PRACTICES

Intro Chapter	Cross-Contexts	Self Context	One-to-One Context	Team Context	Organizational Context	Alliance Context
Prepare Ch 6	Chs 7–10					
Envision Ch 11		Ch 12	Ch 13	Ch 14	Ch 15	Ch 16
Initiate Ch 17		Ch 18	Ch 19	Ch 20	Ch 21	Ch 2
Assess Ch 23		Ch 24	Ch 25	Ch 26	Ch 27	Ch 28
Respond Ch 29		<----- Included on this book's companion Web site. ----->				

The five practices create the engine that drives Contextual Leadership's fully integrated approach to leadership. If leadership geniuses are made as well as born, then this part is a crucial link to that genius.

PART THREE—THE PROMISE AND THE CHALLENGE OF CONTEXTUAL LEADERSHIP

The two chapters in Part Three give you a theoretical and historical foundation for Contextual Leadership, introduce the graphic representation of the model, and provide a greater perspective, ultimately posing an important question—*How much are you willing to commit in the pursuit of effective leadership?*

BIBLIOGRAPHY

It's important you realize that the development of leadership theory and practice isn't a passing fancy, but a legitimate field of study. Just glance at the Bibliography to get an appreciation for the thought leaders and scientists who have contributed to making you a better leader.

APPENDIX: BENEATH THE WATER LINE

As mentioned earlier, one of the greatest challenges in publishing today is to satisfy the need readers have for a quick read and the need authors have to substantiate their ideas and provide depth to those who require it. The Appendix will expand your learning, help satiate your quench for understanding, and provide a couple of how-to techniques. You can find this valuable resource on the book's companion Web site.

THE PROBLEM WITH SIMPLE

Our fervent wish is that you will not feel as though we are asking you to take on too much. It is one of our goals, however, to help everyone realize that many approaches to leadership taught in the past were oversimplified to the point of uselessness. If there's one overarching lesson we've learned in recent times, it's that the practice of effective leadership is neither simple nor easy. If it were easy to achieve, we would be able to look around us and see numerous examples of healthy, vibrant organizations that nourish their people, produce high-quality outcomes, and contribute to society on a number of levels in a sustaining and positive way. That's not what we see. And we don't think you see it either.

The overriding vision that animates our passion and inspired us to take on this challenge is that someday we might be surrounded by truly vibrant, productive, and healthy organizations comprised of people realizing their potential. That's genius—leadership genius.

ENDNOTES

1. For research linking leadership and employee satisfaction, see Tett and Meyer 1993; Eby, Freeman, Rush, and Lance 1999; Lundby, Fenlason, and Magnan 2001.

2. For research linking customer service and employee satisfaction, see Schmit and Allschied 1998; Johnson 1996; Adsit, London, Crom, and Jones 1996.

3. Bennis and Nanus, 1985.

4. Kouzes and Posner, 1985.

5. *The Five Dysfunctions of a Team* is by Patrick Lencioni, 2002; *Self Leadership and the One Minute Manager* is by Blanchard, Fowler, and Hawkins, 2005; and *Leading Change* is by John Kotter, 1996.

6. Authors of this book have authored or co-authored the following "short" books in addition to their other more substantive publications: Drea Zigarmi—*Leadership and the One Minute Manager* (with Ken Blanchard and Pat Zigarmi); Dick Lyles—*Winning Ways* and *Winning Habits*; Susan Fowler—*Self Leadership and the One Minute Manager* (with Ken Blanchard and Laurence Hawkins), *Empowerment— How to Sustain Peak Performance Through Self Leadership* (with Ken Blanchard), and *Good Leader; Good Shepherd* (Lyles, Zigarmi, Fowler, and Flannigan).

PART ONE
THE FIVE CONTEXTS

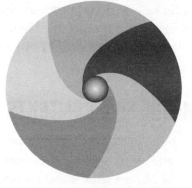

For thousands of years from prehistory until 396 BC, the ancient Egyptians communicated through a creative written language that became known as hieroglyphics (Greek for *holy inscriptions*). Hieroglyphics could be found on public buildings, government decrees, and art until the Roman occupation when Latin was mandated, with occasional Greek. Within a hundred years, the Egyptian hieroglyphics were no longer used or understood by anyone. Virtually all understanding of this mysterious script was lost. Hieroglyphics was a dead language. But the enigmatic characters still fascinated. For 1,400 years, scholars unsuccessfully tried to translate the forgotten language. It took a remarkable discovery in 1799 to unlock their mystery.

THE ROSETTA STONE—KEY TO UNDERSTANDING

Napoleon's soldiers digging near a fortress in the Egyptian city of Rosetta unearthed a granite stone almost four feet long declaring a royal decree. It turns out that the great Greek dynasties of pharaohs had the habit of making their decrees bilingual in territories they occupied—including both Egyptian and Greek languages. But this seemingly humble stone had a decree written in *three* ways: The top band contained hieroglyphics, the middle band was an Egyptian script called Demotic (meaning *popular* script), and the bottom was ancient Greek. A young, brilliant, French linguist named Jean-François Champollion used known versions of Egyptian and Greek to compare and contrast to the hieroglyphics, and in 1822 brought the mysterious writing to life. The Rosetta Stone had given him and the world the key to understanding an unknown language, and thus, one of the most fascinating cultures in history.

Today, the Rosetta Stone is a metaphor for a critical key to a process of decryption, translation, or a difficult problem. Though not as dramatic, but perhaps more pragmatic for you, Contextual Leadership could prove to be the Rosetta Stone of leadership.

BREAKTHROUGH: THE FIVE CONTEXTS OF LEADERSHIP

Contextual Leadership helps make sense of the past hundred years of leadership study and application—integrating the most significant leadership perspectives together in a comprehensive framework. The result is a practical model for leadership behavior.

The cornerstone of Contextual Leadership is the realization that who, what, where, and when you lead should determine *how* you lead.

SOTOA

The five contexts of Contextual Leadership are best remembered through the acronym SOTOA, which represents the Self Context, the One-to-One Context, the Team Context, the Organizational Context, and the Alliance Context.

The foundation for Contextual Leadership is the identification of these five unique leadership settings, but the breakthrough is describing how the contexts are *different*. Each context has its own distinct characteristics. Each context requires its own relevant leadership approach. There are a few key leadership practices that are common across all the contexts, but true leadership genius takes shape when you adapt those practices depending on the context.

To see the face validity of the five contexts and how they demand a variety of different skills from you as a leader, just observe your day. We did, and here's what we found. Sometimes you are a self leader, setting your own goals, making action plans, solving a problem, or considering how to propose a new idea. Sometimes you are engaged in one-on-one conversations with an individual who reports to you, setting expectations, outlining his or her plan of action, teaching a new skill, or listening to a person's problems before passing along your hard-earned wisdom. Other times, you are leading a team of people with a common purpose, helping them work through group dynamics, and holding one another accountable for achieving mutual goals. At times, depending on your role, you are addressing a large all-unit meeting, implementing an organizational initiative, or instigating a change. Sometimes you are leading an alliance, working on a big idea that will mutually benefit your organization and external partners.

Contextual Leadership begins with an awareness of the five contexts, but the devil is in the details with the skills and leader behaviors required to successfully lead in each context. Because leadership approaches in the past have not given the five contexts significant consideration, much of the advice given on how to be an effective leader has resulted in generalizations that are confusing at best, and harmful at worst. When context is not considered, the advice and training you receive on "how to lead" is typically muddled, and applicability is diminished—rendering you helpless or confused especially when you shift your leadership efforts from one context to another.

Different contexts demand different skills. However, there are *some* skills that are commonly applied across all five contexts—envisioning and goal setting, for example. But even these skills need to be applied differently *within* a context. Setting goals in the One-to-One context for a staff member's performance plan is challenging. But goal setting becomes even more complex in the Team Context when you are called on to set interdependent goals that can only be achieved through the unified effort of team members. By understanding that leadership is contextual, you can address leadership challenges with a unique logic; by mastering Contextual Leadership, you lead effectively through the behavior and skills most appropriate for the circumstances.

CONTEXTUAL LEADERSHIP BY ANY OTHER NAME . . .

We should note that in leadership conversations, the term *contextual leadership* sometimes takes on a meaning different than the one we have described thus far. The term has been used to describe the social-cultural environment in which leaders find themselves—from a given organization's internal culture to the country or region in which the organization operates.

Given the rash of mergers and acquisitions at the beginning of the new millennium, it's understandable that people have needed a term for what a leader does to perceive, interpret, and adapt to the demands of sub-cultures within merged organizations. There have been major snafus when a leader failed at what has been called contextual leadership. Look what happened, for example, when Carly Fiorina took the helm at Hewlett Packard and was undone by her failure to recognize or appreciate the historic traditions and culture of an established organization. Or when John Sculley naively assumed his marketing experience at Coca Cola could be transferred to Silicon Valley and slammed into the dynamic high-tech industry and counter-culture of Apple Computers.

Contextual leadership has also been used to express geographical leadership questions such as *How does Starbuck's manage the cultural variables of selling Frappacinos in China's Forbidden City?* or *How does Pfizer maintain its sales standards when selling pharmaceuticals in Malaysia?* Contextual leadership has been used to describe the attempts by an organization to transfer not only its products and services, but also its culture, overseas. Given the global scope of organizations today, *geographical* context is not just an important consideration—it's vital.

But as important as these particular applications of contextual leadership are, they are only one aspect of what we consider to be contextual leadership. As we define it, *Contextual Leadership is the consideration of who, what, where, and when you lead.* By definition it incorporates the social-cultural environment, geographical dilemmas, and the challenges of leading in a particular sector such as military, manufacturing, government, education, nonprofit, or public.

So for Firorina, Sculley, Starbuck's in China, and Pfizer in Malaysia, the ability to read and respond to the *cultural* demands of an organization is a *specific* skill required for leading in the *Organizational* Context. But what if you are a mid-level manager in China who needs to motivate, teach, and develop an individual who is unfamiliar with Starbuck's Western-style of doing business? You are then leading in a different context—the *One-to-One* Context—and need a different set of skills to do it well. So whether you are in Peoria teaching the tricks of your trade to a staff member who is new to the ways of your particular company culture or managing an individual in China who is new to the ways of Western culture, you are leading in the One-to-One Context. The content of what you are teaching may be different, but the requisite leadership skills are the same.

To be an effective contextual leader you must recognize the context—not just the culture—you're leading in. Why? Because the skills for leading in the Organizational Context are different than in the One-to-One Context; leading in the One-to-One Context is different than the Team Context. The different skills needed to be effective in each context have been identified, defined, and organized in the Contextual Leadership model. Contextual Leadership as described in this book is at once more complex and yet more ordered and easily prescribed to than the more non-descript definitions often used in leadership literature that raise the question of context but have no unifying framework or methodology for practical leadership application.

IN WHICH CONTEXT ARE YOU LEADING?

Before you can actually take leadership action, you must first identify the context in which you are leading. The context will determine your next move. How do you know when you are leading in one context or another? Knowing the characteristics of each context is the beginning of deciphering the mysteries of leadership and is the focus of the next five chapters.

CHAPTER 1

THE SELF CONTEXT: YOUR ROLE IN CREATING MEANINGFUL WORK

Close your eyes for a moment and imagine your work life five years in the future. What are you doing and where are you doing it? Now answer this question: *Would you be satisfied doing the same job, contributing at the same level, using the same degree of education and level of skill, and making the same amount of money in five years as you do today?*

The most frequent answer to this question is a resounding *No*. Not surprising. But what may be a surprise is the answer we hear when we change the question to: *Would you be satisfied doing the same job, making the same contribution, using the same degree of education and level of skill, but* making more money? The answer is still *No*.

We discovered that most people express a need to improve their competence, enhance their level of contribution, and experience personal and professional growth—regardless of the money issue. Contrary to a popular belief that people resist change, perhaps even fear it—most people *embrace* the prospect of change. We are willing to bet that *you* aren't resisting change either—and may even be *hoping* for change to happen! (Perhaps sooner, rather than later.)

Consider this: *People don't resist change; they resist being controlled*. People don't fear change; they fear not having a hand in creating the change they realize must happen over time. Most people desire development, growth, and an opportunity to be an architect of the change they know is inevitable. So why the big deal over change in the workplace? Unfortunately, too many people don't realize that being an architect of their own change requires determination and skills—so rather than taking the initiative to forge their own future, they often flounder as their boss, their organization, market conditions, and industry ups and downs determine their fate. The workplace is filled with victims waiting for a rescue that may not come. This is why learning to lead in the Self Context is critical for acheiving leadership genius.

> *Leading in the Self Context is having the skill set and the mindset to accept responsibility and take the initiative for succeeding in your work-related role.*

The first essential acts of leadership take place in the Self Context. Mastering self leadership enables you to establish positive conditions in the present and design a future that lives up to your aspirations—no matter what your position in the organization. It will also provide a foundation of understanding to lead direct reports, teams, organizations, or alliances more effectively. How can you expect to effectively lead others toward their vision and in pursuit of their goals if you are not effectively leading yourself? Leading in the Self Context begs the question: *How do I, as a self leader, empower myself and get what I need to succeed in my role?*

THE SIGNIFICANCE OF SELF LEADERSHIP

Don't get the idea that self leadership is self-serving. It is your energy to initiate, motivation to learn, commitment to succeed, desire to contribute, ability to produce, and your passion for work that enables your organization to fulfill its potential and sustain its success. Unfortunately, many organizations don't *get* the importance of self leadership.

SELF LEADERSHIP AT WORK—THE KEY TO ENGAGED EMPLOYEES

A popular bit of recent research reveals that only 20 percent of almost two million workers in the U.S. claim their strengths are in play every day, indicating that most organizations operate below 20 percent capacity.[1] It's even more dismal for workers in countries outside the U.S.[2] The research claims that fewer than 80 percent of workers are engaged in their work—19 percent are *actively disengaged*—signifying that their contributions are significantly diminished and they may thwart or even sabotage organizational efforts. The remedies recommended most often for re-engaging workers rely on organizations and managers to do something different. But consider what might happen if the focus shifted to fostering self leaders who make it their *own* responsibility to put their strengths in play every day. Imagine a workplace full of self leaders finding ways to contribute in spite of being hamstrung by bad systems, coping with organizational dinosaurs, or suffering with an incompetent manager.

It just makes sense that every organization *should* develop self leaders—yet this is usually the most underfunded and undervalued aspect of leadership training. (Is this a result of believing that training efforts are most valuable when directed to those who hold formal leadership roles or based on a fear of employees knowing too much? An interesting, but divergent question.) The fact is the lion's share of money and effort in most organizations is earmarked for training high-potential leaders who are taught how to delegate responsibility—to pass the ball, so to speak. But woefully little is allocated to teaching the rank and file how to catch the ball and run. (Let alone, how to *take* the ball and run!)

Unwittingly, organizations are paying a high price for failing to appreciate and respect the significance of the Self Context. Our stance is this: Employee engagement suffers because organizations depend on managers to engage employees, rather than developing self leaders who recognize their responsibility and have the skills to take initiative for success in their role. What if employees didn't wait to be empowered—but empowered themselves?

SELF LEADERSHIP AT WORK—THE KEY TO EMPOWERMENT

If more employees had the skill set and mindset to accept responsibility and take the initiative for success in their work-related role, they wouldn't have experienced the painful failure of the empowerment movement of the '80s that lingers even today.[3] Organizations intent on reducing overhead, purging dead weight, and becoming lean and mean use downsizing, rightsizing, and too often capsizing, to eliminate layers of bureaucracy with the hope of pushing decision-making and autonomy down the ranks. They still call it empowerment and promise you power, authority, and a sense of ownership in your work. Organizations still trust that empowerment is a way to meet the demands of being fast, flexible, and competitive in the new world marketplace.

But almost everyone discovers an interesting paradox as they cope with the chaos that ensues in the wake of their organization's latest empowerment movement: Although you may live in a democracy, you don't necessarily work in one. Despite the intentions to empower people, grant decision-making, and grant autonomy, most organizations don't come close to honoring the democratic approaches that enable empowerment.[4] Many military can probably relate to the adage, "We are here to defend democracy, not practice it!"

The bottom line is: You won't find empowerment thriving in most of today's organizations—no matter how you define it. If you define it as managers' willingness to give up control and decision-making authority—it's clearly not alive and well. Define it as the organization creating systems and best practices that decentralize controls and embrace self-directed teams with true power—you'll find it's clearly not supported. Define it as individuals feeling autonomous; free to do their best work, and control how their job is performed—it simply doesn't exist.

The significance of self leadership is this: *Empowerment is a concept; self leadership is what makes it work.* Empowerment can't exist, won't work, and is meaningless without self leaders—people who possess the ability, energy, and determination to accept responsibility for success in their work-related role. And when formal empowerment systems are nonexistent, a self leader will innovate, produce, and thrive by taking initiative. But, empowerment often dies from neglect because leaders don't foster, focus on, or follow through on self leadership training. Skill development is necessary for empowerment to be realized.

Managers and others in leadership roles are not the only ones to blame for the lack of self leaders in the workplace. Individuals—would-be self leaders—failed to embrace the opportunities and possibilities of empowerment. Why? Too many of them are still waiting for someone else to give them the power. For empowerment to take hold, potential self leaders must overcome the victim mentality, take responsibility for their own success, and ask for what they need. They must stop blaming systems, managers, or circumstances for creating unfavorable conditions. The victim mentality is the greatest obstacle to empowerment.

At lunch one day, a high-placed colleague of ours was complaining that the goals set by his boss were unfair and uninspiring. We chastised him for being a victim—in a loving way, of course. We reminded him that even though he was a leader of others, he also had the responsibility and the skills to be a self leader. He could and should challenge or reframe the goals. That afternoon, he knocked on his manager's door and made a case for reframing the goals. The manager not only agreed, but expressed relief because he had been stumped on how to deal with other sales managers who had the same issues with their goals.

Our colleague experienced the old axiom that *authority is 20 percent given and 80 percent taken.* When you practice self leadership, empowerment is the by-product.

THE CHALLENGE OF SELF LEADERSHIP

Of course, the greatest challenge of leading in the Self Context is being willing to master the skill set and mindset required to accept responsibility and take initiative for your own success—that's one-fifth of the reason we wrote this book.

It's also a challenge to hold the tensions of your own needs in balance with the expectations of your manager (or board of directors), teams, organization, and alliances. A creative instructional designer tells the story of having her innovative training designs rejected by the company's CEO with the following explanation, "Your problem is you keep creating nine-ton elephants and we only have two-ton cages." With that feedback, the designer realized she had three choices—she could push the envelope and create "out of the cage" designs that would get rejected; she could recognize the limits of the organization and work within them; or she could meet the organization's current needs while trying to help it begin to build bigger—and better—cages. Eventually, she found herself taking all three approaches, depending on the project, the risks involved, and her frame of mind.

Self leadership is a constant balancing act between your needs for expression and your organization's need for productivity; your need for autonomy and control and your organization's need for you to be a follower; your need to pursue a vision and goals that are meaningful to you and your organization's need to have a workforce dedicated to its vision and goals. To develop as a self leader, you need to have the skill set and the mindset to meet both your needs and those of the organization you serve.

Truth is, as a self leader, you will eventually face those three choices: do it your way, do it the organization's way, or do it in a way that helps the organization grow, change, and improve over time. Self leadership ultimately comes down to the famous Serenity Prayer—you need the serenity to accept those things you cannot change, the courage to change the things you can, and the wisdom to know the difference.[5]

THE PROMISE OF SELF LEADERSHIP

A common lament is: *The problem with being a self leader is that when something goes wrong, there's no one else to blame.* It's true. The burden of responsibility for self-development and success in your role falls on you, the self leader. But, the personal and professional rewards of being able to respond to challenges through your insights, skills, and actions are worth the effort—that's the *promise* of self leadership.

As a self leader, you will benefit from increased marketability (because you have the skill set and mindset to tackle and master new skills faster); you will benefit from diminished dependence on an ineffective manager (because you have learned to manage up to get what you need); and you will benefit by becoming a better leader of others (because you learned by leading yourself that good leadership comes from the inside out).

We have the testimonials of hundreds of self leaders who are enjoying the fruits of their self leadership—from the young author who took the initiative to set goals and create the conditions necessary to land her first book deal and an $80,000 advance; to the shy, introverted lowly-placed computer geek (his own description) who took the initiative to set up a training course on computer graphics and now manages 26 people in the graphics department of a major printing company; from the woman who expressed her desire to help physically abused women and was rewarded when her company and co-workers gave her support financially and emotionally to make the leap to managing a half-way house; to the young man with dreams of being a filmmaker who now runs an in-house media center for his company. We also have the simple stories of self leaders who now find it easier to relate to their boss, or who have accepted the reality of their organization and found ways of coping without losing their souls, or who have discovered how to appreciate opportunities for growth wherever they find them on a daily basis.

For your organization, the promise of self leadership is a rejuvenated and re-energized workplace that is living up to its people's potential. The promise to you as an individual is experiencing your vision and possibilities for your work-related role as you pursue self-determined goals.

But the most compelling reason to take on the mantle of self leadership is to live a more meaningful, purpose-filled existence—at least as it relates to your career. Nearly 75 percent of the time that you are awake is connected to work. It is critical to be conscious and conscientious about what work is and how it's done. What a shame to fall victim to circumstances—*I can't get what I need, my boss doesn't understand me, the organization's systems don't work, I don't have the resources I need, my job doesn't use my strengths, they don't appreciate me, there's no room for me to grow, they don't know what I could be doing if only given the chance.* Master the skills of self leadership, and you experience liberation from the perceived tyranny of organizational life. The good news is that what's good for the organization can be good for you and vice versa.

A fundamental belief of Contextual Leadership is that excellence in one context creates a positive ripple effect in the others. Learning to lead in the Self Context is like dropping a small stone in a still lake and eventually hearing the gentle waves break on shore. Our message to you is this: In a world desperate for effective leadership, you need to begin in the most obvious place—yourself.

ENDNOTES

1. Buckingham and Clifton, 2001 (6); Buckingham and Coffman, 1999 (28).

2. Flade, Peter, "The Workforce Lacks Inspiration" (New York: *Gallup Management Journal*, 2003).

   This article reports that the United States has a sadly disengaged workforce (56% not engaged; 17% actively disengaged) but still leads most industrialized nations such as Canada (60%; 16%), Japan (72%; 19%), Great Britain (61%; 20%), and France (57%; 31%).

3. The *Journal of Applied Behavioral Science*, Volume 37, Number 1, March 2001, Special Issue: *History of Workplace Empowerment.*

4. Ibid.

5. The Serenity Prayer is often attributed to Reinhold Niebuhr. Sydney
    Hook, author of *Out of Step: An Unquiet Life in the 20th Century* (San
    Francisco, CA: Harper and Row, 1987) names German philosopher
    Friedrich Christoph Oetinger (1702–1782) as the author of the
    original version *Tranquilitat*.

CHAPTER 2

THE ONE-TO-ONE CONTEXT: YOUR ROLE IN DEVELOPING INDIVIDUAL EXCELLENCE

Nothing reveals your credibility, authenticity, and true intent more than interacting with another human being. This is especially true when you are working with someone whose progress and success in the workplace relies on your leadership. The first "O" in SOTOA represents the One-to-One Context, which could be the most important context for demonstrating leadership genius. No organization can function without the self-sufficient high achievers you are charged to develop and nurture. It could also be the most illuminating context, for here you must openly demonstrate your character.

> *Leading in the One-to-One Context is developing the abilities and focusing the energy of individual direct reports so they can attain and sustain independent achievement in their work-related roles.*

In the One-to-One Context, your leadership thought, effort, and primary action is focused on teaching, encouraging, guiding, and supporting a direct report—an individual assigned as your responsibility. Keeping this focus does not diminish organizational results—indeed, it is within the framework of the organization's welfare that development of your direct report takes precedent.

The One-to-One Context prompts the question: How do I create a motivating environment for the individual I lead that encourages and promotes productivity and satisfaction in the moment—and over time?

If you have more than one direct report, your challenge is multiplied according to how many people you have reporting to you. Don't panic yet; the rewards and gratification for successfully leading an individual usually outweigh the challenge. In fact, it is the satisfaction of watching people grow and succeed that makes a manager's job worthwhile. Rarely is it the money!

THE SIGNIFICANCE OF ONE-TO-ONE LEADERSHIP

One of our favorite musical albums of recent years was *Genius Loves Company*, duets between Ray Charles, the old master himself, and a host of great partners from relative newcomers such as Nora Jones to pop stars Michael McDonald and Elton John; from country-tinged Bonnie Raitt and Willie Nelson to soulful Gladys Knight. Whew, what a treat! Duets have always been a popular form of music, and no matter what your age, you can probably name your favorite duet performers: Jeanette MacDonald and Nelson Eddy; Louis Prima and Keely Smith; Simon and Garfunkel; Hall and Oates; the White Stripes; Usher and Alicia Keys; or anyone with Frank Sinatra, Nat King Cole, or Carlos Santana.

We ask you to think about great duets because they are apt metaphors for leading in the One-to-One Context. Not as intricate or complex as performing in an ensemble (Team Context) or in an orchestra (Organizational Context), the duet still requires a great deal of shared focus, concentration, and effort. A duet seems to bring out the best in both performers, resulting in something extra special. A duet is a partnership, subject to an ebb and flow of music and energy, as two performers collaboratively interpret the music to a final expressive ending.

Consider the metaphor: Performing a duet requires that you first have music (the job description of your direct report's role, organizational rules, and the department's expectations, for example). Of course, you need an audience (external and/or internal customers). And, a duet dictates a joint effort in order to perform the piece well (goals and standards).

Now think about your work with a direct report. As the two of you move progressively toward your mutual and organizational outcomes, you will experience an ebb and flow of activity. Like a duet, your partnership is collaborative—each of you must do your parts to ensure an effective and successful outcome. When successful, you will both experience a sense of equality and common focus; your direct report will not suffer a sense of oppressive control, paternalism, or unreasonable servitude. Just listen to Ray Charles and Nora Jones—it's obvious that they are both enjoying each other's talents and gifts; each ultimately is honored by the other. And the audience? Well, we experience magic.

THE CHALLENGE OF ONE-TO-ONE LEADERSHIP

Most of your leadership opportunities in the One-to-One Context take place in face-to-face interactions between you and an individual you lead. These meetings are the springboard for trust, respect, and mutual understanding. When you are up close and personal, who you are, what you value, and what you stand for will become apparent to those you serve and lead. To be effective, you must clearly know yourself, be aware of how your intentions might be perceived by your direct report, and when necessary, adapt your behaviors so they are suitable to the conditions.

Your first and foremost priority when leading one-to-one is to effectively build the ability and focus the energy of a direct report so he or she can independently accomplish their role-related outcomes. Knowing how to develop a person from novice to master is the essence of one-to-one leadership and also one of your biggest challenges. How do you . . .

- Develop the follower's ability and energy to become an independent, excellent performer?
- Guide someone you lead toward their goals while promoting the vision and long-term health of the organization?
- Overcome your own potentially obstructive instinctive behaviors and ego needs to focus on the needs of the person you lead?
- Embrace and demonstrate that service is the primary reason for the leader-follower relationship while achieving service and profit motives of the organization?

Your organization probably requires you to do other things besides teach and develop your direct reports. It may expect you to allocate resources, recruit, prepare budgets, and generate reports; demand you be a team player, peacemaker, spokesperson, and all-around jack-of-all-trades; and call on you to represent and implement the organization's vision, values, and processes. You might complain about all those managerial duties and not see them as helpful in your mission to teach and develop your direct reports. However, it's important to realize that these processes are geared specifically to *support* your one-to-one leadership efforts. For example, employee performance appraisals, recruitment guidelines, dismissal policies, salary requirements, and other HR procedures help you strike a fair, middle ground for both your direct report and the organization.

There are ample resources within your organization or industry associations to help you with these management aspects of your role, but it falls on your shoulders to acquire the skills and master the role of a leader-teacher.

TEACHING SOMEONE TO SING

If your direct report is new to a goal or outcome taken on, your relationship will initially be more like a duet involving a teacher and a student. When a student plays a duet with a teacher an amazing synergy occurs. They learn through comparing their efforts with yours, through your timing, and from the harmony that occurs when two people are synchronized in their thoughts and actions. A music teacher not only provides a second musical voice—a sounding board for comparisons by which the student can express their skills—but also helps the student master the technical and interpretive parts of the musical expression. The relationship can and should ultimately become a true duet where each player takes the lead, depending on the requirements of the music. The true duet permits both players to experience more than they could alone. Each experiences interdependence, not co-dependence. Everyone—musicians and audience alike—experiences the beauty of the music, not the technical problems of playing the piece.

AN OVERLOOKED ROLE

Your role as a teacher may be the most important and overlooked aspect of leadership in organizations. As a leader-teacher, you are a developer of people; you are shaping the skills and energy of each of your direct reports so they can play their part—but always with the purpose of helping them to be solo virtuosos.

Imagine you are a parent whose children never become competent or motivated to live their own lives by taking full responsibility for their actions. Your job as a leader is not dissimilar to that of being a parent—*you want to develop autonomous, engaged, and productive individuals who respect and trust you enough to take your counsel when needed, but who are not dependent on you.* In the workplace, employees will always be learning something new and need you to fulfill your role as teacher, but at some point they also need you to let go and let them demonstrate their own mastery.

Only when your student progresses from learner to master can your organization begin to function at capacity. Only when your direct report has high ability and energy focused on their assigned goals can you empower him or her. It is foolish to empower people who lack the competence or confidence to sustain high performance on their own. Both your direct report and your organization depend on your teaching ability for success and long-term health.

GOOD LEADER; GOOD TEACHER

You don't find many leadership approaches that reinforce adult learning theory as a priority for effective leadership. But we're convinced that to be a good leader in the One-to-One Context, you need to be a good teacher. To be a good teacher, you need to be aware of the factors that positively support adults as they learn and create the six conditions that structure your direct report's adult learning experience.[1]

Encourage the Need to Know

The foremost factor for adult learners is the need to know why the learning is important.[2] You need to introduce learning as part of his or her job, making it legitimate to make certain mistakes as part of the learning process. Involve the learner in deciding what should be learned—and how the learning takes place.[3] It is crucial to be a learner yourself and model learning through your actions.

Build Self-Confidence for Learning

Building your direct report's self-confidence when it comes to learning is time well spent on your part. The most effective learners have high self-confidence in their ability to learn, which leads to their belief that they should be responsible for the decisions in their own work life. Ironically, your job is to lead your way out of a job. Learners who go on to be independent, excellent performers develop a deep psychological need to be seen by others as capable of self-direction. Most independent workers will resent and resist situations in which they feel others are constantly imposing ideas and behaviors on them. The more your direct reports take control of their own goals and assume ownership of their learning, the more effectively they will learn.[4]

Even when learners take responsibility for their own learning, they may still choose a highly teacher-directed approach for its convenience, speed, or because of their learning style.[5] Savvy learners understand the importance of the role you play as leader-teacher. But the highly teacher-directed approach is more effective if *chosen* by the learner. To foster their self-confidence for learning, it is essential you help the learner demonstrate his or her autonomy by providing choices throughout the learning process.

When you are helping your direct reports learn new job skills, offer as much choice as possible regarding when the learning will occur, how what they've learned will be demonstrated, and how quickly they want hands-on experience. At minimum, you should ask your direct reports for the best way to present information to help them learn. For example, a manager at a company we work with recently offered a mandated course in two forms— a day-long classroom training or a virtual experience using interactive computer training. She gave her direct reports the choice of which learning method best suited them. The learning was not up for grabs, but how the learning took place was the choice of the learner.

Tap Prior Experience

A notable difference between teaching adults and teaching children can be found in the deep and varied experiences brought by the adult to the learning opportunity. To enhance and enlist the adult learner, this accumulated experience must be acknowledged and tapped. To become more effective learners, adults must link new knowledge and skills to existing experiences and firmly plant the new knowledge and skills in their memories.[6] Of course, existing knowledge can challenge or limit the acquisition of new knowledge and become a giant barrier to the new knowledge to be learned.

You need to ask learners if they have prior knowledge or experience with what you are teaching them. If they have had some exposure with the topic, discuss it and see how their knowledge or experience applies to the skill or goal at hand.

Increase the Readiness to Learn

Adult learners usually show a readiness to learn when the situation creates a need to know something new. That need to know is contingent on the goals and competence the learners bring to the job or role-related outcomes they or others want accomplished. However, most adults show a motive or need to understand and master their environment, to feel free and in control of their actions, and to have feelings of competency and worth.[7]

Even though most adults have a built-in need to demonstrate competencies in roles of their choosing,[8] it is your obligation as the leader-teacher to induce readiness by providing learners with models and examples of superior performance, career counseling simulations, exercises, case studies, and on-the-job training. You can accelerate their readiness by communicating an organizational vision and goals that are so compelling and meaningful that learners are inspired to be involved in something greater than themselves.

Generate a Life-Centered Orientation to Learning

Adults are motivated to learn information, skills, and competencies that will help them perform tasks or deal with problems that they face in their lives.[9] New knowledge, understandings, and competencies are most effectively learned and retained by adults when presented in the context of real-life situations.

Much life-centered learning is centered on problem solving.[10] Because the adult learner is interested in solving real-life problems, you as the leader-teacher must continually use an inquiry-based method of teaching. You must see adult learning as an interactive process of mental inquiry, not one of passive reception of transmitted content or ideas—that means guiding the transfer and application of concepts to real-life work problems that require solutions.

Sustain a Motivation to Learn

The adult learner expects there will be a positive payoff from solving real-life work problems. In other words, learning adults expect the learning effort will lead to better outcomes. The adult learner also expects internal payoffs to the learning. This does not mean that external rewards (money, praise, advancement, and so on) are not relevant, but rather internal payoffs (joy in learning, a sense of esteem through mastery, a challenge met, and so on) are more potent motivators in the long run. Helping learners sustain their motivation over the course of time it takes them to master what they are learning is one of your greatest challenges as a leader-teacher—but it will ultimately yield some of your greatest returns.

Research indicates that adult learners can be motivated to keep growing and developing throughout life, but they often feel blocked by a negative self-concept as a learner, lack of resources, or programs that violate the principles of adult learning.[11] Your leadership challenge is to constantly point out the opportunities for the joy of learning as well as the growth and sense of mastery. As their skills develop, you must help them appreciate their growth.

A question that inevitably arises in *leader as teacher* conversations is: *How can I teach something I can't do?* This question often becomes the excuse for not teaching. First of all, teaching is a process that you can learn. After mastering the process, you can, at a minimum, *oversee the learning process* of your people. Secondly, some of the best teachers are those who weren't (or aren't) the most naturally gifted or successful at their trade. Because of their natural ability, they may not appreciate or understand what it takes to build skills and overcome a lack of natural ability. It's rare for great natural athletes to become great coaches. On the other hand, *good* but *not great* players, such as Pat Riley and Phil Jackson in basketball, have become great teachers, coaches, and mentors. Surely you have known a golf pro at a country club who was a wonderful golf instructor but didn't make it on the tour; an inspiring music or dance teacher who never made a hit album or danced on Broadway; or a motivating sales manager who didn't break all the sales records as a rep. There's that old thought that those who can't do, teach. Thankfully, sometimes that is true because in some cases, the individual had a different gift or skill—teaching. And in the long run, as a leader in the One-to-One Context, perhaps that is the greatest gift or skill of all.

THE PROMISE OF ONE-TO-ONE LEADERSHIP

Perhaps you can relate to the old saying, *When you are up to your neck in alligators, it's hard to remember that your primary mission is to drain the swamp.* Many leaders are so preoccupied with work and organizational demands, so focused on bottom-line progress, and so tied up getting reports and work done for their boss that they often don't have time left to serve those who will accomplish the outcomes. When in doubt, serve those who are most responsible for doing the greatest amount of work. Your main function when leading in a One-to-One Context is to serve those who must get the work done.

When you develop the abilities and maximize the energy level of each individual you lead, they will independently and consistently produce excellent results for the organization. Your most important payoff comes when those you serve are performing independently at outstanding levels.

If the thought of a workplace where employees take responsibility, are masters at their key responsibilities, actively pursue new ways to contribute, and take the initiative to make the workplace more efficient frightens you, then you may want to question why you're leading in the One-to-One Context. Great leaders within this context understand that competent and motivated direct reports are not a threat, but the answer to the nagging problems that keep you up at night.

Question: *Thinking back over your educational and work experiences, who would you name as the best boss, coach, or teacher you ever had? Who is the adult, aside from your parents, who most inspired the positive attributes you exhibit today or contributed the most to your current success?* After you have the answer to that question, consider why that particular person comes to your mind. What was it about their leadership, their guidance, their influence that was so affective?

Now consider this: *There are few jobs you will do, roles that you will embody, or rewards you will garner as important or satisfying as being someone else's best boss, coach, or teacher.* You have the opportunity to be the most inspiring and influential contributor to another's success. Perhaps that is what will motivate you to practice leadership in the One-to-One Context.

ENDNOTES

1. Knowles, Holton, and Swanson, 1998.
2. Reber and Wallin, 1984; Clark, Dobbins, and Ladd, 1993.
3. Hicks and Klimoski, 1987; Baldwin, Magjuka, and Loher, 1991; Tannenbaum, et al., 1991.
4. Brookfield, 1986; Candy, 1991.
5. Grow, 1991.
6. Merriam and Cefarella, 1991; Jonassen and Grabowski, 1993.
7. See White 1959 to review or Ford 1992 for an in-depth view of the origins of the concept of competence.
8. Deci and Ryan, 1985; Deci, 1995.
9. Knowles, Holton, and Swanson, 1998.
10. Kolb, 1984.
11. Tough, 1982.

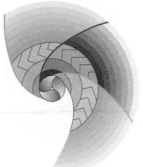

CHAPTER 3

THE TEAM CONTEXT: YOUR ROLE IN FACILITATING HIGH-IMPACT TEAMS

Bring four people together in a team, and you have 11 possible relationships; bring eight people together, and you have 247 potential groupings; 16 people result in the possibility of a stunning 65,519 subgroups! Leading a team can be exponentially more complicated than leading in the One-to-One Context—making it a stumbling block on the way to achieving leadership genius.

The complexity of leading in the Team Context demands a different focus that many leaders fail to recognize and requires different leadership behaviors that many leaders fail to master and use.

> *Leading in the Team Context means gathering, structuring, and developing the collective abilities and energies of a team of people with a common purpose, and guiding them to the achievement of interdependent goals and sustained high performance.*

Leading in the third context of SOTOA, the Team Context, triggers the question: How do I elevate my leadership skills to guide and respond to the needs of the unique team dynamic as well as individual team members?

ARE YOU LEADING A GROUP OR A TEAM?

Are you leading a team, or are you fooling yourself? Here's a quick quiz. Determine which of the following examples represents a team and which represents a group.

- District sales reps
- San Diego Padres Baseball Club
- The U.S. Women's Gymnastics Team
- Board of Directors for a publicly held company
- White House Staff
- Night-shift piece workers
- Claims clerks in an insurance office
- Employees brought together to create the organization's purpose statement

As you check your responses for which examples represent a team and which describe a group, also consider how this distinction might affect your leadership approach.

A team is three or more people associated in a joint action whose interdependent goals cannot be achieved without mutual cooperation and effort. A group is a collection of people who are related in some way.

The sales reps are a group, not a team, because there is no interdependency. Their individual goals are similar, but they go about their work individually—goals are individual rather than collective. Even if they have a district goal, the way they achieve that goal is every man and woman for himself or herself. One of the greatest misnomers is *sales team*. If you are a *sales team leader*, you are probably leading a group of individual salespeople, and your focus should be in the One-to-One Context—focusing on developing an individual's sales competencies and performance. If your sales folks have interdependent goals, are rewarded interdependently, and *must* function as a *one for all and all for one* team in order to be successful, then in addition to having the responsibility to make sure each individual lives up to his or her goals and expectations, you are *also* leading a team. The dynamics of a team demand different leader behaviors from you than either an individual or a group of people (thought to be a sales team) who come together because it's a more convenient way to share and receive sales information.

The San Diego Padres are a team because the members have a common vision, goals, and outcomes that cannot be achieved without the contribution of each individual's specialized talent and skill.

The U.S. Women's Gymnastics squad is a group when each young woman is vying for an individual title, but they come together as a team when vying for the team medal and each performance contributes to team points.

The White House Staff is a team, interdependent with an appointed leader, assigned roles and responsibilities, and common purpose and goals. The Board of Directors is a team for the same reason.

The night-shift workers are a group unless working together on a special task force with expected outcomes, or they are structured so that each person's job influences the performance of another. The claims clerks are a group given the same circumstances as the night-shift workers.

The employees brought together to create the purpose statement are a team because they share the duty to create a product or deliverable (the organization's purpose statement) and interdependence in carrying it out.

Why take the time to make the distinctions between a team and a group? The distinction is critical because one of three things could result if you misjudge who you are leading:

1. You may be wasting team-building efforts on a group that doesn't need them—groups usually don't have common goals that require interdependent actions and shared knowledge in order to achieve goals over a sustained period of time.

2. If you assume you are leading a group and fail to provide the team leadership needed, it is almost guaranteed that the team will fail.

3. You don't want to employ team leadership skills on a group of people at the expense of one-to-one leadership that individuals may need. Although groups may require certain team skills, you should never let this cause you to overlook or underestimate your role as a leader of individuals—you could be neglecting the one-to-one leadership your group of individual followers need.

COMPARING TEAMS AND GROUPS

Observe the team or group you lead and see which column from Table 3.1 best describes their beliefs, attitudes, and behaviors. It could be that you have a group of people who should or could be a team, or vice versa.

TABLE 3.1
COMPARING TEAMS AND GROUPS

Team	Working Group
A number of people who convene, work, and decide together because of their passion for a common vision and outcomes.	A number of people who work together and make decisions to further their own or departmental goals.
All members see the effectiveness of the group as their responsibility.	Specific people are responsible for the effectiveness of the group.
Individual issues are subservient to team issues.	Individual issues take precedence.
People you lead want and create cross-functional relationships.	People are skeptical of cross-functional relationships because they fear a reduction of individual or departmental power.
People you lead see challenges as a group issue.	They see challenges on an individual basis.
The team and the work the team is doing are equally important and enjoyable.	The group is not as important as the issues.
Interdependence is high.	Interdependence should be kept to a minimum because it breeds dependence.
The individual sees own success or failure in terms of the group's success or failure.	Individuals judge their own performance in relation to the group.
Lack of interpersonal skills is pointed out through open feedback and discussed.	Interpersonal and team skills are not valued or discussed.
Collaboration and synergy are typical.	Collaboration and synergy are infrequent and not seen as necessary for success.

THE SIGNIFICANCE OF TEAM LEADERSHIP

As the leader of a team, you may begin to question why a team is necessary and find your enthusiasm waning. Oftentimes, leaders who have been put in charge of teams are not aware of, or appreciative of, the market trends and cultural forces pushing more organizations to a team-based approach to getting work accomplished.

WHY TEAMS? WHY NOW?

Quality Customer Service Demands Teamwork

The tremendous emphasis on building a closer relationship with the customer necessitates quality, speed, and sensitivity to customer demands. This kind of customer service must be done through a seamless set of activities by more than one person. We were recently impressed by the team approach of a hospital in Hawaii. Each patient is assigned a team that consists of a doctor, two nurses, accounting representative, and patient-care advocate. Specialists are assigned as roving team members based on need. The medical and administrative members formed a team whose responsibility it was to take care of the patient from admission to release—including all communication, billing, and follow-up care. We weren't surprised to learn that the hospital has won numerous awards and recognition for customer service—important when operating in a competitive marketplace.

The Increased Span of Control (The Number of People a Manager Manages)

Downsizing and the efficiency efforts of the 1980s drastically left frontline people with more responsibilities and fewer managers to act as coaches and teachers. The lack of quality coaching resources demands that people help each other in a spirit of teamwork.

Specialization Requires Collaboration for Solving Complex Problems

The cross-fertilization of ideas and information will happen more naturally in teams. Technology and information sharing demand teamwork.

Globalization Requires an Appreciation of Other Cultures That Are Collaborative

Three-fifths of the world population values a collective approach to living and working. The cultures of Africa, Asia, the Middle East, and Latin America show a strong preference for loyalty to a group, tribe, or family.

With the globalization of organizations, the need to work in teams has increased. Cultural preferences may demand teamwork.

Unions Are Demanding Teamwork

Unions are advocating the adoption of employee involvement systems as a way for companies to become more competitive.[1]

Knowledge Workers Want More Say in Decision Making

Workers today are more highly educated, come from affluent backgrounds, and expect involvement. They want participation, autonomy, and responsibility, which can most readily be fostered in a team setting. A more sophisticated workforce is demanding genuine teamwork.

WHY TEAMS FAIL

What drives people crazy about teams? Unfortunately, when people answered this question, they didn't interpret crazy in a good kind of way—*I'm just crazy about teams because* . . . . Instead, the number-one response was *What drives me crazy about teams is poor leadership.*[2] The other nine things that drive people crazy are things influenced by or within the control of leadership: unclear goals; unmotivated team members; disorganized or unfocused meetings; lack of decision making; lack of follow-through and commitment to promises made; uneven contribution by team members; no communicated plans of action; hidden agendas; and the lack of acceptance by the organization of the team's recommendations.

Is there a correlation between what drives people crazy about teams and the leading causes of why teams fail? You guessed it: *Leadership is the common denominator.* According to research, the causes for failing teams include unclear goals (again), changing objectives (this could be an organizationally based problem, but when better managed by the team leader, is not a critical issue), lack of accountability, lack of management support, lack of role clarity, low priority of the team, not being rewarded, and—most crucial— not knowing how to deal with team dynamics.[3]

CHOOSING TO LEAD A TEAM

If you choose to master team leadership and deal with issues such as those listed previously, you will find teams are more than worth it. Research is clear that major gains on quality and productivity most often result from organizations with a team culture.[4] Individuals acting independently can make a big difference in an organization, but they rarely have the knowledge, experience, or skill equal to individuals working in a well-led team.

To be a competent team leader means being efficient at solving complex problems that require diverse, in-depth technical knowledge that can only be found among several subject matter experts. In fact, complexity mandates teams.

You must help team members develop a faith in the group's power to achieve their outcomes. The research is abundantly clear that team efficacy—or the team's confidence in itself—will result in significantly increased productivity.[5]

When you foster an environment where team members share the same degree of focus, passion, and excitement, you also foster creative ideas. Leaps from conventional wisdom most often occur through the tension of differences. As the team leader, the safe environment you create stimulates the dynamic tension that spawns unconventional wisdom.

Even though there is ample research linking good team leadership to extraordinary performance and organizational benefits, you should also be aware of the challenges of being an effective team leader. As stated at the beginning of this chapter, leadership challenges increase exponentially when you lead a team of three to twelve people with expectations of producing a common outcome.

THE CHALLENGE OF TEAM LEADERSHIP

Mastering the skills of the Team Context and overcoming the reasons people dislike teams and why teams fail is always challenging—but even more so in cultures where independence is rewarded over collaboration. Research indicates that teamwork is more of a challenge in Western cultures (the U.S., Australia, Great Britain, Canada, the Netherlands, and other Northern European nations), where individualism predominates over collectivism.[6] In a simple, but fascinating, example of the different perceptions of team involvement between the East and the West, people were asked to estimate what percent of the whole they think they contribute to their team's overall effort.

In Asia, the total for the team added up to less than 100 percent—in other words, if there were ten people on the team, you might expect each person to contribute 10 percent on average, totaling 100 percent. But the

Asian team members consistently estimated their contribution to be less than their equal share.

In America, however, the total of all the team members was consistently higher than 100 percent. Unlike team members in Asia, team members in America and other Western nations consistently *overestimated* how much they contributed to their team's overall effort.[7] It seems that in the West, team members consistently feel that their teammates don't work as hard or contribute as much as they do.

Teamwork does not come naturally in cultures that place greater emphasis on individual contribution than team effort. But before you renew your team leadership efforts by planning the team picnic, ropes course experience, or activity-based event, it's important for you to understand the difference between *team bonding* and *team building*.

BEYOND TEAM BONDING TO TEAM BUILDING

Team bonding experiences are helpful as ways to promote interpersonal connection—but they should not be confused with team building. Team building begins with considering what type of team is best suited for achieving your expected outcomes and deciding what number of people and mix of personalities, skills, and expertise best serve those outcomes. Team building requires crafting a charter so all the team members are clear and committed to the team's purpose, goals, and processes; and managing the team's ability and energy over time as they pursue the team's goals. Team building is formalizing ground rules and operating guidelines to handle conflicts and the internal and external forces that could impede the team's progress. Ultimately, team building means providing the team with the guidance and support it needs as it matures and then letting go—sharing leadership with the team members so they become self-managing.

THE DUAL NATURE OF TEAMS

Every team leader—indeed, every team member—must maintain a dual perspective:

- ■ You must be both a leader and a member.
- ■ You must be both a participant and an observer.
- ■ You must be concerned with both output and process.

Leader and Teammate

In your role as team leader, it is obvious that you need to have the skill set to focus and inspire the team, as well as the individuals within the team. You must know enough about team dynamics to set up processes that promote an efficient working environment and help the team grow and develop over time. But over time, a successful team will develop revolving leadership that demands each member be able to assume the role of team leader, depending on their expertise and the team's focus on output and process. As the original or official team leader, you must ultimately be willing to let go and let others lead. Otherwise, you will stifle and smother the team's potential, creativity, and initiative. Great coaches know when to let other members of the team take the lead around both output and process issues—as Phil Jackson, then coach of the Chicago Bulls basketball team, would (for the most part) watch quietly from the bench during games while Michael Jordan led the team on the court. *Pares inter pares*—a first among equals—describes the leader/member duality of team leadership.

Given the challenges of leading effectively in the Team Context, you may need to be reminded why it's worth the effort!

Participant and Observer

Because output and process are equally important, each member of the team must maintain the dual focus of participating in producing team results, and still be mindful of how team members are treating each other. To be a contributing team member, you must be fully engaged as a participant in helping the team achieve its goals (output). At the same time, you must be detached enough to observe what's going on and respond to the team's needs regarding both process and output.

Output and Process

On one hand, you need to always ask output questions: What is the team supposed to do? What products, services, and outcomes are expected of the team? On the other hand, you need to also be concerned with process questions: How is the team doing what it is doing? How is the diverse expertise of team members being integrated? How are conflicts resolved, problems solved, and decisions made? How do team members relate to each other as work is being accomplished? If you focus on output without process, you may achieve short-term success, but inevitable disharmony and disillusionment will ultimately sabotage results. If you focus on process at the cost of output, your team may seem to be functioning well, but its lack of productivity and success will ultimately destroy the spirit and motivation of the team.

THE PROMISE OF TEAM LEADERSHIP

Hearken back to a time when you were on a winning team. By winning, we mean a team that produced results and whose members were dedicated to a common purpose and motivated to succeed. You may have been on a high-performing sports team that ultimately came in second in the tournament, but you and your teammates could rejoice in the combined and sustained effort as much, or more, than the eventual outcome. Maybe it was a little league baseball club, a church choir, a project or event team, a software conversion task force, or a jury.

That memory of a positive past team experience may be all you need to realize the promise of team leadership. It was through the team experience where you realized it is possible to feel more joy when it's reflected in the face of another. The team is where you found it stimulating to have ideas generated from the synergy of diverse-thinking people. You discovered that by teaming with people who are as talented—or more so—than you are, you can accomplish things you cannot achieve alone. There is something profound about celebrating success with others who share your understanding of the meaning of success. It was through a team experience that you may have sensed the intrinsic reward that comes from contributing to something greater than yourself.

Hopefully, the promise of teams will compel you to master the leadership practices in the Team Context.

ENDNOTES

1. Bluestone and Bluestone, 1990.
2. Fowler-Woodring and Zigarmi, 1997.
3. Why teams fail, according to studies by the Hay Group as reported in *USA Today*, February 25, 1997: goals unclear (55%); changing objectives (55%); lack of accountability (51%); lack of management support

(49%); lack of role clarity (47%); ineffective leadership (45%); low priority of team (40%); no team-based pay (30%).

4. Katzenback and Smith, 1993; Bennis and Biederman, 1998.

5. Osborn and Hagedoorn, 1997; Khana, 1998; Callister and Wall, 2001; Ring and VanDeEn, 1992; Kogut, 1998.

6. In a worldwide study of 116,000 employees of IBM in 1980, Dutch psychologist Geert Hofstede was able to rank 40 cultures according to the strength of individualism or collectivism. The five nations with the highest level of collectivism were Venezuela, Columbia, Pakistan, Peru, and Taiwan, as reported in the *Straight Times*, January 28, 1999, "Individualism vs. Eastern Cultures."

7. Psychologist Shinobu Kitiyama from the University of Oregon, as reported by the *Straight Times*, January 28, 1999, "Individualism vs. Eastern Cultures."

CHAPTER 4

THE ORGANIZATIONAL CONTEXT: YOUR ROLE IN GENERATING THE ORGANIZATION'S VITALITY

Even though you may never be the president of an organization or owner of your own company, understanding the Organizational Context will help you appreciate the challenges and efforts of those who do lead the organization; empathize with and help implement decisions and changes initiated from the top of the organization; and be a more valuable member of the organizational community by being able to act locally but think globally. It is impossible to master leadership genius without understanding and appreciating how leading in the fourth context of SOTOA, the Organizational Context, impacts everyone's leadership efforts in the other contexts.

> *Leading in the Organizational Context means directly and indirectly influencing and aligning individual and team efforts toward fulfillment of the organization's purpose through systems, processes, and structures.*

The Organizational Context includes the leadership required to lead a company, corporation, agency, or institution (any of which might be either proprietary, not-for-profit, or governmental in nature). It could also mean leading a business unit or even a department, division, or section of a larger organization.

If you are the leader of the organization now, or plan to be one day, you may have made your way to the top by demonstrating leadership in the Self, One-to-One, or Team Contexts and being promoted through the ranks. But exemplary as your leadership record may be, expertise in the other contexts does not qualify you or guarantee your success for leading in the Organizational Context. Outcomes are subjected to more variables, and the time required to achieve the outcomes is generally longer than in the other contexts. You will need another set of skills and behaviors to answer the question: *How do I focus systems and inspire people to move together toward a strategic outcome?*

THE SIGNIFICANCE OF ORGANIZATIONAL LEADERSHIP

Thousands of companies die every year for myriad reasons. Sometimes it's because the opportunities or demands that led to their formation disappeared, but the most prevalent reason is poor leadership. Either the company leaders lacked vision, experienced a breakdown in values, or failed to implement the changes necessary to stay competitive in emerging markets. Quite often it's simply because the leaders didn't understand the basics of how organizations work, let alone how to lead in the Organizational Context.

UNDERSTANDING THE BIG PICTURE

Before you master *how* to lead an organization, it is essential to grasp *what* it is you are leading. Each of the aspects of an organization shown in Figure 4.1 not only demand your attention, but also your ability to integrate them into a cohesive, highly functioning whole.

All organizations—small or large, well run or languishing—have these aspects in some form or another. First, an organization is created in response to either a demand or an opportunity. For example, a *demand* might be when a company forms a subsidiary company to guarantee the availability of necessary parts at a competitive price, say an automobile firm starting a company to build tires. An example of an *opportunity* might be a group of software engineers who develop an idea for productivity enhancing software and then form a company to develop the new software product and take it to market.

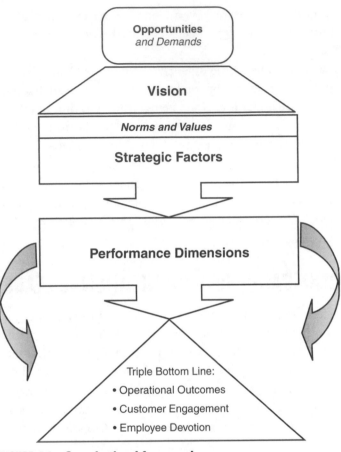

FIGURE 4.1   **Organizational framework**

A vision focuses the energy and efforts of all involved. Every organization has a vision—or, as the case may be, visions. In fact, it may be that every individual working in the organization has his or her own vision about what the company is and what it could or should do. Because so many leaders leave the vision to chance and fail to develop a vision into a clear, compelling, and energizing force, their organization flounders and finds itself at the mercy of whatever prevailing forces are at work. Similarly, all organizations have values or guiding principles. Often the espoused values are different than the values in use. Alas, if these values are not developed values, carefully chosen and operated upon, they will fail to optimize the energy of the workforce. The vision, with its values and norms, creates the direction and boundaries for the organization; they create the heart and soul of an organization and need your attention, focus, and mastery.

Strategic factors provide the framework for performance, including processes, systems, and infrastructure to support performance. Performance dimensions include initiatives and goals that determine the organization's day-to-day activities.

Every organization has outcomes and outputs that we refer to as the *triple bottom line*. The triple bottom line includes measuring achievement against organizational outcomes, customer devotion, and employee engagement. It's obvious that financial measures are part of an organization's bottom line, but it's also important to consider that customer satisfaction and retention are outcomes, as are employee satisfaction and morale.

Leading in the Organizational Context takes on greater significance when you realize that it is your role to take responsibility for every aspect of the organizational structure. As a leader in the Organizational Context, you are in a position to create the vision, values, norms, initiatives, systems, and processes, as well as use management practices that engage employees, satisfy customers, and ultimately lead to high performance that can be sustained over time.

THE CHALLENGE OF ORGANIZATIONAL LEADERSHIP

As organizations grow, they create different challenges for leaders at each stage of their growth. The leadership requirements in each category shown in Figure 4.1 are different for a small, new entrepreneurship than from those that are required to lead a large, complex, mature bureaucracy to success. The elements are still needed, but they will be more informal and less structured with smaller, newer organizations than the more structured and formal practices required in larger, more established organizations.

Ichak Adizes created perhaps the most popular and detailed documentation of the growing and aging phases of organizational evolution. His Corporate Lifecycle Theory describes how organizations start with a Courtship phase, and then progress through Infancy, Go-Go, and Adolescence to reach Prime. After reaching Prime, if not led properly, they become Stable, and then pass through the phases of Aristocracy, Early Bureaucracy, Bureaucracy, and then Death.[1]

In an article entitled "Evolution and Revolution as Organizations Grow," Larry Greiner laid out another paradigm that detailed five distinct phases of evolutionary change that growing organizations must work through, interspersed with four distinct crisis phases that must be responded to with revolutionary changes if an organization is going to continue to grow.[2]

The work of Greiner and Adizes is useful in helping leaders to understand why certain dynamics exist in their current organization and what might be needed to take the organization to the next level. For example, if you—as a leader of a relatively small and growing entrepreneurship—were to observe recently that deadlines were being missed, follow-through and accountability have become a problem, and information is falling through the cracks on a regular basis, you might reasonably conclude that you have passed through Greiner's first evolutionary phase of growth—a crisis of leadership—and are now facing the crisis he calls *the crisis of autonomy*. The appropriate revolutionary changes you'd make as a leader would be to introduce stronger and more explicit management systems and use a focused and inspirational approach to leadership that would guide the organization out of its state of chaos and confusion.

Seems obvious, doesn't it? Then why don't more leaders do it? The answer comes in two parts. First, many leaders don't think strategically in terms of leading their organization to its optimal future. Even though they think about what markets they want to penetrate, the higher-level financial returns they want to produce, or the businesses they want to acquire, they most often overlook the strategic demands of the organization itself. They fail to ask: *Is my organization functioning the way it should, given our current size and level of operations?* They fail to realize: *There are natural, predictable phases of organizational development that must be understood and managed.* If your organization functions the same as it did five, three, or maybe even one year ago, and it has changed in size, market focus, or operations, you are sub-optimizing.

The second reason most leaders don't lead their organizations to the next level is because they lack the skills needed to identify and implement the specific initiatives to take their organization where it needs to go. They don't know how to manage the changes they must make. Today many people talk about managing change. They should talk about managing *a* change. The pre-eminent challenge for leaders in the Organizational Context today is to identify the specific changes needed to carry the organization forward and then to be able to implement the particular nature of each of those changes successfully.

Watching many executives try to implement changes in their organizations today is like watching a goose trying to get butterflies to fly in formation—lots of honking, without much resulting precision.

But, one of the greatest challenges leaders face today is a failure to grasp the fundamental purpose of their organization—thinking it is more about making money than serving the customer by responding effectively to specific opportunities and demands, or serving their people who *are* the organization.

If you are shaking your head in denial at this moment, please be patient. Profits are important: They buy you tomorrow. Revenues are important: Without them, you have no profit to grow and sustain the organization. But if there's one important lesson we've learned during the past 50 years about corporate leadership, it's that leaders whose focus is primarily on operational output and financial measures—without first focusing on employee passion and customer devotion—will lose their way and ultimately be ineffective.

Are you aware of where your primary focus as a leader should be? Do you know the primary predictors of your organization's long-term success?

PREDICTORS OF ORGANIZATIONAL PERFORMANCE

Employee passion is the most reliable predictor of long-term organizational performance.[3] When employees are engaged in their work and have low intention to leave, when turnover is low and organizational citizenship behavior and morale are high, and when employees trust their leaders, there is a greater likelihood of high performance.

However, the opposite is not true. Organizational performance does not predict employee engagement. You *can* have high organizational performance and disengaged employees—but your organization's high performance will be short-lived. So even if your organization has high performance, a majority of your employees could be disengaged, actively looking to leave, sabotaging, stealing, and wasting company resources. If this is the case, your long-term organizational success is endangered. An organization cannot sustain high performance without the active engagement of a majority of its employees over time.

The same is true regarding customer devotion. When you have repeat customers who recommend, or have intentions of recommending, your products or services; when customer complaints are low, and customer satisfaction index measures are high, your organizational performance measures will most likely also be high.[4] Another striking research finding is that measures are correlated with measures of customer devotion.[5] The higher the employee passion, the more likely you will see high customer devotion.

How do you challenge the belief, drummed into leaders over many centuries, that the way to make money is to focus on making money? It seems such a natural truth that if you don't focus on making money, the company will cease to exist and the people and the customers will perish. But, there's a big difference in using financial and economic factors as indicators of output, *versus making them your leadership focus*. In other words, the way to make money is to change your leadership priorities from making money to leading people and serving customers effectively.

That's the challenge that confronted Jim Despain, head of the once-failing TTT Division of Caterpillar.[6] The company was in dire financial trouble. He turned it around by choosing to shift the focus of leadership from the age-old battle cries regarding revenue and productivity to the alarmingly warm and fuzzy measures of leader-employee relationships and living the organization's vision and values. Despain, long considered a bull-of-the-woods-type leader who would just as soon kill the messenger if he didn't like the message, seemed the least likely candidate to become the role model for leading by values. But he made a hard-nosed decision to shift away from the paradigm of *it's all about the money* and was rewarded with success that included the bottom line, but went well beyond it. Profitability and morale were restored using people-based versus power-based principles built on values of trust, teamwork, and empowerment. Not only did he turn around the division, but he also did it without a union contract during a time of bitter union-management strife. The paradigm shift from focusing on output measures first, and people engagement and customer satisfaction second, to focusing primarily on employee engagement and customer satisfaction first and foremost resulted in employee commitment, customer satisfaction, and superb operational and financial results.

THE PROMISE OF ORGANIZATIONAL LEADERSHIP

Leading organizations is often like navigating a whitewater river with its turbulence and unforeseen obstacles. Sometimes organization leaders must navigate through turbulence and unforeseen problems. But the whitewater analogy has its limits. Sometimes leaders must react to forces and problems beyond their control. But most of the time, an organizational leader must operate more like the conductor of an orchestra rather than the pilot of a whitewater raft. Similar to the One-to-One Context, where you play the role of teacher-leader as your direct reports learn to play their own music and eventually to solo, you are teaching and leading your organization to manage the initiatives you have implemented. You have chosen the music (an initiative), and you are coordinating all the different sections of the orchestra (the big five systems[7]) to work in perfect harmony.

For example, suppose you have a vision that customer service is the piece of music you want your organization to play. Everyone in the organization must understand their part in the piece and how their contributions fit in the larger whole. Their priority is to play their part. Notice it will be hard to play many other pieces while playing the customer service piece. From a systems perspective, what must be in place for everyone to play the piece well?

The more difficult the music you have chosen for the orchestra (the more complex the initiative), the more challenged you will be as a conductor-leader, and the greater the dedication of the musicians will need to be. It is a privilege to lead an organization; it is your duty to have the skills and behaviors to lead it effectively. The promise of leadership comes at a price—you must master the practices of leadership in the Organizational Context and learn to respond to the needs of the organization. Your reward will be commensurate with your effort when you have created a workplace where people feel privileged to work and customers feel privileged to buy and use your products and services.

ENDNOTES

1. Adizes, Ichak. *Corporate Lifecycles: How and Why Corporations Grow and Die and What to Do About It*, Prentice Hall, Englewood Cliffs, NJ. 1988.

2. Greiner, Larry E. "Evolution and Revolution as Organizations Grow," Harvard Business Review (July–August 1972), 37–46.

3. Toronow and Wiley, 1991; Ryan, et al., 1996; Schneider, 1991; Tett and Meyer, 1993.

4. Johnson, J., 1996; Schmit and Allschied, 1998.

5. For analysis of research linking employee passion, customer devotion, and organizational vitality, refer to *Perspectives: The Leadership-Profit Chain* by D. Zigarmi, S. Blanchard, and Essary. Available through the Ken Blanchard Companies, Escondido, California. Item #MK0483 033006.

6. Despain and Converse, 2003.

7. The big five systems are generally agreed to be accountability, data, feedback, reward, and learning systems.

CHAPTER 5

THE ALLIANCE CONTEXT: YOUR ROLE IN FOSTERING STRATEGIC RELATIONSHIPS

One of the most significant business changes during the last several decades is the shift from hierarchically-based, unilateral power within the organization to a reliance on alliances and partnerships.[1] These alliances represent the fifth and final context of SOTOA and another challenge to achieve leadership genius.

> *Leading in the Alliance Context means using networks and bilateral relationships to create a third entity that extends beyond corporate boundaries and achieves the goals and serves the mutual interests of all the members of the alliance.*

The idea of strategic alliances prompts the question: *How do I forge, nurture, and manage collaborative relationships that expand and leverage my organization's assets, services, and potential?*

Alliances can occur on any of several levels—as a partnership between two individuals or between an individual and an organizational unit, although these are rare, or more likely between two organizations or two organizational units. If the alliance is created between two different corporate bodies, it is an *external alliance*. While an alliance of two or more entities belonging to the *same* corporate entity—say between the marketing and sales departments of a single company, or between two brands within a company—might be considered an *internal alliance*, these usually don't have the complexity that external alliances experience.

Market forces—including specialization, globalization, and the need for economies of scale for competitive advantage—have contributed to organizations relying less on hierarchies and more on networks that cross traditional organizational boundaries to drive performance and achieve results. Despite discomforting controversies about some of Wal-Mart's operating practices, one aspect of its commercial success is undeniable: The partnerships between its buyers and vendors are examples of strategic alliances that significantly improved communication, ordering processes, and pricing, which have resulted in millions of dollars in savings and one of the most efficient and envied warehousing systems in the world of retail.

ALLIANCES ARE DEFINED BY PURPOSE

The major difference between a strategic alliance and a simple relationship is that strategic alliances are defined by purpose, while simple relationships are usually defined by proximity or emotion. You have a relationship with the people in your neighborhood because you live in close proximity. You only create an alliance with each other if you join forces to accomplish a mutually shared objective, such as getting a stoplight installed at a dangerous intersection nearby. You have a relationship with your friends because you like each other. Your friendship becomes an alliance if you decide to go into business together or to focus your collective energy on some other mutually shared goal.

Although alliances may be formed to accomplish an immediate purpose such as the completion of a task or project, such short-term outcomes are typically the purview of project teams or task forces. Alliances are generally formed to accomplish longer-term aims that bring a significant major advantage to the parties involved for an extended period of time—for example, an alliance formed between an airline and a hotel chain to serve the ongoing needs of a certain market segment of tourists.

THE SIGNIFICANCE OF ALLIANCE LEADERSHIP

The director of sales for a company that manufactures and sells cardboard boxes to many of the maquiladora[2] plants along the U.S./Mexican border realized that strategic alliances might be a business solution and opportunity after he attended a university course delivered by the authors. A prime market for his company's cardboard boxes was manufacturers of electronic components that must ship their products around the world.

The electronic component firms often put the squeeze on the cardboard box manufacturer, forcing the young sales director into bidding wars. Facing the intense competition and small profit margins, the sales director sought a competitive edge. He noticed that even if he won the business by offering the lowest prices, his customers still faced a dilemma—the foam inserts they bought from other vendors to position the electronic components properly inside his cardboard boxes often didn't fit. Because the processes and technologies used to create foam inserts is radically different from those used in creating the cardboard boxes, the cardboard box suppliers are different from the suppliers of foam inserts.

It seems the primary reason the electronic component manufacturers were demanding such low pricing on the cardboard boxes was because they had to be reconfigured so the foam inserts would fit. There was absolutely no cooperation between the cardboard box manufacturers and the foam insert manufacturers, and everyone was suffering from the inefficiency. (Maybe you can relate when you buy hot dogs and buns from different food vendors who obviously have never cooperated. Either the dog is sticking outside the bun, or there's so much bread you can barely find the dog.)

The young sales director realized he was losing business and money because his cardboard boxes didn't integrate with the foam inserts the way the customer wanted. He approached the CEO of the leading foam insert company and proposed a strategic alliance. The two companies combined forces to offer an integrated solution to their customers. In six months' time, they virtually cornered the market and doubled the revenues and profitability of both companies!

ALLIANCES—A PREDICTABLE PHASE OF ORGANIZATIONAL DEVELOPMENT

Probably the earliest to prophesy that all of this would happen is Larry E. Greiner. In his seminal study on the growth of organizations, Greiner documented various phases of transformation successful organizations must complete in order to achieve sustained success over time. The highest phase of transformation he called the *collaboration phase*, which emphasizes spontaneity in management action through teams and the skillful confrontation of interpersonal differences. Social control and self discipline take over from formal control.[3]

Although Greiner had a sense of what this phase should look like, he acknowledged that he didn't have a clear model in mind, so the leadership model he chose for this collaborative phase was a model based more on interpersonal relationships than on inter-organizational relationships. We believe that during the ensuing decades since the publication of Greiner's work, it is safe to say that this collaborative phase should be formulated through spontaneity in leader action through the skillful formation of both internal and external alliances more than merely on team formation alone. Further, we believe that the skillful confrontation of interpersonal differences, although important, is not the key at this level. We believe that the skillful integration of core competencies that exist in separate corporate bodies (or in the case of internal alliances, sub-sections of the same corporation) is the more relevant key to mastering this level of organizational development. An organization simply won't reach this level of development if its members haven't already demonstrated interpersonal competence on a fairly broad scale.

In the early 1990s, IBM was for the most part a stand-alone company. *We're Big Blue and everyone else can follow in our wake* was how many people perceived the attitude at IBM. Today, just the opposite is true. Leaders at IBM will tell you that IBM has more than 90,000 strategic alliances—formal relationships with other companies without whom IBM feels they could not adequately serve their customers.

Nowhere is the need to understand how to lead strategic partnerships more obvious than in the alliance-crazy cyber world of the Internet and the volatile world of entertainment. As our culture moves from mass media to individualized media, the opportunities for strategic advantages will come through alliances that meld the newest technology with the most desirable entertainment content. Consider this posting appearing on Variety.com at the beginning of 2006:[4]

> The Walt Disney Co. has turned a digital spigot into a fire hose, broadening its offerings on Apple's iTunes to include sports, news and animated shorts from the Walt Disney library.
>
> Expanded offering comes as NBC Universal trumped ABC's groundbreaking iTunes deal for "Lost" and "Desperate Housewives" by inking

a much broader deal with Apple that has bombarded the service with NBC network fare such as "The Office" as well as content from NBC U cable properties Sci Fi and USA and the Universal syndie library.

Disney's ESPN and ABC Sports will be the first to test the viability of sporting events on the service by offering condensed versions of the Fiesta, Sugar, Orange and Rose Bowls the day after they air.

Just two days later, this posting appeared:

AOL soon will launch its previously announced In2TV, a free, ad-supported online library of shows from Warner Bros. In addition, the portal is expected to start selling shows online, similar to Google and iTunes, by the end of 2006.

"The fastest way to grow this market is via free, ad-supported content," Kevin Conroy, AOL's exec VP of media networks, said Thursday at CES. "We expect to launch transactional video-on-demand later this year."

In a keynote address Thursday morning, Sony CEO Howard Stringer outlined his company's broad suite of products uniting technology and content. He also brought along helmer Ron Howard, producer Brian Grazer, and star Tom Hanks to promote upcoming Sony pic "The Da Vinci Code."

No matter what your industry, or whether you're in a key staff position or a leadership position at any level in your organization, chances are you'll find yourself in the position of having to make an alliance succeed. When alliances fall short of achieving their objectives, it is usually because alliance leadership failed to ensure compatibility, the strategic purpose was unclear, or the alliance charter was not explicitly defined. But the challenges of maintaining alliances are many and varied.

THE CHALLENGE OF ALLIANCE LEADERSHIP

After alliances are formed by overcoming the challenges associated with defining purpose, they face significant operational challenges. Because alliances are created between different organizations, the biggest challenge they face is often that of accountability.

To effectively lead an alliance, you need to answer questions such as . . .

- How will the members of the alliance hold each other (and themselves) accountable for performance?
- What steps will be taken or what recourse will alliance members be able to rely on in the event their partner fails to follow through?
- How does the alliance itself maintain its vibrancy and commitment when it ages?
- What happens when some members of the alliance team leave and are replaced by newcomers who don't share the same enthusiasm and values as their predecessors?

Alliance leadership team members need to know how decisions will be made, how problems will be solved, how they will communicate, and where the authority related to their operations lies.

The greater the degree of ambiguity around management processes and the activities of leadership, the greater the likelihood the alliance will fail to meet its expectations.

THE PROMISE OF ALLIANCE LEADERSHIP

When the challenges are met and alliances are properly led, there is perhaps no better leveraging tool available to leaders in organizations today to maximize the performance of their companies. There's a reason IBM has taken the time to create more than 90,000 strategic alliances. The reason is return on investment.

Companies around the world are finding that they are able to sustain growth during economic declines, accelerate the rate of growth during good times, and achieve gains more efficiently through alliances than any other strategy. As a result, leading in the Alliance Context may very well prove to be one of the most critical competencies leaders need to master during the next several decades.

SUMMARY—THE RIPPLE EFFECT OF CONTEXTUAL LEADERSHIP

Contextual Leadership reinforces the dynamic in-depth nature of leadership and how leading in isolation without regard to the ripple effect among contexts can lead to inefficiencies that waste time, squander resources, de-motivate, and confuse you and those you lead.

Regardless of good intentions, action (or inaction) in one context can create negative consequences in another: For example, an unclear company-wide vision or a poorly communicated corporate vision (Organizational Context) makes it difficult for you to set or align goals for yourself or your direct reports (Self and One-to-One Contexts); team members expected to contribute to a team's success (Team Context) are difficult to motivate when the organization's overall incentive and reward systems are aligned to reward only individual efforts (Organizational Context).

Contextual Leadership provides you with a new language, not unlike the famous Rosetta Stone, that helps you unlock the mystery of the various and sundry leadership approaches you've been exposed to over the years. Finally, you will know how to integrate leadership practices that are *common* across all the contexts and apply the distinct leadership skills that are appropriate *within* each context.

ENDNOTES

1. Gibson, Randel, and Earley, 2000; Paskevich, Brawley, Dorsch, Weidmeyer, 1999; Gully, Incalcaterra, Joshi, Beaubien, 2002.

2. Maquiladoras are U.S.-owned and -operated facilities located close to the U.S./Mexican border that employ Mexican labor and resources.

3. Greiner, 1972.

4. Variety.com postings: January 3, 2006; January 5, 2006.

PART TWO

THE FIVE PRACTICES OF CONTEXTUAL LEADERSHIP

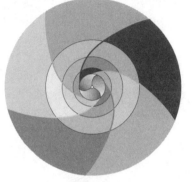

L eadership is a wonderful notion. But until leadership is practiced, it remains simply a notion—tantalizing us with its possibilities and frustrating us with its elusiveness. A doctor practices medicine, a CPA practices accounting, an attorney practices law, and a leader *practices* leadership. Leadership is not just a concept. Leadership is something you *do*.

> *Leadership is the repetitive acts of arousing, engaging, and satisfying the values and needs of followers in an arena of conflict, competition, or achievement that result in followers taking action toward a mutually shared vision.*

In Contextual Leadership, five essential practices guide *what you do* as you lead in each of the five contexts: 1) Prepare, 2) Envision, 3) Initiate, 4) Assess, and 5) Respond. Part Two is devoted to each of the practices and how you carry them out in the Self, One-to-One, Team, Organizational, and Alliance Contexts. A snapshot of each of the five practices is provided next.

PREPARE—THE FIRST LEADERSHIP PRACTICE

What you *do* as a leader is shaped by who you *are*. So, the first leadership practice is to Prepare by *understanding yourself*. What does Bill Clinton understand about himself now that he didn't when he was President of the United States that almost cost him the presidency? What could Martha Stewart understand about her basic nature that in part led her to a prison term? What if all leaders chose to overcome their inherent weaknesses, as Gandhi and Churchill did, to become not perfect, but heroic leaders?

> *You Prepare for leadership when you recognize, control, and adapt your disposition-driven behavior; develop personal values; and investigate your persona, so your leadership behavior does not predispose you to act in ways that may sabotage your effectiveness.*

As a leader, it is especially important to take responsibility for your behavior. Your actions *directly* influence those you lead, but because of their *symbolic* nature, they also influence indirectly. For example, when you impatiently snap at someone, you might get the immediate response you desire. But you have also acted *symbolically*—your behavior sets the tone for those who work for and with you, providing an example of the way you want to be treated and expect others to be treated. When you ask or tell someone to do something you wouldn't do; when you tell someone that we are all equal, yet you have or take special privileges; when you tell someone to make sacrifices and yet you don't; when you don't walk your talk, don't be surprised if your behavior results in disloyalty, poor performance, or even sabotage in the long run. Whether you know it or not—and whether you like it or not—people interpret your intentions and values through your behavior.

Chapters 6–10 will help you Prepare by giving you the insights and tools you need to understand where your leadership behavior comes from and how you can adapt it to better serve those you lead.

ENVISION—THE SECOND LEADERSHIP PRACTICE

An irrefutable principle of leadership is that all leadership, regardless of context, starts with vision. If leadership is the repetitive acts of arousing, engaging, and satisfying the values and needs of followers in an arena of conflict, competition, or achievement that result in followers taking action toward a mutually shared vision, then without vision there can be no leadership.

You Envision when you visualize an inspirational ideal one can aspire to, craft a statement of purpose one can be dedicated to, proclaim rank-ordered values that act as a noble guide for behavior and decision making, and align the vision across contexts.

In the Self Context, you Envision by creating a clear vision of *your ideal* work-related role. It is important as a self leader that your vision for your role be compatible and integrated with your overall life purpose and values, as well as the visions of the manager, teams, organization, and alliances you serve. As a leader of others, it is your responsibility to also guide your direct reports, teams, organization, and alliances in the creation of *their* visions. Your vision motivates you through the inevitable challenges of achieving and sustaining high performance; leading others through the envisioning process will do the same for them.

While envisioning takes place in each context, you can't hope to sustain the passion and performance of others unless you and those you lead share a *common vision for the whole* and how each person contributes through their specific role. Chapters 11–16 provide the framework for envisioning in each context so that visions are linked and complement one another.

INITIATE—THE THIRD LEADERSHIP PRACTICE

After you have created a vision, you must ensure that initiatives are created to actualize and sustain it.

You Initiate when you establish and facilitate the goals, expectations, ground rules, operating guidelines, and steps for implementation that embody, enable, foster, and sustain a work-related vision.

The most significant way to support a vision is to initiate goals that are specific, motivating, attainable, relevant, and trackable. The format and criteria for setting goals is similar for each context, but as you will see, the complexity increases as you move from setting goals for yourself, to guiding your direct report, to chartering teams or alliances, to setting goals for an organization.

Contextual Leadership emphasizes that the goals you initiate in one context should reinforce goals in the other contexts, and stimulate collaboration, coordination, and synergy. How you do this is explained in Chapters 17–22.

ASSESS—THE FOURTH LEADERSHIP PRACTICE

With a vision and goals established for those you lead, you must then determine what they need to successfully and responsibly pursue and achieve the goals that have been set. The assessment you make—especially the ability and energy level of those you lead—should guide your leadership behavior.

You Assess when you appraise the Ability and Energy of an individual, team, organization, or alliance to achieve a specific outcome.

Suppose you assess that it is well within the ability of your direct report to achieve a particular goal. It would be a waste of your time to explain in detail how to do it if he or she already knows how to do it. On the other hand, if your assessment reveals that the skills and understanding required for your direct report to achieve the goal is completely outside the scope of anything the individual has ever tried before, then your priority becomes to explain in specific detail what is expected and how to achieve those expectations. Understanding how to assess the ability and energy of individuals, teams, organizations, and alliances to perform to agreed-upon expectations is a critical component of being a Contextual Leader and is explored in Chapters 23–28.

RESPOND—THE FIFTH LEADERSHIP PRACTICE

With a vision in place, goals initiated, and the ability and energy of those being led to achieve the goal assessed, it is time for you to Respond—the fifth leadership practice.

You Respond when you take the appropriate leadership action with individuals, teams, organizations, or alliances to develop their abilities and energies to achieve specific outcomes.

For you to respond to the different demands of each context requires you to have great *versatility*—the skills to lead in the Self Context are very different from the skills you need for leading in the Organizational Context. For example, a skill you need in the Self Context is to *solicit and receive* feedback; in the One-to-One Context, that skill's complexity is heightened to *giving* effective feedback; in the Team and Alliance Contexts, the skill level rises exponentially as you need to master group dynamics; and in the Organizational Context, you have to be able to scan the environment and pick up on indirect signals that give you input and information.

But that's only the beginning! You also have to be adaptable, because the skill you use within a context needs to be adapted to a particular situation. You will respond within a context depending on the needs and performance level of those you are leading. For example, when you are giving feedback in the One-to-One Context, you might give someone who is starting the learning process on a particular goal very detailed feedback about *how* he could get better results. On the other hand, if an individual has proven capabilities or has mastered the goal in the past, your feedback would be focused on providing information on progress or *what* results—the quality and quantity of the results—the person produced. As with teaching a child to ride a bike, the feedback you give the child climbing on for the first time will be quite different from the feedback you give the child once the training wheels are removed and he or she can ride faster than you can run.

Chapters 29–34 outline the skills you need for meeting the different kinds of leadership challenges you'll face in responding to different levels of performance in each of the contexts.

SUMMARY

The practice of Contextual Leadership means you must . . .

- Identify the context in which you are leading: Self, One-to-One, Team, Organizational, or Alliance.
- Apply the five leadership practices within and across all contexts: Prepare, Envision, Initiate, Assess, and Respond.
- Adapt how you respond to those you lead within a context based on the individual's, team's, organization's, or alliance's level of performance.

The road to leadership mastery is indeed paved with good intentions, but intentions are made real through practice, practice, practice, practice, and practice.

CHAPTER 6

PREPARE: THE FIRST LEADERSHIP PRACTICE

It is so easy to see the folly of others. As you read about Dennis Kowalski's rampant misuse of millions of dollars of Tyco stockowners' money; or the conspiracy of fools at Enron, you think: *That could never happen to me.* You watch otherwise seemingly decent people falter in their leadership roles because of personal issues—Bill Clinton, Martha Stewart, and Steve Madden, founder of a shoe empire who pulled in an annual salary of $700,000 as he continued to act as creative director for his company while serving his prison term and admitted he was guilty of stupidity, arrogance, and greed.[1] But do you think: *There but for the grace of God, go I?* Probably not. Maybe you've wondered why Jimmy Carter is more revered now than when he was President of the U.S.; how Nelson Mandela transcended his 28-year purgatory to rule again with such grace; or how Oprah Winfrey manages to bare her life to millions daily and gain more respect as time goes on while running one of the most successful entertainment companies in the world. *But can you relate?*

The temptation when writing about leadership genius is to use well-known personalities so that readers will have a common frame of reference. The problem is that you may read these stories with interest, but not relevancy. You will likely find many reasons why *their* story is not *your* story.

So, here's our compromise. We'll use famous examples from time to time to illustrate a point, but we need you to be willing to use yourself as the example when the time comes. Leadership begins with self-preparation, and self-preparation begins with introspection. Have you taken the time to get to know the person you spend the most time with? Well, it's time you get to know yourself. Trust us. You're fascinating. But more important, knowing your personality and the part it plays in your leadership role is every bit as important to your effectiveness as understanding market conditions, economic factors, employee issues, or the competition.

This book is about *you* in relation to those you lead. Your learning and growth will be limited unless you are able to transfer meaning from the academic research we cite and the familiar examples we use, to your specific situation. Nowhere is this transference between the written word and personal action more important than in the first practice of Contextual Leadership: Prepare.

When you do the inner work of leadership, you will find it guiding your behavior and impacting your effectiveness in all five contexts, as shown in Table 6.1.

When you Prepare for leadership, you ultimately need to affirmatively answer this question:

Have I gained knowledge from observing my personality patterns, and do I use what I've learned to adapt my leadership behavior in service of those I lead?

PERSONALITY MATTERS

Gaining knowledge begins with observing your personality. *Personality* is one of those words used without much regard to what it means. It's often used as a broad term describing intangibles about someone—*I don't like his personality; she has a nice personality; I can't help it, it's just my personality.* In Contextual Leadership, the term *personality* includes every factor that describes your values, sensitivities, fears, goals, habits, and inclinations for coping with stressful as well as nonstressful situations.[2] Your personality is made up of inner thoughts, impulses, and emotions held over time, and expressed outwardly as you go about the business of living and leading.

TABLE 6.1

QUICK REFERENCE GUIDE: PREPARE WITHIN AND ACROSS CONTEXTS

You Prepare for leadership by recognizing, controlling, and adapting your disposition-driven behavior; developing personal values; and investigating your persona, so your leadership behavior does not predispose you to act in ways that may sabotage your effectiveness.

Self Context	One-to-One Context	Team Context	Organizational Context	Alliance Context
Prepare by reconciling your disposition-driven and values-motivated behavior as a means to fulfill your work-related vision and achieve your individual goals.	Prepare by reconciling your disposition-driven and values-motivated behavior as a means of leading your direct reports as they fulfill their work-related visions and organizational initiatives.	Prepare by reconciling your disposition-driven and values-motivated behavior as a means of leading your team as it fulfills its charter.	Prepare by reconciling your disposition-driven and values-motivated behavior as a means of leading your organization as it fulfills its vision and achieves its initiatives.	Prepare by reconciling your disposition-driven and values-motivated behavior as a means of leading your alliance to fulfill its Big Idea.

It is important to distinguish four components of your personality—your subconscious self, disposition, values, and persona—because even though each is a separate aspect of your personality, they interact and can be contradictory, can cause internal conflict, and can confuse the heck out of people trying to understand you.

SUBCONSCIOUS SELF

Your *subconscious self* is the unknown, esoteric aspect of yourself that emerges through your dreams and fantasies; it has inspired religions, philosophies, and self-reflection since the beginning of mankind.

Your subconscious self is often called your core, collective unconscious, or even the spirit or soul—terms used to describe the indefinable aspect of your humanness that may connect you to something greater than yourself.

Thomas Merton wrote, "At the center of our being is *le point verge*, our all but ineradicable point of nothingness which is untouched by sin and by illusion. The pure glory of God in us. If we could but see it emblazoned in each other all the time, there would be no more war or cruelty. I suppose the big problem would be that we would fall down and worship each other."[3]

The exploration of your subconscious self could have a significant influence on your personality, and thus, leadership of yourself and others. While we don't directly address how to examine your subconscious self because it is so highly personal and esoteric, by teaching you to better understand the other aspects of your personality—your disposition, values, and persona—you'll be more likely to examine and reveal more of your subconscious self, illuminating all that you do.

DISPOSITION

Your *disposition* is reflected in your instinctive thoughts and impulses. It is your gut-level, physiological reaction to circumstances and events—your unconscious tendency over time to fight or flight, confront conflict or avoid it, control your environment or accept it, or act extroverted or introverted, for example.

You will discover more about your disposition in Chapter 7, "What's Driving Your Leadership Behavior?," where the basic tenet is: *There's a difference between disposition-driven and values-driven behavior.*

VALUES

Your *values* are premeditated, cognitive standards of thought and emotion about what you believe to be good and bad. Your Values Point of View is a set of beliefs you've chosen to accept as guidelines for living your life.

You will have the opportunity to explore your values in Chapter 8, "Leading with Developed Values," where the basic tenet is: *Every leader leads by values—unfortunately, many are influenced by programmed rather than developed values.*

PERSONA

Your *persona* is the social mask you present to the world. It is your historical view of yourself—a fleeting, conscious sense of yourself that vacillates between all that you ideally could be, should be, and yet are, at any given moment.

You will be provided with the tools for investigating your persona in Chapter 9, "Investigating Your Persona," where the basic tenet is: *Your persona can be used as a tool for understanding and adapting or changing your leadership behavior.*

AWARENESS, UNDERSTANDING, AND CHANGE

We are often dismayed in our work as leadership coaches by how many leaders are unaware of how their behavior sabotages their intended outcomes. Sometimes they lack awareness of how others see them, so that even their good intentions get misconstrued. With so much riding on your actions, you must behave in a way that is appropriate for the circumstances and your good intentions. Too often intentions and behavior are not congruent. Consider an individual who wanted to challenge the office bully, but didn't; or someone who wanted to give advice to a co-worker, but instead became frustrated with the co-worker's incompetence; or the leader who intended to take the back seat in a project, but couldn't help imposing personal ideas on the group. Can you think of a time when your own behavior wasn't congruent with your hoped-for outcomes?

Sometimes the behaviors of leaders *are understood by others*, but unfortunately the leaders themselves haven't examined their own behavior, motives, or values. The more aware you are of the dynamics of your personality, the more *intentional* you become. Without self-awareness, your behavior will often be unconsciously dysfunctional. Without self-knowledge, you may have the opportunity, title, or authority to lead yourself, direct reports, teams, organizations, and alliances, *but you will not be a leader in practice.* Without self-understanding, you become preoccupied with your own needs and myopic to the needs of others—the very needs you seek to arouse, engage, and satisfy through a common vision.

You may have to face the fact that to lead the way you want to lead means making some changes. You will learn how to use the tools of your personality in Chapter 10, "The Challenge of Change," where the basic tenet is: *People can and do change.*

ENDNOTES

1. "Genius of Capitalism: Steve Madden," by Rob Walker. Posted Wednesday, April 10, 2002, at 12:43 PM ET on www.Slate.com.

2. Kahn, et al., 1964.

3. Merton, 1968, page 158. Thank you to Dominic Perri for sharing his insights on Merton.

CHAPTER 7

PREPARE: WHAT'S DRIVING YOUR LEADERSHIP BEHAVIOR?

Contextual Leadership tenet: There is a difference between disposition-driven behavior and values-driven behavior.

Comedian Flip Wilson tapped into our inner psyche with his popular catchphrase *The Devil Made Me Do It!* It may be convenient to blame counterproductive behavior on something else—like that little red guy with horns sitting on your shoulder whispering in your ear—but it isn't very productive. Instead, acknowledge that some of your behavior may be inappropriate or dysfunctional in certain circumstances and *choose to consciously* act differently.

Here's the problem with this approach: Much of your behavior is instinctive, and you are probably unaware of it. But, inappropriate behavior is inappropriate whether words and actions are instinctive or deliberate. Because instinctive behavior is without thought or regard for conscious intended outcomes, it can oftentimes be dysfunctional. For example, if your instinctive reaction to a situation is to flight or avoid conflict, the result may be the lost opportunity for a sale or resolution of an interpersonal problem. To make consistently good choices, you must first be able to acknowledge, observe, and then, finally, understand and adapt your instinctive behavior—or *disposition*.

Defining Disposition

Your disposition is reflected in your instinctive thoughts and impulses. It is your gut-level, physiological reaction to circumstances and events—your tendency over time to fight or flight, confront conflict or avoid it, control your environment or accept it, or act extroverted or introverted, for example.

You may have used the word *disposition* to describe someone else: *He has a nasty disposition* or *She has a pleasing disposition.* These remarks are gross generalizations—examples of how people tend to observe or experience someone's behaviors, group those behaviors, and then label them with a predominant or prevailing tendency, or disposition. In these examples, the dispositions were labeled *nasty* and *pleasing.* Our intent is to give you a better way to consider disposition that avoids judgment. The point is, disposition isn't good or bad, but rather compatible or incompatible with the conditions you find yourself in or the requirements demanded of you as you lead yourself and others.

Hopefully our research-based method of helping you observe and group your *own* behaviors will yield a description of your predominant or prevailing disposition that's more helpful to you than being labeled *nasty* or *pleasing.*

WHERE DOES DISPOSITION COME FROM?

Imagine someone invades your body space—they violate your personal comfort level of physical closeness. Without conscious thought, your body has a reaction: to put space between you and the invader by either moving aside or pushing the other person away. Unless you're taught to observe it, you may not have been consciously aware of your internal response—or preference—to *fight or flight*.

A *preference* is a preconscious tendency to react or act in a certain way to an event at *a given point in time*. You don't think about it—you just react to a particular situation. Preference is *would-do* behavior as opposed to *should-do* behavior, which is more conscious, values-laden, and reasoned behavior. *Preference is instinctive, unanalyzed, and unplanned—not premeditated.* It is not necessarily good or bad, right or wrong. It is a behavioral manifestation of *who you are.*

Let's say that more often than not—51 percent or more of the time—your preference when someone invades your space is to push the person away, rather than move yourself out of the way. *Your repeated preference becomes your disposition*—a repeated, demonstrated preference for doing a certain behavior over time. In this case, your disposition is to fight rather than flight.

You may wonder, *Is my disposition always the same?* The answer is *No*. There will be situations or conditions when you flight rather than fight, for example. But because you can't fight and flight at the same time, the preference that emerges as dominant through continual repetitive choice over time is considered your disposition.

A MODEL FOR DISCOVERING SELF

There are a number of models used to understand disposition—some better than others. Most of them are based on the original research of Carl Jung, arguably the greatest psychologist of the twentieth century.[1] Our own research conducted and collected over the past 30 years validates and adds depth to these models, making them practical for application in the workplace. For the sake of easier communication, we will use the DISC Model,[2] where the letters D, I, S, and C stand for four *statistically relevant groupings* of behaviors.

IT'S NOT ABOUT LABELS

It requires skill to observe yourself with a scientific and unprejudiced eye, so it is helpful to have a model to help you sort through your behaviors and make sense of them. What isn't helpful is to jump to judgment based on the labels given the four groupings (D for Dominant, I for Interactive, S for Steady, and C for Conscientious). In fact, even though we've satisfied you if you had a need to know what the letters stand for, we would just as soon you forget the labels and focus on the observable characteristics and behaviors that comprise them.

We are very clear about what we hope you will do with the DISC Model: *Use it as a framework for self-observation, understanding your behavior, and adapting your behavior when appropriate.* DISCposition is not about labeling yourself or anyone else—the DISC Model is a guide for observing and sorting your *patterns of behavior* so you can understand how you react to certain stimuli, and change it if it's not working for you or those with whom you hope to relate. After you successfully DISCover Self, there will be a time for DISCovering Others.

SELF-OBSERVATION

Imagine you are a journalist assigned a story about a very important person: You. What questions would you ask yourself in addition to the standard ones about your age, marriage status, past history, family, and work life? As a savvy observer of human behavior, what would you observe to get the real story?

There are dozens of things you could observe about yourself, but there are four tell-tale behavioral indicators that should become the focus of your self-observation.

Are You Extroverted or Introverted?

How do you interact with your environment—through *extroversion* or *introversion*? If you tend to outwardly demonstrate your thoughts or emotions, your answer would be through extroversion; if you do not show what you are thinking or feeling, the answer would be introversion.

Observe yourself playing poker. To determine if you tend toward extroversion or introversion, notice your nonverbal and verbal behavior during the game. If you have a hard time concealing your hand, if your facial and body movements tend to be animated, if you give others at the table frequent direct eye contact, and if your vocal tones reveal emotion, then you are demonstrating indicators of extroversion. Think of Jodie Foster's character in the movie *Maverick*. Try as she might to hide her hand, she couldn't quite control her behavior—ultimately she revealed her cards by the way she twisted her hair. Extroverts have a difficult time restraining their inner thoughts and emotions.

On the other hand, if you tend to be inscrutable, if your facial expressions are more placid, if your eye contact is infrequent, if your body movements are minimal or subdued, and your voice projection tends to be monotone, you have displayed indicators of introversion. Your friends probably don't like playing poker with you—but, consider that a compliment!

Extroversion not only implies the tendency to outwardly demonstrate your inner thoughts and emotions, but it also implies that you may gain energy around other people. The preference for introversion, in addition to the tendency not to share thoughts and feelings, includes high needs for privacy and alone time. Begin to notice your energy compared to others. Are you like the extroverts who have outwardly directed energy that can be felt as soon as they enter a room, or more like the introverts who have softer energy that allows them to easily slip into a room undetected?

Here's another potent way to grasp extroversion or introversion. Imagine that you are a radio receiver. If you are an extrovert, when you turn on the radio switch, the reception is low. It's as if you're in that cell telephone commercial, *Can you hear me now?* and the answer is *No.* As an extrovert, your lack of sensitivity to the stimuli in the environment is called *low gain,*[3] meaning that you don't readily pick up on all the external signals around you. As a result, you have a high need to explore the external world by interacting with it directly—much like a dolphin or whale uses sonar to bounce off objects to maneuver and adapt their bearings. This is why extroverts tend to speak before thinking—it is their way to hear what they sound like, to check out their ideas. In retrospect, they often find themselves retracting statements or defending statements they wish they hadn't made!

On the other hand, if you are an introvert, when you turn on the switch, you receive incredibly clear signals. In fact, your receiver is highly sensitive, picking up on all the noise and chatter in the atmosphere. This heightened receptivity to stimuli in the environment, called *high gain,* means that you need to create a way to filter in order to cope. In fact, as an introvert, if you didn't have a way to filter the signals, you'd go crazy. This is why introverts take longer to process information—it must go through the filters first. When extroverts ask introverts a question, they often grow impatient waiting for a response. On the telephone, you will hear an extrovert checking to be sure the introvert is still on the other end, *Hello, are you still there?*

Remember, there is merit to both extroversion and introversion behavior—there is no good or bad; just different.

Do You Control or Accept?

The room is cold. The music is loud. The meeting agenda is not being followed. Is your need to control the environment or change it to make it warmer, quieter, or more orderly? Or do you tend to accept what the environment provides and go with the flow? By *environment,* we mean the things, people, and events that create the circumstances you find yourself experiencing.

If your disposition is to *control*, then you have a tendency to act on the environment and change it to meet your inner needs. If your disposition is to *accept*, then you tend to take what the environment gives you and use what's given to meet your inner needs. To either *control* or *accept* is a basic and fundamental dispositional response.

Do you think your preference is typically to control or accept? If you prefer to control your environment, consider whether you do it in an extroverted or an introverted way. If the room is too cold, as an extroverted controller, you will directly change the thermostat or ask or tell someone else to do it—assuming that everyone must be cold as well. As an introverted controller, you will attempt to indirectly control the cold room by questioning why the maintenance team hadn't adjusted the thermostat or wonder aloud why the organization is wasting so much money on air conditioning that isn't needed. Eventually someone will hear you, get the idea, and the temperature will get changed—you have just controlled your environment, even though you didn't do it directly!

If you tend to accept what the environment gives you and are extroverted, you will probably talk to everyone about how cold the room is, joke about it, or call for a group hug to get warm. The cold room is seen as a way to make friends, create community, or make a lemon out of lemonade—after all, misery loves company. If your preference is to accept and you are an introvert, you might not even notice it is cold, or simply put on your jacket, or quietly *will* yourself warm.

Putting It All Together

Now take a look at the DISC Model, as shown in Figure 7.1. Research shows that the behaviors in each of the four groupings *hang together*. If you are *extroverted*, you will probably also be *direct, risk taking, and change-oriented*. If you are *introverted*, you will tend to also be *indirect, risk assessing, and continuity-oriented*. If you *control* your environment, then you probably also prefer to *fight in the face of conflict, judge, and act pessimistically*. If you *accept* your environment, then you probably also prefer to *flight, perceive, and act optimistically*.

Even though you may be able to relate with aspects of all four groupings, or what we call DISCpositions, you will probably find yourself identifying more strongly with one of them.

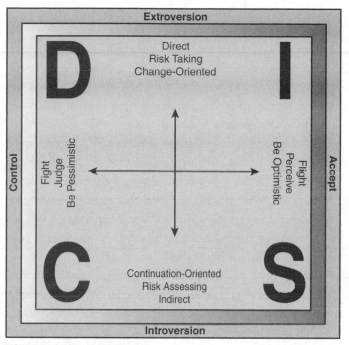

FIGURE 7.1 The DISC Model

A central premise of the DISC Model is that you are *prone* to use certain behaviors and disposed *not* to use others. You instinctively present yourself to others through your frequently used behaviors—and through the absence of certain behaviors as well. To change or adapt your behavior, you must allow yourself the possibility of acting in ways *other* than your natural preference.

Understanding your DISCposition through self-observation and reflection is a major step in preparing for leadership. But leadership implies action. What matters next is what you *do* with your understanding. The old adage from Wall Street also applies to self-knowledge: *To know and not to do is not to know.*

One of the authors was in a client-meeting with a colleague who claimed to know the DISC Model, yet continued her controlling behavior—shutting down many people in the meeting who found her energy too overwhelming to combat. The woman sensed what was happening and announced, "Sorry. It seems I've taken over; my natural DISCposition is to control." Two weeks later, the client asked that the woman be taken off the account. When she heard the news, she rationalized, "They wouldn't have been a major account anyway."

The obvious downside to this case is that the woman wasn't willing or able to overcome her inappropriate controlling behavior and rationalized it by putting the client down. But the story behind the story is that over the years, the woman had gained financial and professional success by virtue of her hard work and determination. She was able to justify her often-inappropriate behavior because of those successes. What she and her organization missed were the opportunity losses that come when inappropriate behavior is justified because it works some of the time. They missed the opportunity for leadership at a higher level that would benefit the organization and its clients. Sometimes inappropriate behavior in a work setting will be tolerated because of the financial results, but not so in our personal lives, where quality of time and relationships are at stake.

Understanding both your *natural* modes of responding and the ways in which you do *not* naturally respond allows you to choose your response more consciously—rather than reacting to a situation or *wishing* you had behaved differently. This self-knowledge enables you to be more versatile when the situation demands such versatility.

DISPOSITION-DRIVEN VERSUS VALUES-DRIVEN

Research shows that managers use both disposition (natural energy) and their values (sense of right and wrong) when influencing others.[4] But some managers are more disposition-driven than values-driven—and the difference can be startling. *Do you know if your leadership behavior is typically more disposition-driven or values-driven?*

The car you are driving could give you interesting insight into the dynamic between your disposition and values. *How* you go about buying the car will reveal your disposition: Did you study the data in *Consumer Reports*, compare government studies, and then make a choice based on careful analysis of the facts? (This is the "C" DISCposition—introverted controller.) Or did you go with your gut decision—and then use data to justify it? (This is the "D" DISCposition—extroverted controller.) Maybe you conferred or consulted with knowledgeable friends and experts to get their opinion, and then made a conservative choice that guaranteed longevity and long-term performance? (This is the "S" DISCposition—

introverted accepter.) Or maybe you noticed that cool actors in Hollywood like Leonardo DiCaprio are driving environmentally-friendly cars and bought a certain model because of his endorsement? (This is the "I" DISCposition—extroverted accepter.)

But what if you, the Leonardo fan, were more concerned with image and popularity and bought the car only because of Leo's endorsement—with no concern for the environment? Then you would have fallen prey to your disposition rather than making a values-based decision. If Leo had purchased a Hummer, you would have been willing to consider one, too—given you could afford it.

However, let's say you decide to buy an ecologically-friendly hybrid car that uses solar power or non-petroleum-based fuel *because of your commitment to the environment.* That is clearly a values-based decision—thoughtful and premeditated. *The way you go about buying* your car is usually a reflection of your DISCposition; *what* car you buy is usually more a reflection of your *values.* If you have a value around economics, you may buy a Volkswagen. If you value safety, you may buy a Volvo. If you value status, you may buy a Jaguar.

Your instinctive, preconscious *would do* behavior is your DISCposition—demonstrated in the manner in which you go about buying the car. Your thoughtful, premeditative *should do* behavior reflects your values stance—what you think is good or bad; right or wrong—demonstrated in the reasoning behind which car you buy:

- Your DISCposition—instinctive behavior that *is not* premeditated.
- Your values—thoughtful behavior that *is* premeditated.

As you have probably discovered over the course of your life, most conflicts of conscience were caused when your actions were not congruent with your values. If you want a quick values check, consider *your emotion* regarding a car you bought. For example, what if after buying the car, you suffered buyer's remorse? By reflecting on the cause of your crisis of conscience, you might discover that you breeched a personal value.

A friend of the authors bought a sexy, little, baby-blue sports car. Within a month, she had it up for sale. She had bought the car because a friend recommended it, but she realized that ultimately her choice breeched her values around economics, safety, and practicality (so she sold the baby-blue sports car and bought a powder blue Volvo). When you languish over money spent, get in touch with the emotion behind it. If you realize you could have used the money charitably, planted a new tree in your yard, or repaid a debt you owe, perhaps you've triggered a value of giving, ecology, or financial freedom.

Too often you don't realize you've breeched your values until after the fact. Not that big a deal with a car—you can return it or resell it. But it's much more difficult to undo words and actions that betray your values and good intentions when leading and dealing with people. Being aware of the difference between your disposition-driven behavior and values-driven behavior is a start toward deliberate behavior you won't regret later.

CHOOSE HOW TO BEHAVE

Mahatma Gandhi's introverted *disposition* was diametrically opposed to the demands of being a revolutionary leader. His tendency was to avoid conflict and accommodate the needs of others. His natural inclination was not to speak out, not to deal with media, and not to attract attention. But Gandhi's *values* drove him to overcome his natural tendencies and do what was necessary to achieve his goal of liberation of people through peaceful means. Gandhi was a man who had an obvious disposition, but he was values-driven.

Interestingly, when Gandhi asked his followers to meet violence with nonviolence, he was asking them to do the *unnatural* thing. Using the vision of self-determination, he compelled people to counteract their natural disposition to fight or flight. Through nonviolence, he led the most successful *peaceful* civil disobedience in history. He appealed to people's values to overcome their disposition.

Understanding the difference between *your* disposition-driven behavior and values-driven behavior provides new alternatives for behaving that may be much more appropriate, productive, and rewarding. It is brilliant when you can evaluate a situation, grasp what the circumstances are demanding from your personality, and determine what you are prepared to give in order to achieve your desired outcomes. You are challenged to do this every day as a leader. Circumstances may demand behavior that is not natural or comfortable for you, but is necessary for success. We want you to recognize that *when values are absent, your behavior defers to your disposition*—and that may limit your alternatives.

There are otherwise good leaders whose values get sabotaged by their disposition-driven behavior. Martha Stewart comes to mind. She's a woman with exemplary values concerning work—especially her own work ethic. Many Martha fans praise her *values* of not only making homemaking popular, but also raising it to an art. Martha's primary *disposition* is toward control and introversion. In fact, her preference for perfection is one of the characteristics that make her an easy mark for late-night jokesters. Ironic for a person in the public eye, her natural tendency is to protect her privacy and not reveal personal information—much like Ross Perot, who abandoned his run for the presidency to avoid media scrutiny. It was Martha's need to control her environment and her introverted, private nature that caused her to block the initial investigations into her stock dealings.

Martha is a woman with obvious values, but whose disposition-driven behavior at critical junctures may have been her undoing. What if she had thought about her values, put them in perspective, and monitored her instinctive behaviors to determine if they supported her values or sabotaged them? Would she have acted as she did? In the end, Martha's preferences for results and outcomes over people and relationships led jurors to judge her as *cold* and *aloof*, and may have resulted in a no-sympathy vote.

Of course, if you've seen Martha being interviewed by Barbara Walters or read accounts of her life, she doesn't see herself this way at all. She is very proud of relationships with her family and long-time employees. Despite her claims to the contrary, the energy she presents to the world does not engender warmth and intimacy. Here is a case where a woman's persona—her concept of herself in relation to the world around her—is very different than what most others perceive.

Martha is not alone. Most of us live inside our heads looking out at the world with our own set of glasses that often distort the way others view us. We have seen leaders go into states of shock when they receive objective feedback from direct reports that is in direct opposition with their own self-view. Our data suggests that 42 percent of the thousands of managers we assessed see themselves differently than their direct reports on written 360-degree questionnaires.

You now have information to help you find answers to the question posed by this chapter on whether your leadership behavior is disposition-driven or values-driven: *Are you aware of how your instinctive, dispositional behaviors either support, or sabotage and impede, your efforts to lead by your developed values?* This question ultimately leads to another question to be answered in Chapter 8, "Leading with Developed Values": *Are you leading with developed values or programmed values?*

ENDNOTES

1. The origins of the concept of disposition comes from the work of Carl Jung. See Jung, 1923; Marston, 1929; Kiersey and Bates, 1978; Kroeger and Thuesen, 1988; Eysenck and Eysenck, 1985; Alessandra and O'Connor, 1996; Merrill and Reid, 1981; Myers and Myers, 1980.

2. The authors wish to thank Michael O'Connor and Life Associates for allowing the inclusion of the proprietary DISC Model within this text and acknowledge that the appearance of the model herein has no impact on their exclusive ownership. Also see Zigarmi, Blanchard, O'Connor, and Edeburn, 2005.

3. Ornstein, 1993, page 51.

4. England, 1967; Deci, 1995; Zigarmi, et al., 2005.

CHAPTER 8
PREPARE: LEADING WITH DEVELOPED VALUES

Contextual Leadership tenet: Every leader leads by values—unfortunately, many are influenced by programmed values rather than developed values.

You will not be surprised, if you are like other leaders we have met and studied, that your values influence your approach to leadership.[1] What may be a revelation, however, is how much your values—and especially your follower's *perceptions* of your values—influence the motivation and morale of those you lead. Our research shows that the commitment followers have to their leader and the organization are profoundly shaped by their *perceptions* of what the leader values.[2]

To be an effective leader, you must not only be clear about the values you hold, but also how your values are being perceived by others. Leaders often forget that they earn the right to lead by representing the dreams of those who follow.

The president of a company takes his young V.P. of Sales to a posh new housing development. As they stand on a bluff overlooking the impressive development, the president points to a spread closest to them, "Look at that house down there—it must be an acre and a half, 5,000 square feet, perfect for building a horse corral." Pointing to another house he exclaims, "That one is even better. Six thousand square feet, two acres—room for a swimming pool." Then he turns to the V.P., puts his arm around the young man's shoulders, and tells him, "If you keep working as hard as you've been working and continue to exceed your numbers, someday all of this will be mine."

> ### Defining Values
>
> A value is an enduring belief that a particular end or mean is more socially or individually preferable than another end or mean.

Your *values* are premeditated, cognitive standards of what you consider to be better or best versus what is bad or not good. Leadership problems in organizations attributed to *miscommunication* are often just the opposite—they are problems that arise from *clearly communicated differences* in values.[3]

Perhaps the most important reason to explore your values as a leader is because values influence the reasons you want to lead and ultimately the legacy you leave.

BEGIN WITH BELIEFS

A key word in the definition of values is *belief*. Because values are built on an underlying foundation of basic beliefs, the exploration of your values must begin with your beliefs.

A belief is the *mental acceptance* that some idea or perception is true. A belief is not just the idea or concept, but also the *conviction* that the idea or concept fits a patterned reality. *The sun always rises in the morning and sets at night* is a belief. You formed this belief through observation, and your direct experience watching the sun rise and set daily confirms the validity of your belief. It helps that there is consensus among others that the belief is true. But as solid as this belief is, it probably didn't lead to a value. All values are beliefs, *but not all beliefs are values*. Some beliefs are more central or core to your values than others. So in the exploration and development of your values, you won't be analyzing at all your beliefs—just those that are underlying key values.

The quality of your values will ultimately be determined by the source of your beliefs. For example, when your beliefs are tied to an expert or authority—whether it's a religious leader, *The New York Times,* or your parents—your beliefs and values are only as solid as that authority. When doubt is cast on the source of your beliefs, your derived beliefs are cast in doubt—and so too, any values associated with those beliefs. Fallen role models and discredited authority figures often cause shaken values.

You should question your beliefs to determine if they are valid and appropriate through your direct experience and deductive conclusions, but also by examination of what others experience. Have you ever watched the auditions for television's *American Idol* or the international equivalents? What you witness are people with beliefs based on their own experience—*I believe I'm a great singer*—that have absolutely zero consensus among others. Their belief in their singing ability is the most difficult type of belief to challenge. It is a belief that comes from personal experience that doesn't seem to include the consensus of others. Imagine their disillusionment when their beliefs are held up against overwhelming differences of opinion. Some seem stunned at the verdict; others are unwilling to acknowledge that their belief may be invalid and attack the judges who issued the verdict. This is why it is important to test your beliefs and be uncompromisingly dedicated to the truth from several trusted sources of verification.

Your first challenge as you explore your values will be to examine your underlying *beliefs* that have led to those values by questioning: *How did I come to this value? Is the value based on my experience? Have others validated my value?* You will most likely discover that not all values are created equal— some are programmed and some are developed.

PROGRAMMED VALUES

Programmed values are taken for granted without the benefit of conscious and conscientious reflection. A programmed value is a value that you have acted upon over time without direct experience with the value or conscious examination of other alternatives. You may have many programmed values derived from your upbringing and life experiences. But programmed values can fall apart when challenged because you have never bothered to get beneath the surface of the value.

Let's say you grew up with vegetarian parents in a communal environment surrounded by a vegetarian lifestyle where you were never fed meat or meat by-products as a child. While being a vegetarian may be central or core to your being, if you have simply accepted the lifestyle without conscious examination, the value must be considered programmed. If you simply followed what your parents dictated, then being a vegetarian should be considered programmed.

A risk you face with programmed versus developed values is that when faced with alternate choices—in this case, different ways of eating and living—your so-called values might not hold up over time, and you may not continue to act on them.

As part of a women's studies course she was taking in college, a bright young woman we know found herself asking: *Where did I get my values?* She found herself wondering where her stances on issues such as race, gender, sex, marriage, and other pithy issues had been planted and cultivated. She set up interviews with her parents, siblings, longtime friends, and babysitters to collect stories and anecdotes that could help her ultimately determine what she had come to believe as a result of others' prompting versus her own volition. What she did is a healthy exercise for any adult—revealing the distinction between her programmed values and her *developed* values.

DEVELOPED VALUES

A developed value is formed through direct experience with the object of the belief, examination of the alternatives, and the anticipation of possible consequences. Your value is only a developed value if it meets five criteria:[4]

1. **A developed value is freely chosen.**

   When a value is freely chosen, it means it is not coerced. You have had the opportunity to freely question the source of the underlying belief and trust that it is valid and appropriate for you.

2. **A developed value is chosen from alternatives.**

   In order to make values conscious, they must be weighed against other alternatives. Gandhi was raised as a vegetarian in India. As a young man, he noticed that the Brits, who were the ruling class, ate meat. Perhaps this was the source of their power, he reasoned. One night, he and a friend pilfered some meat, and in a secret tryst, ate it.

Even though he became violently ill, Gandhi continued to eat meat, hoping to experience the strength and vitality that he believed was required for his people to overcome British tyranny.

You don't have to literally try or experience the alternatives to your values—certainly if you value life, you don't need to experience murder as an alternative! However, you do need to have given thoughtful consideration as to why you value life and what might happen if you don't. If more people truly considered alternatives to their current values, they might discover an entire world of opportunity for living and working at a higher level. What if more organizations considered the alternatives of existing for profit and explored servant leadership or embraced a vision that served the welfare of the whole? They would find organizations prospering and flourishing beyond expectations.[5]

3. **A developed value is chosen with an understanding of the consequences of the alternatives.**

   After years of experiencing the alternative to being a vegetarian, Gandhi came to realize that eating meat had nothing to do with the political issues that were the source of his passion. He reconsidered his values on the matter. He understood the consequences of both alternatives. In tribute to his people and lifestyle, Gandhi consciously embraced vegetarianism—he realized that to lead his people to freedom, he must embody their common values. Gandhi had elevated his eating habit from a programmed value to a developed value through consideration of the alternatives and its consequences.[6]

4. **A developed value is acted on over time.**

   All developed values have a behavioral component. You may claim to have a value, but a developed value is backed up by your behavior over time. While there may be exceptions, it is a major contradiction to say you value something but then not act on the value over time. Your credibility as a leader is at stake if you say you value teamwork, but reward individual performance over team effort; if you say you value promptness, but always arrive late; or if you say you value life balance, but work 80 hours a week and expect others to follow suit. You risk not being seen as a values-driven leader when you don't act on your espoused values.

5. **A developed value is prized or publicly owned.**

A developed value can stand the light of day. You may not relish having a particular value blasted on the evening news, but do you really value something if you can't share it with your loved ones? In the work setting, declaring a value allows you to test your value in light of others' perceptions—giving them a chance to help you examine possible alternatives and anticipate consequences. This can also be uncomfortable. Have you ever given an employee a bonus but been afraid to admit it to others? Have you ever worried that co-workers would discover that you agreed with a decision your boss made, fearing they'd consider you a traitor? Prizing or public affirmation of a value allows you to test your emotional attachment or conviction to the value.

KEY QUESTIONS TO SHIFT YOUR VALUES

How do you begin shifting from programmed values to developed values? Ask these four key questions to sort, organize, and better understand values on a specific issue:

1. **What is the end value?**

An *end value* describes a future outcome or final state that is desired for you or others.

2. **Is the end value others-focused or self-focused?**

Others-focused end values focus on what future end state is best *for others.* With an others-focused end value, the concern is what a particular group requires rather than what is required for a given individual.

Self-focused end values focus on what is best for you and do not imply the inclusion of others.

3. **What is/are the means values?**

Means values describe the way you want to go about achieving an end value—it is your belief about the best way to bring your end value to fruition.

4. **Are the means values social or personal?**

Social means values focus on the best way to accomplish or bring about an outcome for others involved, advocate the way others should accomplish an outcome, and implies how you will treat others.

Personal means values focus on the best or right way for you to accomplish or bring about your particular outcome and achieve your end values, but does not imply the best way for others to achieve their ends. Means values that are personally focused are not particularly concerned with the moral or social *shoulds* for others.

UNDERSTANDING EACH OTHER—A MATTER OF ENDS AND MEANS

Distinguishing between ends and means values is not only helpful for understanding your own values, but also for discovering the source of most values dilemmas and conflicts.

For example, let's say that you and your spouse both have a value to raise honest children. This is an *end value*—it describes a future outcome or final state that you desire for yourself or others. An end value is something you want to achieve, or cause to come about, or work toward—an outcome you want for yourself or others over a period of time.

So, the fact that you and your spouse agree on an end value of raising honest children is a good thing. But, ends values do not dictate means values. A *means value* describes the way you want to go about achieving an end value—it is your belief about the best way to bring your end value to fruition. This is where you and your spouse could get into conflict, especially since means values may not be understood, obvious, or discussed. For example, you believe that the best way to raise children to be honest is through strict adherence to established rules and boundaries. Therefore, you punish, spank, and hold them accountable whenever they lie. Your spouse, however, has a different set of means values and believes the way to raise honest children is through demonstrated tenderness, tolerance of the natural unfolding of the innate goodness of a child, and thoughtful dialogue about why certain behavior isn't acceptable.

Matching values is the greatest determinant of lasting and meaningful relationships; mismatching values is the greatest determinant of interpersonal conflict.[7] If you and your spouse don't distinguish differences between your means values, you could endanger the relationship. The discrepancy between the means values concerning *how* to produce the shared end value may result in you and your spouse having many unclear disagreements until the difference between means are understood. From your perspective, it's difficult to believe your spouse wants to raise honest children when he or she doesn't uphold rules, hold children accountable, or care enough to do the hard work of tough love by an occasional, appropriate spanking. If your differing means values lead you to believe that your spouse and you have differing ends values, the relationship is at risk of unraveling.

In the workplace, comparing ends and means values is a critical component for understanding yourself in relation to others. For example, if your primary end value is to create an organization that makes the world a better place, and your business partner's primary end value is to create wealth for all senior-level executives within five years, you may not want to be in business together—there's an obvious mismatch in ends values that will influence what long- and short-term decisions are made.

Let's say that you and your partner both agree on an end value—to create products and services that exceed the expectations of the customers. The issue then becomes: How do you propose to go about doing that? *You* mean to organize the workplace by following traditions and policies that hold employees responsible for the welfare of the customer. But your partner means to organize the workplace based on employees' rights that encourage them to take initiative and act on their own conscience to create customer satisfaction. You are both working hard to create a successful organization, but you believe in very different approaches. Over time, you get irritated because your partner seems to ignore or bypass the traditional paths of communication and decision making and embraces what you consider situational standards; your partner gets irritated because you appear attached to dogma and are loyal to traditions that may seem outdated for the circumstances.

Sorting through ends and means values will reveal the operating *values point of view* that you and others bring to a particular issue. The clarity that results from determining your and others values point of view leads to the understanding and empathy needed to resolve potential or existing conflict.

FROM ENDS AND MEANS TO A VALUES POINT OF VIEW

To determine a values point of view on a particular issue, plug the answers to the four key questions posed earlier into an organizing framework. This simple framework, with ends values as the vertical axis and means values as the horizontal axis, results in four values points of view, as shown in Figure 8.1.

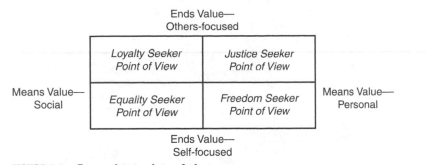

FIGURE 8.1   **Four values points of view**

Notice that the name given to each point of view describes the primary stance of its combination of ends and means values.[8] These names are generalized ways to capture the focus of that point of view:

- Loyalty Seekers find meaning in the values of the group to which they belong.
- Equality Seekers pursue equal opportunity to have their ends met through social means.
- Justice Seekers desire to serve the welfare of the whole through their own individualized actions.
- Freedom Seekers attach great worth in exercising their unrestrained rights and options.

We'll help you understand more about the qualities inherent in each values point of view, but for now the titles will simplify your use of the model.

As these different points of view are clarified, try to *suspend judgment* about what is good or bad and right or wrong. Don't allow potential prejudices to cloud your understanding and appreciation for the best aspects of each point of view. Otherwise, you may reject certain types of values before truly understanding them or their attributes. Each has produced history makers, great leaders, and notable men and women.[9]

You have the opportunity here to bring your programmed values to light, reflect on them, determine if they are still relevant, and potentially develop new values. Figure 8.2 gives you additional insight into the four Values Points of View and their requisite ends and means values.

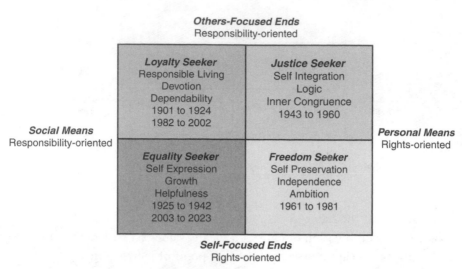

FIGURE 8.2   Values Points of View Model

USING THE VALUES POINT OF VIEW MODEL

Building off the Gandhi example described earlier, let's say you are considering becoming a vegetarian. In and of itself, "vegetarian" is not a values point of view. However, answering the four key questions and applying the Values Point of View Model in Figure 8.2, you can explore and identify your value(s) on the issue:

1. What is my end value?

   Let's say your response to the question is: *To stop the ill-treatment of animals.*

2. Is my end value others-focused or self-focused?

   You have expressed an others-focused end value (*It's about the animals*).

3. What are my means values?

   Let's say your response is: To join an animal rights group that advocates abstaining from meat.

4. Are my means values social or personal?

   You have expressed a social means value (*I'm loyal to a particular group of like-minded people*).

The combination of *others-focused end* and *social means* puts you squarely in the *Loyalty Seeker Point of View*. Different ends and means values regarding a vegetarian lifestyle play out differently on the model, as seen in Figure 8.3. Notice that each point of view may have the same result—a vegetarian lifestyle—but the motives (ends values) and methods (means values) are different in each case.

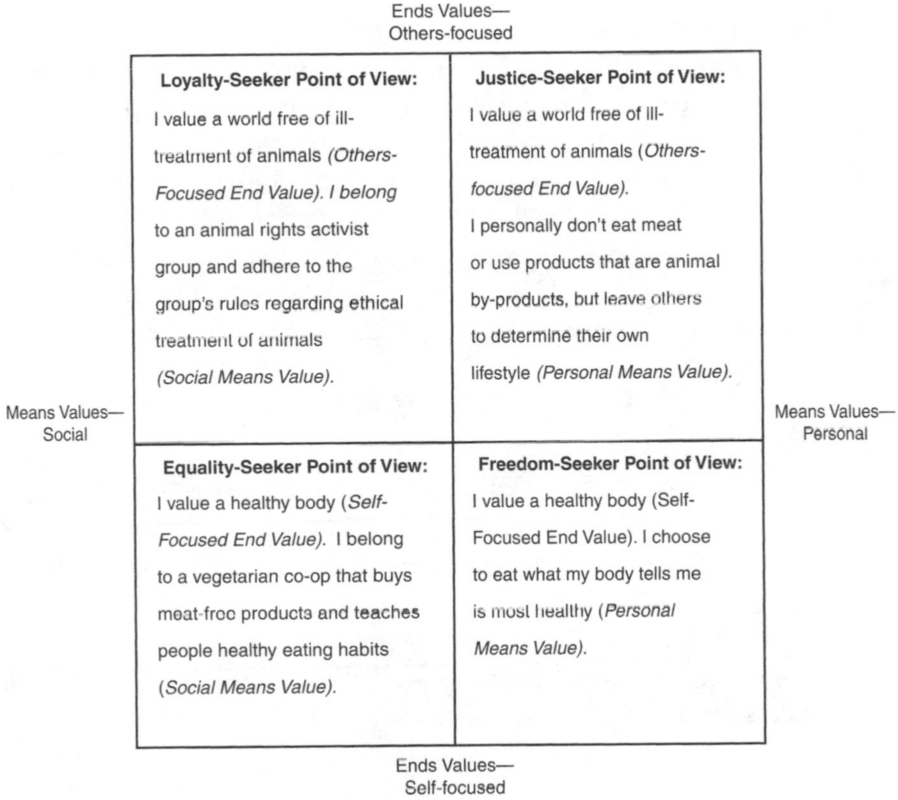

Ends Values—
Others-focused

Loyalty-Seeker Point of View:	Justice-Seeker Point of View:
I value a world free of ill-treatment of animals *(Others-Focused End Value)*. I belong to an animal rights activist group and adhere to the group's rules regarding ethical treatment of animals *(Social Means Value)*.	I value a world free of ill-treatment of animals *(Others-focused End Value)*. I personally don't eat meat or use products that are animal by-products, but leave others to determine their own lifestyle *(Personal Means Value)*.
Equality-Seeker Point of View:	Freedom-Seeker Point of View:
I value a healthy body *(Self-Focused End Value)*. I belong to a vegetarian co-op that buys meat-free products and teaches people healthy eating habits *(Social Means Value)*.	I value a healthy body (Self-Focused End Value). I choose to eat what my body tells me is most healthy *(Personal Means Value)*.

Means Values—
Social

Means Values—
Personal

Ends Values—
Self-focused

FIGURE 8.3   Values Points of View Example

To understand a co-worker's underlying beliefs that led to her vegetarian lifestyle, interview her and discover her rationale, motives, and intent, from which you can deduce her values point of view:

1. What is her end value? *To have a healthy body.*

2. Is her end value others-focused or self-focused? *It is a self-focused end value.*

3. What is her means value? *I eat what my body tells me is good for it, so I'm refraining from eating meat in order not to pollute my body.*

4. Is her means value social or personal? *It is a personal means value.*

Your co-worker has a Freedom Seeker Point of View with self-focused ends and personal means when it comes to her vegetarian lifestyle.

As you become aware of your values, determine if they truly reflect the way you live or *want* to live. Do you have an Equality Seeker Values Point of View in a Loyalty Seeker workplace and wonder why you feel disconnected from the goals and mission of the organization? Would your programmed values stand up under scrutiny or challenge? Do you have a Loyalty Seeker Values Point of View you inherited from parents you deeply respected, but with little appreciation for the historical merit of the values? If your values are developed, how do they serve you and your leadership aspirations? Do you have a Freedom Seeker mindset in a Loyalty Seeker setting that causes you to question the rules, policies, and procedures that the organization expects you to uphold? Are the beliefs that led to your values still valid?

GENERATIONAL VALUES

Generational values easily translate into programmed values. In a fascinating study, researchers William Strauss and Neil Howe were able to track the Values Points of View through generations. They found that the combination of ends and means values repeat sequentially in a fixed pattern over time—and have documented it from 1584 in America![10]

You may have noticed that the Values Point of View Model in Figure 8.2 depicts a set of dates representing a cohort group of people born within the same generation. These cohort groups share a history and significant cultural phenomenon that help shape their beliefs—and thereby their values. Together, each generation lived by values derived from their common experiences. It's important to realize that just because you were born into a particular generation doesn't automatically mean you share their values—but chances are you do, unless your values were conscientiously determined by forces more persuasive than the collective experience of your peer cohort group.[11]

Understanding the potential of programmed values in each generation can help you better understand the different motivations of workers in your organization and develop strategies for communicating and appealing to all four values types. Programmed values are also heaven-sent for advertisers needing to appeal to the values of a particular generational group. But as discussed in the earlier section on the risks of programmed values, it is wise to remember that such values can be easily shaken. It is especially imperative for you in a leadership role to not stand on potentially tenuous programmed values, but to embrace values that have been developed through thoughtful consideration.

THE CHALLENGE AND PROMISE OF DEVELOPING YOUR VALUES

We encourage you to begin a conscious and conscientious effort to develop values through self-observation. Monitor your everyday decisions—they are an expression of the values you hold. Consider decisions you've made just this week: to exercise, or not; to attend church, or not; to eat that extra piece of cake, or not. Look at the decisions you have made regarding your time and money: How did you spend your time while your boss was out of town? Did you put that in-room movie on your expense report? Did you fudge on the mileage you reported? Did you attend the town meeting to oppose the new development? Did you take the time to mentor a colleague? Did you pay off this month's credit card balance? Did you give a handout to the homeless person who approached you on the street? What percentage of your paycheck did you donate to charity?

Leadership requires that you are conscious and conscientious about the values you declare, and more importantly, the values you live. This doesn't mean you become inflexible, dogmatic, or unreasonable when faced with alternative values. It does mean that you have a position to push alternative ideas against—to compare and contrast other points of view in search of your best truth. Values give you a way to make decisions that feel right for you and the circumstances. It means that you are clear about which issues are worth fighting for, dying for, and living for.

Leadership also demands awareness of how your *values and disposition both influence your leadership behavior*. It is more likely that your instinctive, disposition-driven behavior will override underdeveloped or unexamined programmed values and sabotage your outcomes; inappropriate disposition-driven behavior is less likely to rule if you are guided by thoughtfully developed values that enable you to act, live, and lead with intention. To be a values-driven leader, you need to answer a resounding *Yes* to the following statements or know how to use the four key questions and the Values Point of View Model to get to *Yes*:

- *What motivates me to be a leader?*
- *What ends do I want to accomplish as a leader?*
- *What means will I use as a leader to achieve those ends?*
- *I have examined the alternatives, prioritized, and considered how my values contribute to my leadership effectiveness.*
- *I am aware of the impact my values have on the people I lead.*

ENDNOTES

1. See Zigarmi, et al., 2004, Chapter 7; England, 1972; Reynierse, et al., 2000; Macy, 1995; Murphy, et al., 1997.

2. See Zigarmi, et al., 2004, Chapter 7.

3. England, 1972.

4. For a more extensive treatment of these criteria, see Raths, Harmin, and Simon, 1966; Rokeach, 1972, 1973, 1979.

5. Collins and Porras, 2002.

6. See Fischer, 1950.

7. One side of the values coin is that the greatest determinant of lasting friendships and meaningful relationships is having a values match. For example, a black man and a white man are more likely to be friends when their values match than two black men (or two white men) whose values do not. People seem to be more fair-minded about race than they are about beliefs that are different from their own (Rokeach, 1972).

   But the other side of the values coin is how values differences lead to misunderstandings, acrimony, divisiveness, and a lack of an agreed-upon focus. A perceived similarity or dissimilarity between people's belief systems is the basis for rejection or acceptance of others. This principle of perceived beliefs has direct implications for the way you approach people. You are constantly evaluating—whether you realize it or not—if another person's beliefs are similar or dissimilar to your own.

8. These titles have been used differently depending on the authors, yet the four points of view have been firmly researched. Massey, 1981; O'Connor, 1986; and Zigarmi, et al., 2004 use the terms Traditionalist, Inbetweener, Challenger, and Synthesizer. Strauss and Howe, 1991, 1997; and Howe and Strauss, 1993 use the terms Civics, Adoptors, Reactors, and Idealists.

9. Strauss and Howe, 1991.

10. Ibid.

11. **Loyalty Seekers born 1901–1924.** People with this values point of view grew up during the founding years of the Boy Scouts; they came of age together with Charles Lindbergh's transatlantic flight; and were the generation most affected by Pearl Harbor Sunday and the subsequent world war. Cohort members include Walt Disney, Bob Hope, Walter Cronkite, Billy Graham, and Lee Iacocca. This is the generation responsible for John Steinbeck's *The Grapes of Wrath*, John Kennedy's *Profiles in Courage*, and *The Honeymooners* television show starring Jackie Gleason—all of which reflect a generation characterized by their allegiance to civic duty and which experienced the striving of upward mobility, which resulted in the greatest leap in home ownership in the twentieth century. All but two of the presidents of the United States over the past 50 years came from this generation: Lyndon B. Johnson, Ronald Reagan, Richard Nixon, Gerald Ford, John F. Kennedy, Jimmy Carter, and the first George Bush.

Equality Seekers born 1925—1942. People such as Marilyn Monroe, Andy Warhol, Woody Allen, and Clint Eastwood grew up watching *Snow White* set box office records while the Great Depression lingered, and were young men and women when the atomic bombs were dropped. Their contributions to culture surely reflect something about their values stance—from the introduction of *Playboy* magazine that fostered a social means to achieving very personal ends for self gratification, as well as *Sesame Street* reflecting their social means for achieving education for the young via mass media. This is the only generation in the twentieth century that did not produce a president of the United States, but it also spawned virtually every major figure in the modern civil rights movement—from Martin Luther King, Jr., to Malcolm X, from Cesar Chavez's farmworkers' union to Russell Means' American Indian Movement.

Justice-Seekers born 1943–1960. People with this values point of view had Benjamin Spock to thank for their upbringing; were impressionable youngsters when the TV age began; took the first polio vaccine; shaped and helped shape the free speech movement; and fought, died in, and protested the Vietnam War. Cohort members include Oliver North and Angela Davis, Donald Trump and Oprah Winfrey, and Steven Jobs and Bill Gates. Gary Trudeau's *Doonesbury* cartoon strip reflects this generation's questioning of the traditional political landscape, and Spike Lee's *Do the Right Thing* reflects their value to serve others through their own efforts. This generation has produced two presidents of the United States thus far: Bill Clinton and the second George Bush.

Freedom Seekers born 1961–1981. People with this values point of view were born the same year as the birth-control pill was approved; were young children when Roe v. Wade was judged; and watched the *Challenger* spacecraft explode on takeoff. Their cohorts include Michael J. Fox and Eddie Murphy, Tom Cruise and Mary Lou Retton, and Mike Tyson and Michael Jordan. Their cultural contributions reflect their desire to reinvent traditional social constructs, from *Liar's Poker* by Michael Lewis, Steven Soderbergh's *sex, lies, and videotape*, and *As Nasty as They Wanna Be* by 2 Live Crew.

CHAPTER 9
PREPARE: INVESTIGATING YOUR PERSONA

Contextual Leadership tenet: Investigating your persona can be used as a tool for understanding and adapting or changing your leadership behavior.

To borrow again from the great philosopher Flip Wilson, your persona screams *What You See Is What You Get!* One reason that line was such a brilliant farce is that you knew it wasn't true. Everyone puts on a public face—and some faces are obvious masks that either intentionally or unintentionally obfuscate the person beneath. Your *persona* is the fourth aspect of your personality, and when you investigate it, you are breaking through the façade, or mask, that you present to the world as *you*.

What you see is rarely what you get. Instead, what you show to the world is represented in everyday life through your behavior, but inwardly it is an ever-evolving complex set of rationalizations, historical precedents, diminished interpretations of events and experiences, and needed self-delusions—not to mention potentially conflicting DISCpositions and Values Point of View.

> **Defining Persona**
>
> Persona is the social mask or façade you present to the world generated from a historical accumulation of the disposition-driven and values-driven behavior you draw from to cope with daily experiences.

Your persona is expressed at a moment of time based on your historical experience with your disposition and values. But history does not have to repeat itself if it is understood. Your persona is ever-evolving because you have the capacity for introspection; you have the capacity to shape the future. With reflection, you can investigate the functionality of your behavior (your expressed disposition and values), recognize historical patterns, and then either continue them or decide to change them.

For example, suppose your most comfortable disposition has been as an introverted, reserved, and, some might say, aloof person. Others see few displays of emotion or demonstrations of affection from you. You tend to keep your opinions to yourself and value learning and personal quests. You will support the common ways of doing things and want others to have the same opportunity. These characteristics can be described as your introverted, controlling disposition ("C" DISCposition) and your self ends and social means values (Equality Seeker Values Point of View). This combination of disposition-driven and values-driven behavior conspire to create a persona that you present to others as *you*.

What others see from the outside is a human being acting in an instance, but which is actually a result of life experiences that reveal a pattern over time.

THE PERSONA TRIAD—THE REVELATION OF YOU

What if you could begin to see the connections between your introverted disposition, a historical pattern of important people in your life belittling your ideas at critical times in your past, and your tendency not to speak up and express your views directly during team meetings?

Your persona is like a composite mask you show the world, but behind the mask is a set of *multiple selves*:

A. *The person you think you are* (including the physical and psychological personal traits, characteristics, and beliefs as reflected in your disposition and values that shape your capacity to achieve your ideal self).

B. *The person you want to be* (the ideal self to which you aspire).

C. *The person you think others expect you to be* (your perception of the social and functional demands on you).

To become more intentional, you need to understand the three forces at work behind the scenes of your persona, as illustrated in Figure 9.1, the Persona Triad.

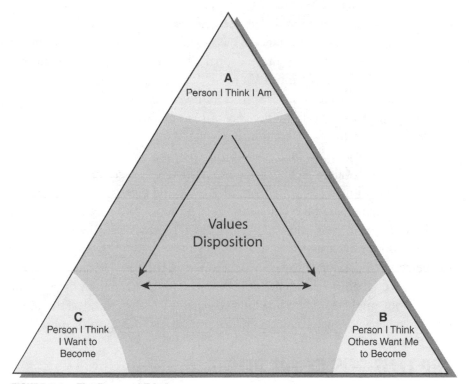

FIGURE 9.1 **The Personal Triad**

When any of these three forces are not understood, you can become imbalanced, rigid, or unresponsive to the requirements of work, family, and society. Have you ever known someone with a dysfunctional habit or pattern that is rigidly frozen in who they think they are? They know the pattern doesn't work; you know it doesn't work. But, for that person, nothing changes.

Take Tom as an example. His professional success has come at the expense of his health, as well as his personal and professional relationships. He doesn't make the connection between his driven lifestyle and his ill-health. He doesn't view himself as others see him—in fact, even though he's been given feedback to pull back on his controlling energy, he dismisses the feedback and seeks ways to justify or rationalize his behavior.

He is a natural extroverted controller who is risk-taking, change-oriented, and direct in his communication ("D" DISCposition). He intuitively tends to fight rather than flight, make judgments about how things do or don't meet his preconceived expectations, and looks at the world pessimistically—as a place full of challenges that need to be overcome. Sometimes his values can be others-focused, but more often than not, his self-focus ends form the basis for his rights-oriented stance. To others, Tom's actions appear to be for reasons of self-preservation and personal pleasure. He appears to have a Freedom Seeker Values Point of View.

If Tom were aware of his disposition, he might decide to adapt it in a situation where it is getting in the way of his outcomes. For example, when his direct controlling and confronting style is preventing resolution to a business deal, he could back off and let the customer come to their own conclusion. If Tom's values were developed rather than programmed, he might understand the impact of his self-oriented ends and means values on his lack of long-term, meaningful relationships.

It would be a great improvement and aid Tom's cause if he understood how to monitor his disposition-driven and values-driven behavior and adapt his personal and leadership behavior. However, if he understood the three forces at work behind the scenes of his persona, as illustrated in the Persona Triad, Tom might gain the insight necessary to *change* the dysfunctional, repetitive behavior that sabotages his dreams, goals, and relationships.

THE TENSIONS OF THE PERSONA

Natural tensions exist among the three forces of your persona. The negative implications of being unaware of, ignoring, or refusing to behave in ways that release the tensions between each force are shown in Figure 9.2.

Building on Tom's extreme case, his extroverted controlling disposition, in tandem with what others interpret as self-indulgent values, are incredibly energy draining to those around him. Tom presents a persona that is a direct, blatantly self-interested, self-serving exterior that gives notice to all that consideration is given, first and foremost, to what's most beneficial to him. There seems to be little compromise with environmental demands or expectations.

Even though Tom might say he wants to be more of what others want him to be, he refuses to move from who he thinks he is (A) to (B). His ex-wife, though respectful and appreciative of many of his fine qualities, has continually expressed chagrin at his *I am what I am* attitude and resistance for inner examination. When situations arise, Tom's frequent first response is always in light of how it will affect him, rather than empathizing or examining the needs of others experiencing the situation. Given Tom's self-focus and his overpowering, controlling energy that demands attention at the expense of anyone else's needs, one might wonder why others tolerate him at all. Tom, as others who can justify or rationalize their behavior, can also be incredibly bright, quick, and results-oriented. Sadly, people interact with Tom not because of their affection or fondness for him, but for what he can do or accomplish for them. This is ironic, because one of the things Tom admits is that he is ready for companionship, in need of meaningful friendships, and aching for an enduring relationship.

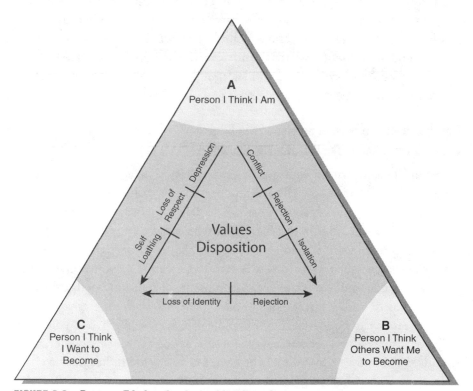

FIGURE 9.2   **Persona Triad—the downside of no change**

Not Resolving Tension Between Who You
Think You Are and What Others Want You to Be

If you say *No* to being what others expect and focus on staying the person you think you are, you may experience conflict, rejection, and if sustained over time, isolation. You run the risk of being a self-indulgent rebel or eccentric.

The tension between points A (the person you think you are) and B (the person you think others expect you to be) comes from deciding whether or not you will put the effort toward changing your behavior to meet the expectations and desires others have of you.

Not Resolving the Tension Between Who You
Think You Are and Who You Want to Become

Another tension exists between the person you think you are (A) and the person you want to become (C). The downside of not moving toward your ideal self can weigh heavily on your psyche. If you continue to live with your limitations, failures, and lack of ability to cope with the demands of living, a feeling of depression, loss of self-respect, and self-loathing can set in. Within everyone's life, a certain amount of effort must be put into self-change and movement toward the ideal self—or a conscious attempt at moving toward your concept of an ideal *leader* if you plan to be an effective leader over the long term.

Not Resolving the Tension Between Who Others
Want You to Be and Who You Want to Become

The third tension within your persona exists between the person you think others want you to become (B) and the person *you* wish you were (C). It is a difficult—almost untenable—position to live an existence in which the person you want to be is in direct conflict with what others expect.

When others want you to be something that is against the person you want to be, especially if the pressure is extreme, it can force you to go against your better inner judgment and act in inhumane, illegal, and unethical ways. If you conform to the expectations of others and forsake acting as your ideal self, the result can be loss of identity and self-esteem—like when you wear a tie because the dress code demands it, but you don't want to; or when your friends convinced you to do drugs or have sex when you didn't want to.

On the other hand, if you ignore or act contrary to what others expect and remain true to your ideal self, you may suffer the loss of others' esteem and rejection in their eyes of the person you want to be.

There can be an upside to resolving the tensions of the persona, as seen in Figure 9.3.

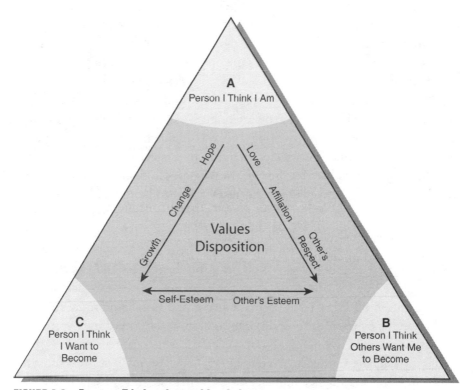

FIGURE 9.3   Persona Triad—the upside of change

The psychic payoff for moving from point A to point B is that other people may respect you more, love you more, and affiliate with you over time. It is reassuring to receive the love, adoration, and respect of others in a leadership or nonleadership situation. The trick here is to be discerning—to be sure those you are moving toward are people you value and with whom you have or wish to have meaningful relationships going forward. There must be a mutual interest in moving toward *their* version of the ideal you.

The psychic payoff for moving from A to C, from who you think you are toward your ideal self, is easily stated: You are filled with hope and the satisfaction that comes from change and growth.

An unbeatable situation is when you find yourself moving toward a point that *both you and others agree is the ideal you.* There's a triple whammy when these forces of your persona are in sync. Two authors of this book had a powerful experience using the Persona Triad. Susan was working hard to meet a publishing deadline when Drea walked into her home office. Immediately Susan started explaining her litany of woes to Drea: "People are counting on me and I'm not sure I can meet their expectations! I've been working night and day and there's still so much to do! It's not like this book is the only thing on my plate, but it's the only thing I can focus on right now, so other things are being left undone!"

Drea looked at Susan with compassion, and in his understated way, asked: "Are you enjoying what you are doing?" At that moment, Susan realized that she indeed loved writing and was living her dream of being an employed author. She was, in fact, merging points A and C—who she was and who she wanted to be. So why was she complaining, whining, and sending off such negative vibes? She also wanted to be more like the person he wanted her to be—to move from A to B—not just to please him, but because it was the best thing for her as well. She wanted to create a spirit-filled home and workplace for herself and Drea. She knew that's what he hoped for her—that her work would bring her happiness and joy, not stress and negative energy. She considered the Persona Triad—the fact that her direct-controlling DISCposition made her prone to take on more than she could handle, over-promise, and get uptight about all the things on her to-do list. At that moment, Susan decided she wanted to be more values-driven; she wanted to overcome her natural tendencies to gain sympathy from others for her immense work schedule and instead imbue her environment with a sense of calm and positive (albeit productive) energy. She wanted to be consciously grateful for the work she was doing and to create a home and work environment where Drea felt good about walking in the door.

When you move from where you think you are (A) toward a place that satisfies the forces of *both* B and C, there's a greater impetus for you to overcome the limitations of your disposition, values, and history and change your behavior. It's like when you work really hard because you actually *want* to go into your father's or mother's business, or when you strive to live your faith and spiritual beliefs as part of a like-minded group of people, or when you let go of a petty irritant to maintain the harmony of a relationship.

Then there are times when you make a conscious choice to *not* resolve the tension between who you think you are and what others want you to be—such as when you protest as a conscientious objector and refuse to go to war. The pain of that loss and rejection is offset only by the pride of maintaining your integrity and upholding your values.

FRODO—A PERSONA IN CRISIS

Despite Tolkien's claim that *The Lord of the Rings* was just a good adventure yarn without political or psychological underpinnings, we keep finding metaphorical meaning behind the story. One of the most enduring insights is the internal struggle—or tensions of the persona—of the central character, Frodo. A handful of enlightened beings entrust pure, innocent, and naïve Frodo with the task of transporting a ring to its source so it can be destroyed. They understand that the ring imbues its wearer with unlimited power and that anyone who possesses the ring is likely to fall prey to its control. It is this power that has made the ring an object of desire since its creation. It is an awesome duty, for it is nearly impossible for one to resist the lure of such power. Frodo's efforts to carry the burden and not succumb to its power is a perfect symbolic example of the struggle each of us has between the person we think we are, the person we wish or hope to be, and the person we think others expect us to be. Frodo wanted to live up to the ideals he had for himself—having seen what the ring did to his friend Bilbo and to the creature Gollum. He also had a need to live up to the expectations of those who trusted him with the duty to destroy the ring. The fate of all mankind (and thus, hobbits, dwarves, and elves) hung in the balance.

Yet with all Frodo's best intentions, the lure of power was great—as is the lure for all of us to behave in ways that bring us (our ego) power. Frodo was not a superhero. He was a humble, mild-mannered, gentle young man. His struggle becomes our struggle. As a leader, how do you resist the allure of power over others? How do you resist the allure of social status and prestige; the payoffs of lots and lots of money and adoration? How do you handle the pressure of making hard choices that seem to please no one in particular, but are for the greater good of all? How do you resist the lure of behavior that feels good in the moment, for behavior that will help you achieve your higher aspirations? How do you use your understanding of your persona to adapt or change your behavior so that it supports your ideals?

In Tom's less-mythical realistic case, there is some alignment between who he wishes he could be and the person others want or need. So what prevents him from moving in the direction of his ideal self and the ideal of others? This is where the Persona Triad can be a helpful tool for gaining insight into patterns of behavior. By investigating the historical tensions that exist in the Persona Triad, Tom could come to realize that his competitive drive, need to overcome obstacles, love of challenge, and his loud, confronting style are patterns begun at an early age and reinforced in some way during critical times in his life.

First, Tom could investigate what he thinks others have expected of him over time and how it influenced his behavior. He was an only child for 12 years before his little sister came into the world. Based on his belief that his parents had certain expectations of him compared to his baby sister, Tom found himself competing with her for his parent's attention—especially his father's. His little sister was the apple of his father's eye, and Tom felt a need to constantly prove himself. In fact, his father promoted the behavior, often pitting child against child by comparing successes and admirable qualities. Tom decided that the only way he could be heard was to shout and control what was happening around him; the only way he could win affection was to compete and take on challenges; and the only way he could be loved was to win.

Historically, Tom's behavior is repeated over and over, based on and reinforced by his accumulated reflections and memories of significant life experiences in his past. His outward manner is a manifestation of his little understood historical self in collusion with his extroverted, controlling disposition and self-focused values.

What if Tom realized that his current behavior wasn't purposeful or the result of thoughtful choices, but repeated historical patterns? Perhaps he would be more likely, able, and prone to change his dysfunctional behavior—which leads to the next chapter and the challenge of change.

CHAPTER 10

PERPARE: THE CHALLENGE OF CHANGE

Contextual Leadership tenet: People can and do change.

A popular story of the Frog and the Scorpion is often cited to demonstrate how people's natures don't change. The Scorpion asks the Frog for a ride across the river. The Frog responds, "Are you kidding? Of course not! I know you, Scorpion, and you would sting me and I'd die. No way will I carry you on my back!" The Scorpion challenges the Frog, "Why would I do that? If I sting you and you die, we both drown. You have nothing to fear by carrying me across the river." The Frog decides that what the Scorpion said makes sense, so he agrees to the request. Midway across the river, the Scorpion stings the Frog. As the Frog gasps his last breath before drowning, he implores the Scorpion, "Why? Why did you sting me, knowing we will both drown?" The Scorpion replies, "It's my nature."

The pity of using this story to describe human nature is that, as with most examples comparing human behavior and animal behavior, it implies that human beings lack self-determination. But, relevant to the topic of change, the story belies the idea that people can and do change. Surely you have witnessed, perhaps firsthand, a person who has experienced a significant emotional event that has changed their point of view, basic beliefs, values, and their personality (for better or worse). Maybe it's the birth of a baby, the loss of a loved one, a near-death experience, a spiritual insight, or a tragedy. Of course, there are examples where significant events have done little to change a person's nature; for example, a convicted felon who continues his illegal lifestyle at the risk of breaking parole.

Life experiences—especially significant emotional events—remain in your psyche as symbols.[1] These symbolic word pictures, or vignettes, serve as a shortcut to help you analyze your current situation, showing you the way you should or should not act. These vignettes provide you with a learned response to similar situations—so you're not always reinventing the wheel in every situation.[2] In this way, your previous life experiences influence your current action.

For example, the vignettes of Winston Churchill's childhood experiences with a remote, philandering father, alcoholic mother, and early political and military setbacks, translated into a remarkable resiliency as the British tower of strength during World War II.[3] As a young man, Gandhi chose making love to his wife over heeding a request from his ailing father. In the interim, Gandhi's father died. A vignette of guilt became the basis for Gandhi's doctrines on abstinence.[4]

IT ALL ADDS UP

Personality is cumulative—that means that over time, the vignettes generated by your life experiences add up to the person you are today. You can either accept the vignettes that make up your personality, or you can choose to consciously shape the vignettes and thereby shape your personality. There is evidence to suggest that the lack of resolution of early life experiences that are not understood and dealt with may contribute to the failure of some executives as they move up the corporate ladder.[5]

Life experiences that stimulate your mind's vignettes provide you with a chance to learn from, and if desired, to change the vignettes or stories you tell yourself in response to current circumstances. It happens when a woman who has suffered abusive relationships throughout her life chooses to be assertive, takes responsibility for her happiness, and lives independently. It happens when a man who has dedicated himself to his work and financial success wakes up alone one morning and realizes the importance of family and intimate relationships. It happens when a shy, inarticulate accountant gets frustrated by the vignettes of his life where he wishes he'd said what he was thinking, and he is compelled by his passion on a particular issue to join Toastmasters, learn the skills of public speaking, and become a spokesman for an important cause. It obviously didn't happen for lottery winners whose vignettes didn't change and who continued to use the same personality characteristics to manage their money as before having the winning ticket.

YOU CAN AND DO CHANGE

It is up to you as to when and how you change.[6] Not to believe this premise is to wonder what our human experience is about—if not to evolve and grow in wisdom. This is, perhaps, one of the strongest common threads of every great spiritual leader throughout history: the belief that human beings can raise their conscious awareness and live life at a higher level. Hope is a belief that things can change for the better; it is what entices you to greet a new day; it is what will propel you to learn from your past and shape your future.

The exciting thing about persona is that it is one of the most illuminating paths for guiding the self understanding that leads to behavioral change. Because your persona is a product of your historical self, accumulated yet diminished reflections, and memories of significant life experiences, it can be altered, upgraded, downplayed, reviewed, and renewed. The human psyche includes two wondrous capacities not afforded many other living organisms (as far as we know)—self-reflection and self-correction. Together they enable you to learn, modify, and pursue your idealized self. By investigating and working with your persona, you can be whoever you want to be. By understanding your behavior in light of alternatives, you can work to change your disposition-driven behavior and/or redefine your Values Point of View; you can recalibrate the person you want to become, independent of what others want; or you can understand and adapt your behavior to incorporate what is required or expected by others.

THE HEALTHY PERSONA

A well-functioning person possesses a persona that is a compromise between the inner psychic realities they live with on a daily basis, the person they aspire to be, and the social functions demanded of them. It is the constant balancing of these three forces that produces either growth and learning, or dysfunctional and repetitive behavior. When you have a healthy persona, you have versatility: You will not preside at a meeting, interact with a customer, talk to an employee, play with your children, or romance your significant other with the exact same persona. But to vary your persona, you must be conscious of it.

To be conscious of your persona, you must clearly understand how others perceive you, and then *own* that as a relevant, truthful part of you. That means constantly seeking feedback from others and weighing that feedback in light of the intended outcomes of your leadership efforts.

There are a number of ways to get information on how others see you, including professional counseling or formal assessments that provide you with others' feedback on specific aspects of your persona.[7] Of course, you can always ask people for their impressions, but be prepared under most circumstances to hear only what they feel comfortable sharing or what they think you want to hear. But if you have intimate relationships based on trust, and you structure the discussion with clear outcomes, you may learn something about yourself that you want to change.

REVEALING YOUR HIDDEN BELIEFS

Carl Jung popularized the concept of *shadow*—hidden beliefs that are manifestations of unexplored, or unresolved, psychological dynamics.[8] Because hidden beliefs operate from behind the scenes, they may be influencing your behavior without your conscious knowledge. Everyone has hidden beliefs—the very idea that you don't could be a hidden belief in action!

In our example, Tom's hidden beliefs might have included statements such as: Unless I prove I'm better than my sister, I'm unworthy of my father's respect; I can never quit at anything or I'll be a loser; The way to get people to love me is to be more competent and productive than anyone else; The only way to get attention is to make yourself heard.

While Tom's hidden beliefs and internal statements led him to admirable professional success, he needs to ask *at what cost?* His very strengths may be results of hidden beliefs, but so are his weaknesses. The behavior that counteracts or sabotages the person he wants to be, or that others want him to be, may be a result of his strengths driven to excess to become his weaknesses. Most truly successful people acknowledge and build on their capacity to use all their possibilities—to become versatile by exploring their fears and unacknowledged needs and values that limit their flexibility and sabotage their dreams. They create the ego-strength, confidence, and self-esteem necessary to be competent in the world. Focus on your strengths, yes. But when your strengths become obstacles and prevent you from advancing toward your ideal self, you will need to develop other skills that will give you the versatility necessary to change or adapt your behavior.

To investigate your persona, ask yourself some deep and potentially difficult questions—then answer them honestly. For example: *Have I rejected feedback given to me because I found it inconsistent with my own self view? Is it possible that what I dislike or even fear in others is a reflection of what I dislike or fear for myself? Have I ever noticed my strengths becoming counterproductive? Is it possible that not doing what I want to do is caused by an underlying fear that is irrational? Is there a historical pattern to my emotional outburst that I need to investigate?*

The answers to these shadow challenges may help you gain the insight necessary to stimulate growth and change. Investigate for the truth behind hidden beliefs that may be subconsciously driving your external behavior—and provide you the paths to change.

PERSONA, INSIGHT, AND CHANGE

As you investigate your hidden beliefs looking for a healthy persona, remember not to damn the shadow, but use it. Again, Frodo from *The Lord of the Rings* fable is a good example of using shadow to help motivate your own behavior. Frodo's shadow is represented by the tormented creature Gollum—the part of Frodo that craves the power of the Ring, or Precious, as Gollum calls it. Toward the end of Frodo's journey, the Fellowship of the Ring has been scattered, with Gandalf, Aragorn, the elves, and the dwarves fighting the armies of Sauron, and his best friend Sam separated from him at the last. It is Gollum, the shadow, who becomes Frodo's surest guide. It is Gollum who points the way to what Frodo must face and ultimately do.[9]

Frodo's dark predicament is: How do I overcome my shadow needs for power and do the right thing? It is a question we must all face every day—especially as leaders. As Jung says, "One does not become enlightened by imagining figures of light, but by making the darkness conscious."[10] Frodo faces his dark challenge on Mount Doom, where the Ring can be destroyed by throwing it into the abyss. The great tension is whether he will give in to the shadow or act on behalf of what others want him to be and the self he wants to be: his ideal self. When finally he throws the Ring into the abyss, the tensions of the persona are integrated, but Frodo is no longer the young man he was at the beginning of the journey. He cannot return to the quiet village with Sam. He is forever changed.

Persona is important to consider—especially in a leadership role—because your persona can either be a source of great delusion or the basis for true change and influence. The persona is like a medium or mask between your real self and the outside world. It exists for reasons of adaptation or convenience, but by no means is the mask a totally accurate representation of the real self.

Much of what leaders perceive about themselves can be an illusion. The illusion gets created and perpetuated by the people and systems leaders have gathered around them. Leaders may misinterpret what is in the eyes of their followers and find themselves using the followers' incomplete truths because their shadow side needs a sense of power; their ego craves a feeling of permanence or power. Don't allow the veil of illusion that results from making decisions based on second- and third-hand information when dealing with issues; take the time and action necessary to examine or test the values being put into play.

As with the emperor and his new clothes, many leaders have people who tell them what they *want* to hear, not what they *need* to hear. People around powerful leaders often will not share their perceptions of the truth. In fact, one of the greatest gifts your followers can give you is their version of the *complete* truth and let you do with it what you will. Create an environment where honest, well-intended feedback is encouraged, honored, and cherished, and the complete truth is valued.

Too many leaders begin believing their own press, buying into titles and entitlements, seeing themselves as separate from or different from those they lead. Unfortunately, when human beings perceive others as different, they can also see them as *less than*. This bloated self-concept only creates further illusions for leaders—adding to the tensions already existing in the Persona Triad.

You must clearly know the person you bring to the opportunities of leading and living. Find a coach, read, and ask for honest, unfiltered, specific feedback about yourself from those you lead. Face what is, and change the behaviors that do not serve others. Then find something worthwhile to believe in, something that others also feel passionate about—and get in front of the parade. In other words, find out what is in the hearts of those you want to lead; and if it is in your heart, then help them get there.

Hopefully you are ready and willing to answer the question posed by the challenge of change: *Do you believe that you can change or adapt your behavior; are you willing to make the effort in order to be the leader you want to be?*

SUMMARY—AN ALTERNATIVE ENDING TO THE FROG AND THE SCORPION

Leadership is not just a role or a title. It is not just a frame of mind. Leadership is ultimately behavior—it is outcome-oriented action that either produces results or doesn't. *Leadership is the act or process of arousing, engaging, and satisfying the motives and needs of followers in an arena of conflict, competition, or achievement that results in the followers taking action toward a mutually shared vision.*

Our definition of leadership has major implications for you, the leader. As you may have noticed, the emphasis is on arousing, engaging, and satisfying the motives and needs *of the followers* toward a mutually shared vision. As a leader, you are obligated to understand the undercurrents of your behavior so you can adapt your behavior accordingly. Hopefully this doesn't strike you as soft. It may offend you if you are a leader who claims *My strength comes from just being myself* or that you must be firm and resolved in your behavior—not changing with the whims of the people or circumstances you lead. We assert that your blind spots are the biggest obstacles to being a good leader. You need to accept and build on your strengths but be willing to change your behavior when necessary to achieve goals for the common good.

This is not *soft* stuff. In fact, introspection and becoming more versatile are hard work. They require conscious and applied effort. They take quiet, reflective time. They demand honesty and the courage to challenge how your inner psychic needs influence the way you meet the demands of your environment.

If you believe that your personality is hardwired, mostly a matter of genetics, and simply who you are—that you can't change your basic nature— then at least take this opportunity to learn how to regulate and adapt your behavior to best serve you and the people you lead. If you're the Frog, learn how to be more discerning; if you're the Scorpion, learn how to get where you're going without hurting yourself or others. Maybe your basic nature won't be changed, but your behavior and the results you get will be.

ENDNOTES

1. Lombardo, 1986.

2. Merriam and Cafarella, 1991.

3. Manchester, 1983.

4. Erickson, 1969.

5. Ket de Vries, 1989. (Especially when executives incur more responsibilities and less control is imposed.)

6. Bandura, 1997; Ornstein and Sobel, 1989; DiClemente, 1986.

7. See the "Resource" section in this book for assessments that provide self and others feedback on aspects of the persona.

8. See Cashman, 1998; Johnson, 1991; Egan, 1994.

9. Raiche, D., 2004.

10. Jung, C.G., 1976.

CHAPTER 11

ENVISION: THE SECOND LEADERSHIP PRACTICE

In 1988, then Vice President George Bush decried the *vision thing* as an aspect of leadership that one "didn't often think about; visioning was initially regarded as the fluffy side of business."[1] Today, it is rare to find an organization that doesn't have a vision. Good thing, because the return on investment for each $1 invested in a visionary company between 1926 and 1990 was $6,356, compared to $955 for nonvisionary companies of the same size and industry, and $415 for the general market.[2]

In your personal experience, you can probably recall when your work was energized by a dream, where your team was propelled to outstanding performance through a common purpose, or how an organization's compelling mission became your own. There have been great organizational visionaries, from Walt Disney to Stephen Jobs and Bill Gates. Books abound on the topic. So why dedicate this and the following five chapters to something everyone is doing and about which so much has been written? Answer: *opportunity loss*.

You are losing an opportunity if you have a personal vision but haven't aligned it with your manager's expectations and your organization's vision. You are losing an opportunity if your organizational vision exists in conflict with—or isolation from—the people the vision was meant to inspire. You are losing an opportunity when a team's vision is out of sync with its members and the organization they serve. Visions that aren't integrated or interconnected among individuals, leaders, teams, and the organization lack the power to inform strategic plans, to guide decision making at the individual contributor and organizational level, and to motivate and *sustain* the people expected to fulfill the vision.

The aim of the second practice of Contextual Leadership, *Envision*, is to tap the power that comes when you *link visions across contexts*. While each context demands distinct approaches, as shown in Table 11.1, it is leadership genius to take advantage of the interactive effect among individual, team, and organizational visions.

It is your responsibility to master (or at least appreciate someone else's mastery of) the skills to envision in each context. It may be one of the most important responsibilities you have as a leader. You can no longer afford to consider envisioning a simplistic, trendy, or gratuitous exercise; you must take it seriously as an integral, vital, and forceful means of unleashing energy in individuals and organizations.

GRAVITY AND VISION

The energy unleashed through a vivid, heartfelt vision is much like gravity—it can't be tasted, seen, smelled, or touched, but it has tremendous influence on the individuals experiencing it.

Gravity is a nice analogy for a vision. Gravity is a process structure—it doesn't have a form in and of itself, but gives rise to material phenomenon—you act and react differently in an environment where gravity exists than in one where it doesn't.[3] One of the hottest tickets in the country is a "gravity-free" ride where people have the opportunity to experience weightlessness. We are so accustomed to living in a gravity-defined environment that the feeling of existing in a world without the process structure we're accustomed to is a thrill—one that people are willing to pay almost $4,000 per ride to experience![4] People experience that same thrill when they work in an organization with a strong vision. Vision acts as a process structure—but *unlike* gravity, which holds people down, a powerful vision creates energy that lifts people up.

You know gravity exists even though you can't see it because you can see it at work and make assumptions, as Newton did with the falling apple. How do you know a powerful vision exists?

TABLE 11.1

QUICK REFERENCE GUIDE FOR HOW TO ENVISION WITHIN AND ACROSS CONTEXTS

You Envision by visualizing an inspirational ideal one can aspire to, crafting a statement of purpose one can be dedicated to, proclaiming rank-ordered values that act as a noble guide for behavior and decision making, and aligning the vision across contexts.

Self Context	One-to-One Context	Team Context	Organizational Context	Alliance Context
Envision by creating a motivating vision for your work-related role that integrates with your personal vision, helps you sustain enthusiasm for your role, and aligns with both your manager's expectations and the organization's vision.	Envision by guiding direct reports to generate a compelling vision of their work-related role that imbues their role with meaning and gives life to the organization's vision.	Envision by designing a blueprint for the team that will inspire and mobilize team members as they initiate their charter, and that aligns with the oranization's vision and expectations.	Envision by establishing an inspiring vision for the organization that becomes a unifying force, informing strategic planning and ultimately acting as a noble guide for people's behavior and decision making.	Envision by developing a stimulating vision for the alliance that capitalizes on the synergy that comes from discovering a common purpose out of the disparate and potentially conflicting agendas of alliance members.

It is vision at work when teams of people unite to raise money and awareness for causes about which they are passionate, as people did after the great tsunami in Asia in 2004 and Hurricane Katrina in 2005; or when you work tirelessly on a project and thrive on the energy generated, as when people chip in to build homes for the needy through Habitat for Humanity.

You can literally feel a vision at work when you walk into a retail store and sense the energy created by the employee's dedication to customer service.

Need more proof? Walk into Google's main campus in Mountain View, California, or Harley-Davidson's headquarters in Milwaukee, Wisconsin. Talk to people who work for Pfizer Animal Health. Have a holiday at the Jumeira Beach Resort in Dubai. Whenever you are bowled over by people's commitment, level of customer service, or longevity to an organization—ask them about it. We bet you'll discover a workforce that has embraced an organizational vision.

At the Jumeira, every waitperson, greeter, van driver, and mid-level manager we spoke with echoed the organization's vision—in their own words and in their own fashion. It came down to considering their property a home away from home and the guests as family. One of their ways of demonstrating their vision was to be proactive with guests. For example, we didn't encounter one employee who waited for us to say hello before responding; rather, they would initiate the greeting. When walking through the property, if you have a perplexed look on your face that you don't even know you have, inevitably an employee will ask you if they can help—even if it's not their job, their area, or their responsibility.

You can detect a vision at work when you come under the spell of a charismatic individual, are swayed by a salesperson, or are unable to deny someone's plea for help or support. When that happens, question that person's personal vision. We're willing to bet they have one they can articulate—even if it isn't formalized, memorized, or written in their day planner. Listen to the music of Bono from the rock group U2, follow his meetings on Capitol Hill, and read the myriad of online news stories about his efforts to raise the public conscience on the plight in Africa; and it is evident that *Time Magazine*'s Person of the Year in 2005[5] is on a personal mission dedicated to peace, ending poverty, and eradicating AIDS.

Like gravity, vision influences your everyday behavior; unlike gravity, it generates an *uplifting* energy that helps sustain you as you pursue your goals.

VISION ISN'T A FUTURE THING

Most people consider vision a linear proposition—an ideal state to be attained at some time and place in the future. Therein lies a problem—*someday* I'll be healthy, happy, and wise; *someday* this person will be a peak performer; *someday* this team will make a contribution; *someday* the organization will be the preeminent provider in our industry; *someday* this alliance will work.

Bono and the people at Google, Harley-Davidson, and the Jumeira Beach Resort aren't waiting for someday—they are living their vision every moment. Instead of thinking of vision as a future thing, we'd like you to consider vision as a force that actually exists now. A powerful vision is not a statement of some future ideal state, but a statement of the ideal present that affects everything and everyone in this moment. The vision may not be realized in every moment, but there's a greater likelihood that it will be. Most people who have had major transformations will tell you that there's truth to the popular saying, "Don't wait to believe it until you see it; believe it and you will see it."

Creating a vision that reflects an ideal present versus an ideal future may seem a subtle distinction. However, we believe this kind of detail will enable you develop something that is powerful, meaningful, and influential—as opposed to trendy and *de rigueur*. It also helps us reinforce the fact that envisioning is a skill. And skills can be learned. That's why the next five chapters are dedicated to providing you with insight into *how* you envision in and across the five contexts. If *the devil lies in the details*, then these distinctions will impact the ultimate effectiveness of your efforts to envision.

ENDNOTES

1. Vice President George Bush made this quip during an appearance in 1988.
2. Collins and Porras, 1994.
3. Wheatley, 1992.
4. Zero Gravity Corporation at research@gozerog.com.
5. *Time Magazine*, "The Good Samaritans, Persons of the Year," December 26, 2005. Cover story.

CHAPTER 12

ENVISION IN THE SELF CONTEXT

Envision in the Self Context by creating a motivating vision for your work-related role that integrates with your personal vision, helps you sustain enthusiasm for your role, and aligns with both your manager's expectations and the organization's vision.

Consider this familiar metaphor:

A man was walking down the street and encountered three laborers. He asked, "What are you doing here?" The first laborer said, "I'm laying bricks, what does it look like?" The second laborer replied, "I'm building a wall." The third laborer looked at the man and said, "I'm building a cathedral. It will be beautiful and thousands of people will come here for inspiration."

The purpose of the story is to help you understand the value of a vision. When it rains or the laborers tire, which of the three will find the strength, will, and desire to continue working? Which of the three will feel a greater sense of accomplishment and satisfaction? Most agree that they would prefer to possess the mindset of the third laborer. All three laborers are completing the same activities, but the third laborer is acting with a higher end in mind, a grander purpose—a vision for his work-related role.

Now consider this twist. What if the laborer is merrily working away to build a cathedral wall only to discover that the actual job is to build a shopping center? It turns out that the laborer was building the wall for one purpose, but his boss had a different purpose in mind. All this time the workman labored under a false expectation—his vision of his role was not aligned with his organization's vision. Envisioning your work-related role provides a way to link and align your vision with the expectations of your manager and organization.

Much to our dismay, despite benefits to managers and the organization, most managers and organizations limit envisioning in the Self Context to self-improvement or self-help categories. Few organizations seem to understand or appreciate the value of personal vision or support it through training.

FOUR GOOD REASONS TO ENVISION YOUR ROLE

Personal envisioning has been left to best-sellers written by ministers who provide effective faith-based approaches, or books such as the highly regarded, but by no means wholly embraced by organizations, *The 7 Habits of Highly Effective People*.[1]

We encourage you to seek out these and other resources; we also encourage you to adapt and adopt the ideas to your workplace environment using the strategies in this chapter. It is our hope that through *your* example, organizations that have embraced the research on envisioning in teams and organizations will come to see the power of personal visions in the workplace.[2]

MANAGE YOUR MANAGER

Back to building cathedrals: Is there a gap between your vision of your job and what your manager or the organization has in mind? For example, do you believe your primary role is to build client relationships for long-term sales that can be sustained over time, but your manager is being held accountable for short-term gain and rewarding the transactional sale? Do you think your primary function is to increase shareholders' wealth, but your employees are disgruntled, burned out, and threatening mutiny? Have you focused on expanding the company's markets and creating new products and services, but the owners of the company are content to stay a small mom and pop shop?

When you create, compare, and contrast your vision with the vision that others have for your role, it will help guarantee less of a gap between what you see as your primary responsibilities and what your manager or organization expect from you.

SHIFT FROM DISPOSITION-DRIVEN TO VALUES-DRIVEN BEHAVIOR

In the first leadership practice, Prepare, you learned that your behavior is influenced by your DISCposition, Values Point of View, and Persona. You also came to understand that your disposition-driven behavior may be sabotaging your desired results. Hopefully, you realize that you can make a conscious choice to demonstrate more appropriate values-driven behavior. One way to kick start a needed behavior change is through a work-related vision that raises awareness of the discrepancy between what you say you want and how your actions undermine getting what you want. *A vision prompts your conscience, guides values-driven behavior, and ultimately influences your outcomes.*

To tweak an old saying,[3]

> *Heed your vision, it guides your actions; Watch your actions, they become your habits; Beware your habits, they become your character; Mind your character, for it becomes your destiny.*

ESTABLISH A WORKPLACE COVENANT

An agreement already exists between you and your organization that, whether you know or understand it, defines the relationship. This informal agreement can take three forms: you take more than you are given; you give more than you take; you are sensitive to the amount of giving and taking and work to make it balanced.[4]

The envisioning process provides you with an opportunity to explore which agreement is most desirable and acceptable and to create a covenant—a formal, conscious, and overt agreement—between you and your organization.

EMPOWER YOURSELF

Wise sages extol the virtue of living in the moment. But what happens when the challenge of the moment diminishes the energy available for moving forward? Your work-related vision acts like an emotional magnet to pull you through the tough times and into a time of possibility. It provides a transition from the potentially threatening current reality to the next step of action. It *empowers* you to overcome the inevitable obstacles, pain, strife, exhaustion, and any number of inevitable de-motivators that could jeopardize success in your work-related role.

HOW TO ENVISION YOUR ROLE IN THE SELF CONTEXT

1. *Visualize your role as if it is ideal*—It stimulates your imagination and generates energy.

2. *Craft a statement of purpose for your role*—It makes your intentions, dreams, and hopes tangible and actionable.

3. *Proclaim the values you choose to demonstrate in your role*—They guide the decisions you make and the way you go about achieving your role's purpose.

4. *Align your vision*—It helps ensure that you have the support of your manager, team, organization, and alliances.

1. VISUALIZE YOUR ROLE AS IF IT IS IDEAL

When you envision, dream.

Don't consider the idea of dreaming a waste of time, too esoteric, or a recipe for insomnia. Stories abound about inventors, cutting-edge thinkers, change-agents, and visionaries who depend on their dreams to guide them. Elias Howe turned a dream into one of the world's great inventions. Howe dreamed that spear-wielding natives captured him. In his lucid dream-state, Howe realized that the spears contained holes in their tips. What could produce a nightmare instead became a curiosity to him. Howe's vision to elevate sewing from a laborious, manual process to a more efficient, mechanized process informed his dream. He and other inventors failed, time and again, to perfect such an invention, but the secret, it turned out, was encoded in Howe's dream. After awakening and reflecting, he realized the meaning of the odd spears. The hole in the needle of the mechanical machine needed to be in the tip of the needle instead of the head, as in a hand-held needle. Elias Howe's dream led to the first successful sewing machine.

But, dreaming is not just a sleep-induced phenomenon. Dreaming occurs through conscious effort such as visualization and guided imagery, and through less formal means such as daydreaming—or affective thinking, as Dutch psychologist Julien Varendonck labeled it.[5]

Consider where the world would be without the dreams of Martin Luther King, Jr., Susan B. Anthony, Rosa Parks, Mahatma Gandhi, Henry Ford, Steve Jobs, Bill Gates, Mary Kay, Martha Graham, Stephen Spielberg, or Elias Howe. For better or worse, their dreams inspired liberation, advocacy, growth, change, profits, art, the mechanical sewing machine, and more dreams.

The fact is, everybody dreams. But, not everybody pays attention to his or her dreams. Tapping your dreams is critical to creating a vision that transports you outside your current reality long enough to help you gain perspective. Oftentimes, that different perspective is all it takes to stimulate your imagination, generate energy, and lift you up when obstacles could hold you back. The more open you are to dreaming, the better your chances of creating a vision that will encourage you, your direct reports, the organization, or alliance when you, they, or it need it most.

If the idea of dreaming—especially within your role—is over the top for you, then consider reading and researching the topic.[6] You may actually need to build your dreaming, visualizing, mental imaging, and affective thinking skills. Plenty of research exists on the power of dream work, visualization, and guided imagery for therapeutic approaches to physical healing, emotional dysfunction, everyday routines for stress relief, and enhanced performance in sales, athletics, music, and the arts.[7] But, scientific data isn't necessary to support the validity of creating vivid pictures in your mind and the resulting physiological and mental changes—it's as obvious as salivating simply by imagining the juice from a plump, yellow lemon squirting in your mouth.

If you are already skilled at visualizing, creative thinking, or daydreaming, you may just need to channel those dreams to your work-related role. After all, it is your dream that will inspire your vision, and when the going gets tough, it will be your vision that inspires you—and perhaps others.

Challenge Assumed Constraints

Reality check: You may have to alter or compromise your vision of your ideal work-related role depending on the realities of the situation or possible unwanted consequences, but don't give in to limited thinking without first giving your dreams a chance. Self leaders challenge assumed constraints by examining and holding themselves accountable for beliefs that limit their dreams and possibilities.

An *assumed constraint* is a belief, usually based on past experience, which limits your current and future experience. An assumed constraint is formed anytime you buy into a fear, give in to limitation, generalize an experience, or take to heart feedback that curbs your enthusiasm. *No woman has ever held that role*; *No one has ever done that before*; and *That's too risky*, are examples of statements that might be offered with love and caring, but only serve to dampen your dream.

The Grasshopper Effect

After years of conditioning, adults are especially prone to the limitations of assumed constraints—despite a few lessons to the contrary growing up. For example, did you ever collect grasshoppers and put them in a jar? Remember how you hole-punched the lid so they could breathe, then watched them, transfixed by their ability to jump? Did you notice that when they jumped, they often hit the lid of the jar with a *ping*? Later, you removed the lid to let the grasshoppers free, expecting them to jump from the jar. You discovered they jumped only as high as where the lid had been. They were *pinged* too many times to jump higher. Finally, you needed to tip the jar over and coax them out. Some were just too tired to go free.

Did the trials and tribulations of trying to break through glass ceilings, pink ceilings, blue collars, corporate politics, hierarchies, or good old boys clubs left you too tired to keep jumping? When you challenge your assumed constraints, you may experience a minor epiphany and realize the lid was taken off and you are free to jump to whatever heights you can; or you may suffer a minor meltdown and realize that you let go of dreams (or never dared to dream in the first place) because you fell victim to assumed constraints.

The Thrill of What If

To challenge assumed constraints at work, ask: *What if* you could do anything at work and knew you could not fail, what would you dare to do? *What if* you tapped into your strengths every day, what would you tap? *What if* you had no restraints, no inhibitions or limitations at work? *What if* you could take the role to where no one else ever dared to take it? What kind of contribution could you make?

After dreams are dreamt and assumed constraints challenged, you are ready to take the next step. You are ready to envision your work-related role by writing a purpose statement that will clarify your choices, help you determine if your work and the organization are meeting your needs, and empower you in the short run by reminding you of the value of your role in the long run.

2. CRAFT A STATEMENT OF PURPOSE FOR YOUR ROLE

There is a simple template for writing an individual purpose statement in the Appendix on the book's companion Web site. The template outlines four steps:

1. Take inventory of your best characteristics (nouns).
2. Identify what you do well (verbs).
3. Describe your perfect workplace.
4. Integrate your responses into a one-sentence purpose statement.

Try it. Construct the first draft quickly, without analysis. Intuition can be your best tool when first attempting to write a purpose statement because envisioning should contain an emotional component. Ultimately, it may take hours to complete a statement of purpose for your work-related role—but you may be amazed and pleased with how far your intuitive effort gets you.

An example of a pragmatic, yet potentially powerful, vision statement is the following:

> *My work-related purpose is to use my real estate expertise (noun) and deal-making skills (noun) to generate sales (verb) and mentor new employees (verb) so that buyers and sellers have faith they are being represented with integrity and fairness at the same time that their investments are maximized to the fullest (perfect world).*

Observe your behavior at work and compare it to your work-related purpose statement. Consider if the statement needs tweaking or amending; consider if your behavior needs tweaking or amending.

Compare Your Personal and Work-Related Purpose Statements

If you don't have a personal purpose statement, adapt the work-related purpose statement technique in the Appendix to create one. If you already have one, then use the technique to validate it. An example might be:

> *My life purpose is to use my communication skills and energy to motivate and inspire myself and others to live and work in ways that are not self-serving but for the welfare of the whole.*

Compare this personal purpose statement with the work-related statement cited earlier. It appears that *generating real-estate sales and mentoring new employees with integrity and fairness* are work-related ideals that are *not self-serving and take the welfare of the whole into consideration.* The two purpose statements seem to be interconnected, reinforcing, and compatible.

If you are not finding a way to fulfill your personal purpose at work, then you are missing a great opportunity for work/life congruence—and the sheer joy to be found by integrating your personal and work-related purposes. The story of the dancing tollbooth operator is a wonderful example of just that. As consultant/author Charles Garfield approached the tollbooth on the San Francisco–Oakland Bay Bridge, he heard loud music. It turns out it was coming from the tollbooth he was about to enter. The operator was dancing. "I'm having a party," he declared. On further investigation, Garfield discovered that the young man's vision was to be a dancer. Rather than seeing his confining booth as a "vertical coffin," as did most of his fellow tollbooth operators, he saw his job as an opportunity to practice dancing. Not only was he entertaining others, he developed a philosophy about his job and created an environment to support his vision.[8]

Reality check: If the dancing tollbooth operator was failing to collect correct amounts or creating backups on the bridge, this would mean that his work-related role and personal visions were not in sync. It would behoove him to integrate the two.

Notice opportunities for alignment of *your* personal and work-related visions. The synergy will generate the energy and passion you need to succeed. The more compatible your personal and work-related purpose statements are, the more likely you are to be living, working, and even dancing purposefully.

The beauty of our approach to writing a purpose statement is that it incorporates your vision of the ideal and jumpstarts you into deliberating on your values.

3. PROCLAIM THE VALUES YOU CHOOSE TO DEMONSTRATE IN YOUR ROLE

The Valuing Points of View Model you used to Prepare for leadership[9] provides a guide to help you explore, sort, and organize your values. By understanding your point of view, you gained insight into the values differences that might exist between you and a co-worker or someone you lead.

These values differences are often the crux of what people call *communication problems*.

Now it's time to Envision, which means consciously choosing the values that will guide your decision making and workplace behavior. In many cases, it may mean developing a set of values that you aspire to follow.

Pretend that you are a man working in a 1940s munitions factory. You have a Loyalty Seeking Values Point of View on social issues—you believe in so-called traditional values where a woman's place is in the home as a wife, mother, and homemaker. It is a family value that you hold dear. Now imagine that with so many young men away at war and an influx of women into the workplace that your new boss is a female. It is difficult for you to take direction from a woman in the workplace; in fact, you resent it.

You are faced with a values-bind. Do you adhere to your Loyalty Seeking values stance or give in to workplace norms? You have a choice. You can choose not to comply with the realities of the workplace and suffer the consequences, or you can choose to have tolerance for women in the workplace and still adhere to your personal values outside the workplace. After hours of evaluation, advice seeking, and personal deliberation, the man in our example chose the latter option.

Obviously, when your work-related values and personal values are congruent, you will be more energized. However, the very act of choosing a value—it is by your own volition that you choose to accept or tolerate a different set of values at work—gives you a sense of autonomy. The freedom of choice may prove to be just as intrinsically motivating and energizing as having congruent values.[10]

The point here is that there is power in a *developed* value—a value that is . . .

- Freely chosen
- Chosen from alternatives
- Chosen with an understanding of the consequences of the alternatives
- Acted on over time
- Prized or publicly owned

Even if the value you choose is a compromise due to the situation, you can experience autonomy, freedom, and energy when you choose the values you live and work by rather than habitually following your programmed values.

Your work-related and personal purpose statements will guide you on the development of your core values at work. In our continuing example, if you are in a real estate sales role, there are dozens of values you might choose from integrity and fairness to making a worthwhile contribution. Donald Trump has said that he values the art of the deal. *Deal making.* It seems a harmless enough value. Of course values always seem positive, noble, and uplifting to those who choose them. What is interesting is how you define them and make them operational.

Are Your Values Defined and Operational?

To witness how important it is to question your values, define them, and determine how you'll make them operational, read the book or watch the documentary based on the book, *Enron: The Smartest Guys in the Room.*[11] It became clear in the last years of Enron that the traders who bought and sold Enron's commodities (real and fabricated) had a primary value of "making the profitable deal." The deal they most valued was called *arbitrage.* This type of deal had the potential for outrageously out of proportion profit. Making the arbitrage deal was so valued that other values collapsed under its weight.

Tape recordings discovered after the fall of Enron reveal a total disregard for the damage, destruction, and human hardships created as a consequence of Enron's traders manipulating California's energy grid as they pursued the arbitrage deals. Traders are heard "yahooing" the rolling blackouts, resulting traffic accidents, and soaring energy prices—reveling in their own power and celebrating the millions of dollars they were generating for the company. In one particularly chilling taped conversation between two traders discussing fires raging in Southern California, one of the traders can be heard encouraging the fires to burn. He knew that the worse it got in California, the more he would profit from escalating energy costs.

A poignant scene in the Enron documentary is an interview with one of those young traders who wonders in retrospect why he allowed himself to descend into such debauchery. He realizes that he should have asked himself: *Why am I doing this? Is this the right thing to do? Is this behavior what I truly value or am I just caught up in the moment?* Had he and others done so, many dollars would have been saved, and more importantly, much human pain, suffering, and hardship would have been prevented.

Enron may seem an exception or exaggeration, but one of the telling aspects of the downfall of America's seventh-largest corporation is how many individuals were implicated—accountants, bankers, investors, reporters, anyone who turned a blind eye to what now seems obviously unethical. What if you had asked any one of them: *What are your values?* It is unlikely they would have replied: *Greed, money, and self-preservation at any cost.* Yet so many individuals failed to stand up for their proclaimed values. What tragedies such as Enron teach us is how important it is that values are demonstrated at all levels of the organization. When upper-level executives lack moral backbone, and there are no checks and balances within the organization's vision and systems, then individual character takes on an even greater importance. An ethically bankrupt organization is not an excuse for individuals to abandon their own morality and concern for the welfare of the whole. Rather, it is a call to self leaders who are willing to constantly question their motives and hold themselves accountable for their values behavior—or lack thereof.

One way to take responsibility for your actions is to clearly define your values and determine how you will demonstrate them and make them operational. The following examples continue the hypothetical real estate scenario:

- **Integrity and fairness**—*I provide honest information and disclose pertinent facts even though it might influence the desirability of a property.* For example, if I know there is a problem in the neighborhood, I will share that information to a prospective buyer; I report actual amounts spent on my expense reports—I do not pad my expense reports.

- **Customer satisfaction**—*I take my client's economic and social welfare into consideration.* For example, if I think the buyer is getting in over her head, even though she qualifies for the property, I will explain why I think it may not be the best financial decision; if I know of impending construction that might influence the buyer's decision, I will reveal the information even though I am not bound by law to do so.

- **Sales success**—*I optimize the revenue and profit for my organization given the bounds of the marketplace and in fairness considerations to my clients.* For example, I exceed the expected quota for cold calls and follow-up meetings; I focus on repeat business and long-term relationships; I continue to improve on my expert negotiation skills so I can help maximize the sales and profits for my company and get the best deal for both buyers and sellers.

Having these three values defined with examples of how you would demonstrate them in your day-to-day work will help you take advantage of opportunities with the conviction that you are doing the right thing according to your own moral compass. Living by your developed, consciously considered values will help you avoid regrets in the future. But, there is still one vital element missing from the values puzzle: When push comes to shove, which value takes precedent?

Are Your Values Rank-Ordered?

Here's the scenario. You are a salesperson for a training and development company who has been working on a potential client for months now, submitting proposal after proposal to train and develop their leadership capacity. Finally, the client agrees—but, under one condition: The regional vice presidents want the assessments being done on their division managers (DMs) sent directly to them, and they will deliver the assessments to the DMs. This provides a quandary for you. In the past your company has advocated that only one copy of an assessment is produced and given directly to the person being assessed. In this case, it would be the DM's responsibility as the receiver of the assessment to share results with their regional vice president (or not).

You know from past experience and research on the topic that there is a high risk that issues of confidentiality, trust, and politics between your client's V.P.s and DMs will be generated by their approach, but the client seems more concerned about giving the V.P.s power than in empowering the DMs. You know there are people inside your company who will strongly disagree with your client's condition, but there are no hard and fast rules. Your choice is between generating tens of thousands of dollars in sales to your company in the short run and hundreds, maybe millions, of dollars in the long run, or telling the client *No*. What do you do?

Our question is actually: *How would you know what to do?* What process would you follow to make the decision? This is clearly a values dilemma. Most salespeople have a value regarding integrity, so you might say *I cannot justify letting my client do what I fundamentally believe is wrong*. Most salespeople also have a value concerned with success, so you might also say *I cannot justify not serving this client and establishing a lucrative account relationship*.

Unless your values are rank-ordered, it will be a very painful decision process. In case you're wondering, in our real-life example the salesperson made the decision based on the integrity value and refused the conditional sale. Ironically, the client was so impressed with the values stance that they began to question their own values and behavior. Over time they became a multi-million dollar, long-term client.

Make a list of your role-related values; define them and how you plan to make them operational; and then rank order them so the next time you're faced with a values dilemma, the right choice has in effect already been made.

4. ALIGN YOUR VISION

This may take some gumption—especially if you have a manager who isn't a great leader in the One-to-One Context, but you need to take the responsibility for making sure your vision, purpose, and values for your role are aligned with those of your manager. As with our example earlier of the brick layer who thought he was building a cathedral, only to discover that his manager and the organization were into building shopping centers, you need to be sure that what you perceive as your job is compatible with the expectations of others.

Consider your role as a piece of a puzzle—one of many in an organization. It is important for you to understand the big picture and your place within it. Your efforts to envision will not only help you understand the meaning of your work, but it will also remind your boss of the vital contributions being made by you and your role.

OPRAH'S LACK OF VISION?

When asked if she and her life partner, Stedman Graham, argue, Oprah Winfrey responded, "Other people might argue about shoes left on the floor or you didn't come home for dinner. We argue about vision versus no vision. All the time. There's not a day that we don't talk about [*imitating Graham*] 'What you need is a greater vision.' Even when we were teaching our [leadership] class together at Northwestern University, he would stand up and tell these graduate students, 'You need to have a vision, there's a process to success,' and I would say, 'Or you don't, 'cause I didn't have one.'"

When asked: *What's next?* Oprah replied, "I don't know because as you know I don't have a vision. [Laughs.] I live in the moment. People are saying to me, how are you going to top this? It's not my desire to top it, my desire is to keep manifesting for myself the life I was meant to live, and so that could take me anywhere."[12]

Sorry, Oprah, at the risk of impertinence to contradict one of *Forbes Magazine's* most powerful women on earth,[13] we would like to argue that you do indeed envision—it depends on how you define vision. We believe you absolutely have a vision of an ideal state—in fact, your idealism is what drives much of your charitable and altruistic work—but also your commercial work. We believe you have a statement of purpose—it is evident in your desire to use television and other media to their highest and best use for doing good in the world. And your values are evident in the choices you make and the way you live consciously—proactively challenging the standards and norms about the way people think. If only the rest of us could have the lack of vision that you have!

Ms. Winfrey, we think you envision in the Self Context better than most other human beings on the planet. Maybe what you (and Stedman) need is a different way of conceptualizing a vision. A vision is not a linear path leading you to some specific place at some distant time in the future, but a set of ideals, purpose, and values that shape each moment in the present—and thereby influence the quality of today *and* the prospect of an enlightened future.

ENDNOTES

1. See *The Purpose-Driven Life: What on Earth Am I Here For?*, Warren, R., 2002; *Your Best Life Now: 7 Steps to Living at Your Full Potential,* Osteen, J., 2004; Covey, S., 1989.

2. See team and organizational sections later in this chapter.

3. Charles Reade, nineteenth century.

4. Zigarmi, et al., 2005.

5. Varendonck, J. *The Psychology of Day-Dreams.* London: George Allen & Unwin Ltd., 1921.

6. To improve visualization skills, see Gawain, 1978; Leichtman and Japiske, 1982; and Benson, 1984, 1996.

7. Research on visualization and mental techniques is plentiful. See in particular, Siegel, 1986; Moyers, 1993; and Benson, 1995.

8. Garfield, 1996 (pp. 276–277).

9. See Chapter 6, "Prepare: The First Leadership Practice."

10. See Deci and Ryan, 2002, especially *Sketches for Self-Determination Theory of Values* by Tim Kasser, pp. 123–140.

11. McLean and Elkind, 2004; DVD, 2005.

12. *People Magazine*. May 30, 2005. Page 109.

13. Oprah is number 14 on Forbe's Most Powerful Women List as of August 31, 2006, at 6 PM EST. Source: Forbes.com/Lists.

CHAPTER 13
ENVISION IN THE ONE-TO-ONE CONTEXT

Envision in the One-to-One Context by guiding direct reports to generate a compelling vision of their work-related role that imbues their role with meaning and gives life to the organization's vision.

There is a marvelous scene in the classic World War II movie *Twelve O'Clock High* where Gregory Peck's character, General Savage, practices envisioning. Savage has been called in to take over the 918th bomb group that has been experiencing heavy losses and erratic bombing accuracy. In this scene, Savage is responding to Jessie Bishop, a young pilot and informal leader in the 918th bomb group. Bishop is discouraged by the high mortality rates, and as the spokesperson for the other pilots is requesting a transfer for himself and the others. Savage knows he cannot afford to lose the commitment of the Medal of Honor winner, but he also knows he is obligated to forward the transfers for consideration. In an impassioned plea, Savage reminds Bishop of their vision. Savage conveys to Bishop the critical nature of his role as a pilot and informal leader—nothing less than his responsibility to help defend the free world.[1]

Despite his best effort creating a vision and sense of purpose, Savage ended the meeting assuming he would lose Bishop and the rest of his pilots. As it turns out in this fictionalized version of a true-to-life experience, Savage's envisioning paid off. Bishop withdrew his request for transfer and was able to convince the other pilots to "hang on." As a result of the commitment turnaround of Jessie and the others, the 918th was able to stay in the fray and contribute to the war effort by proving that daylight precision bombing could be effective.

Envisioning for the individuals or direct reports you are responsible for developing and leading may not be as dramatic as General Savage's, but it can be just as vital to their performance over time. Yet our experience is that leaders in the One-to-One Context find it remarkably easy to *not* practice envisioning. In fact, we find that most fail to envision at all. Why? Because it's twice as hard. You not only have to get agreement from your direct reports on the vision for their role, but you must do your homework beforehand to determine what the vision for the role *should be* given the organization's expectations for your department. General Savage was very clear about the nature of the pilot's work; he was convinced they were playing a strategic role in the war effort. Through his understanding and forethought, he was able to communicate the vision to those he led.

Another reason envisioning in the One-to-One Context is often ignored is because it is too easy to rely on the organization's vision as the energizing, unifying force. It's true: The *organizational* vision lies at the heart of the organization—it is the storyline of organizational life. Every individual should be aware of the organization's vision. But just being aware is *too passive* a connection. As a leader, it is your responsibility to *connect an individual's effort and skills to the organization's purpose and values.*

HOW TO ENVISION IN THE ONE-TO-ONE CONTEXT

Envisioning one-to-one follows the same formula as when you envisioned in the Self Context, but (and this is a big but) it requires an elevated skill level as you act in the best interest of multiple entities: your direct report, your department, and your organization—not to mention your own vision as a leader. The four steps are as follows:

1. Visualize your direct report's role as if it is ideal.
2. Craft a statement of purpose for your direct report's role.

3. Proclaim how the values of your direct report's role embody the organization's values.

4. Align the vision of your direct report's role with the organization's vision.

1. VISUALIZE YOUR DIRECT REPORT'S ROLE AS IF IT IS IDEAL

Challenge assumed constraints and visualize the contribution your direct report is making to your department and the organization as if it were perfectly realized. In essence, you are *positioning* the role of the individual you lead. Where does it fit, how does it fit, why does it exist? If you consider each of your direct reports' roles as a piece of a puzzle, ask *What would be missing if their piece didn't exist or if the direct report didn't show up for work each day? What part of the departmental vision would suffer? How would the organization's vision fail to be complete? What does this role provide that is essential to the big picture?*

Interestingly, we find many leaders who could answer the preceding questions if they related to an individual's role in the achievement of *goals*. Most leaders tend to think of roles as goals—failing to consider the roles of their direct reports from a philosophical approach. When you visualize a role, it means looking at the role in the big scheme of things. For example, a sales manager can tell you what percentage of her division's goals must be made by a particular salesperson; but can she express how that salesperson's role contributes to the vision of organization? If a pharmaceutical company has a vision to improve the quality of life for people; or a real estate firm has a vision to help people find a home, not just a house; if a computer company has a vision to make information accessible to everyone—then how does an individual's role fit into those pictures?

Dana is the manager of the receptionists and greeters at the home office of a mid-sized firm. Despite her efforts to train and monitor performance, turnover was unacceptably high in this crucial position. There were significant complaints and negative comments about the employees who labored in the relatively low-paying, yet crucial positions where phones were constantly ringing and a seemingly endless stream of visitors walked in the front door. Then Dana visualized the role—not as a goal to be achieved someday in the future, but as if it was ideal in the present.

In her vision, Dana didn't see her people as receptionists and greeters, but in a new light—she saw them as the first impressions customers have of the company. As a result, she changed each person's title to *Director of First Impressions* and worked with each person individually to help *them* visualize how their energy, attitude, and behavior contributed to (or damaged) the organization's image and reputation with customers. The effect was almost instant. Improvements were validated by customer satisfaction surveys, but surveys weren't necessary—the changes were obvious to any internal or external client who interacted with the front desk.

Allow yourself the freedom to visualize the ideal role for the people you lead, develop, and teach. Whether the purpose of each role played by your direct report is similar or different, your vision of each in relation to the whole will be like a puzzle, where the pieces come together into a cohesive whole that represents what you hope your department or area of influence stands for.

2. CRAFT A STATEMENT OF PURPOSE FOR YOUR DIRECT REPORT'S ROLE

Adapt the template introduced in the Self Context for developing a purpose statement for the role of each direct report you lead. (The step-by-step process can be found in the Appendix on the book's companion Web site.)

1. Take inventory of the characteristics that best serve the role (nouns).
2. Identify the skills, abilities, or actions that best serve the role (verbs).
3. Describe the perfect workplace when the role is being fulfilled.
4. Integrate the responses into a one-sentence purpose statement for the role.

Use the role of your administrative assistant as an example. Characteristics that best serve the role are attention to detail, interpersonal skills, persistence, flexibility, honor and integrity, ability to keep confidences, and secretarial skills. Your list of verbs that reflect what the ideal administrative assistant is best able to do is to write memos, screen callers, schedule, organize, promote internal harmony, project positive appearance to external clients and vendors, and take dictation. Your idea of the perfect workplace if the role is being fulfilled might be a workplace where documents are always at hand when needed, with clients who are as satisfied having talked to your administrative assistant as they would have been had they actually reached you, together with internal customers who rave about the communication and support they receive. You imagine what it's like to never miss meetings because your calendar is so expertly managed. You picture an administrative assistant who projects the most positive aspects of the organization to external contacts, reinforcing how easy and worthwhile it is doing business with you and the organization. You vision an administrative assistant who has the skills to be excellent at both the task and interpersonal endeavors the role requires. We could go on and on, but the idea is for *you* to do that.

When you combine the first three steps into one statement in step four, it might be something like . . .

> *My purpose statement for the ideal administrative assistant role is where he/she uses his/her attention to detail and interpersonal skills to organize all the office functions, maintain internal harmony, and project a positive appearance to external contacts so that information flows in a timely and efficient manner and both internal and external clients feel well-served by our department.*

With this purpose statement, you will be better able to convey the breadth and depth of the role to your direct report—giving him/her a sense of the responsibility *and* the opportunity in the role.

In the example cited earlier with Dana and her Directors of First Impressions, crafting the purpose statement also served to clarify each individual's contribution to the role and laid the groundwork for their goals and future intentions. In the case of one young woman, Elizabeth was clear that she wanted to focus on presenting the company in a positive light and helping people get the information they needed. As a new wife and soon-to-be mother, she didn't harbor plans for promotions or expanded responsibilities. Kevin, on the other hand, armed with experience and education, came into the role with the idea of improving systems and processes while learning about the company so he could eventually move on to another role with greater potential for growth and earning power. Dana used the purpose statement with her direct reports as a bridge from the present to the future, as a mechanism to springboard future intentions.

The purpose statement also sets you up to proclaim the values inherent in the role, which is, of course, the next aspect of the envisioning process you need to consider.

3. PROCLAIM HOW THE VALUES OF YOUR DIRECT REPORT'S ROLE EMBODY THE ORGANIZATION'S VALUES

Let's say that your organization's top value is ethical behavior. How will the person fulfilling the role of your administrative assistant live that value day to day? What are examples of the decisions that would be made, things that would be done or not done, and behaviors that are acceptable and not if the administrative assistant demonstrates the value of ethical behavior? You might create a values wish list around ethical behavior such as . . .

- Communications are kept confidential; information is revealed only as appropriate given the circumstances.
- Improprieties and unethical behavior are reported to the organizational values check committee.
- Work that appears unethical, unfair, or unjust is not accepted.
- The truth is not obfuscated, and lies are not told just to make communication easy in the moment.

Example: With these values regarding ethical behavior, the administrative assistant wouldn't lie when screening calls and tell a caller you are in a meeting when you are not, but would use telephone skills to simply state the truth—that you are currently unavailable for taking calls, but have times set aside for returning them.

You would work through this process for each of the organization's values. Remember that after you have completed this exercise, you need to rank-order the values according to priority and importance. Your rank order may align with the organization's order, or it could diverge. For example, if your organization has three values in rank order of ethical behavior, success, and customer satisfaction, you might determine that for the role of the administrative assistant that customer satisfaction has a higher priority than success because the role's success is primarily determined through internal and external customer service.

Ultimately, the values you establish for the role will not only dictate the tone of the administrative assistant's future behavior, but reflect the true values of the entire organization. Think about Enron. The company had a stated value regarding ethical behavior and integrity, but in the end it was the behavior of individuals that determined whether that value was in operation or simply a bunch of words on a piece of paper or a plaque in the hallway. Each of the individuals who engaged in unethical trading had a boss leading them in the One-to-One Context who could have, *should* have, monitored and assured that the organization's value was being demonstrated in day-to-day activities.

4. ALIGN THE VISION OF YOUR DIRECT REPORT'S ROLE WITH THE ORGANIZATION'S VISION

It is one thing to envision the role in the ideal; it is another to get buy-in from the person who is fulfilling that role. You might want to try a *parallel* process: Ask your direct report to complete the same steps for the role as you have done and compare notes. Find the commonalities and discrepancies. Through a *collaborative* process, then come to agreement on the final vision, statement of purpose, and rank-ordered values. The characteristics and skills of the person fulfilling the role will determine the final vision, which might be different with another individual filling the role—but the important connections will be intact. This particular role will be aligned with the vision for your department and that of the organization. Contextual Leadership is beginning to spin its mighty web of integration—making the whole much more powerful and effective than the sum of its collective parts.

ENDNOTES

1. *Twelve O'Clock High*, 20th Century Fox, 1949.

CHAPTER 14
ENVISION IN THE TEAM CONTEXT

Envision by designing a blueprint for the team that will inspire and mobilize team members as they initiate their charter and that aligns with the organization's vision and expectations.

Have you ever been on a team that worked hard to develop a new initiative or plan, only to discover you don't have the authority to make it happen? Have you ever been in the position of leading a team only to discover that you don't have the support from the organization you need to be effective? Have you and your team members ever begun work on a project, only to realize the goals and outcomes aren't clear? Have you ever wondered why certain people are on your team and others aren't? If the answer to these questions is *Yes!*, then more than likely your team never had a sponsor to envision the team prior to its formation. We are convinced that one of the primary reasons organizations give up on teams is because teams are conceived ineffectively—if at all.

We hope you have tolerance for a sports story about basketball coach Phil Jackson, bad-boy player Dennis Rodman, and the Chicago Bulls. We recognize that you may be expecting us to keep citing pertinent business or government examples—and we will; we promise. But brilliant leadership deserves to be learned from, no matter what its genesis.

In 1995, Phil Jackson, then coach of the Chicago Bulls, considered recruiting a radical player named Dennis Rodman. Adding a player to the already well-regarded Bulls was not unexpected to ensure long-term excellence, but Rodman was a rebel without a cause, and he certainly didn't fit into Chicago's good-guy team persona. Rodman was eclectic, to say the least. Thought of as beyond difficult—he was unmanageable. People considered him a potentially great talent who was unable to fit into a team structure because of his narcissistic, selfish, and outlandish personality. But Jackson could envision Rodman taking the team's defense and rebounding to another level.

Jackson, with the Bull's owner's consent, met with Rodman. At this point, Jackson had the power and the opportunity to hire Rodman. Instead, he went to the two informal leaders of the Bull's team, Michael Jordan, their on-the-floor general, and Scotty Pippen. Jackson posed the Rodman opportunity to the two young men—making it clear that the hiring decision would be theirs, not his. Hearing Jackson's rationale, Michael and Scotty agreed. It was they who presented the idea to the team. The players voted Rodman in.

What Phil Jackson did was masterful. He didn't act in the role of autocratic team leader, but as team *sponsor*. Acting as the team's sponsor may feel like being a team leader because you are serving the team's outcomes, but the role is very different. As *sponsor*, you are providing the *initial blueprint* for the conception of the team; as a team *leader*, you guide the team in achieving its goals *by responding to its day-to-day leadership* needs.

As his team's sponsor, Jackson had so purely *envisioned* the team, its purpose, and its values and then so clearly *communicated* his vision to the players that they could see the big picture and Dennis Rodman's part in it.

By the way, in the 1996 season, the Chicago Bulls not only won the NBA Championship, they had the best record in the history of the sport with 72 wins. A key factor was Dennis Rodman and his defense, rebounding, and energetic play.[1] (Interestingly, the team had voted that Rodman would be free of the usual team rules regarding off-the-court behavior and expectations such as media interviews. Each team member was willing to follow the rules himself, but allow Rodman to follow his own rules—as long as he delivered at practice and through his performance on the court. Imagine if Phil Jackson had presented that idea or imposed that inconsistent application of rules. It would never have been tolerated by team members.)

HOW TO ENVISION IN THE TEAM CONTEXT

Phil Jackson knew what he needed in order for his team to succeed. His blueprint for the Bulls was well designed, and when there was a gap, he was clear what it would take to fill the gap. We are suggesting that when you envision in the Team Context, your role is to be the *sponsor*[2] who does the initial work of visualizing the ideal team, crafting an initial draft of purpose, proclaiming its values, and aligning the team's vision with that of the organization. Ultimately it will be up to the team's leader and members to embrace, adopt, or adapt what you've created.

Even though the process is similar to envisioning in the Self and One-to-One Contexts, remember that the complexity of leading a team grows exponentially and requires a higher level of skill:

1. Visualize the team as if it is ideal.
2. Craft the team's initial statement of purpose.
3. Generate potential team values.
4. Align the team's vision with the organization's vision.

1. VISUALIZE THE TEAM AS IF IT IS IDEAL

When you visualize the team in its ideal state, it is *your* vision—but your job is to capture and express what you believe is in the hearts of those you hope will eventually shoulder the burden of carrying out the vision.

When you visualize the team, use all your senses to imagine the issues that are being solved, the outcomes being produced, and the contributions being made. See in your mind's eye the difference being made as a result of the team's performance and the positive reactions from those being served.

Also visualize the ideal team of people—between 4–12 (8–10 is considered the ideal size) team members with the right mix of technical talent to accomplish the work of the team, the interpersonal skills necessary to foster the team through difficult times, and representing the plurality of ideas and diversity in thinking so the team can respond creatively to issues. Visualize team members with a passion for the outcomes the team is charged with producing.

When the team is up and running, the quality of its work will be directly connected to its motivation and how meaningful the work is. It was clear in the case of Dennis Rodman and the Bulls that despite his radical behavior (wearing a bridal gown to a book signing, posing nude on a motorcycle, dying his hair outrageous colors, piercing every orifice imaginable), he was aligned with Phil Jackson's and the player's vision for the team and motivated to make a positive contribution. Whether it's a sports team, a political campaign, a special task force, the Twelve Disciples, or Navy Seals—there is enormous power when a team of people share the same mental picture of success.

2. CRAFT THE TEAM'S INITIAL STATEMENT OF PURPOSE

Adapting the same template for crafting the team's purpose statement, as described in the Self and One-to-One Contexts, is a fun and productive exercise when you are sponsoring a team. Later, when the team is initiated, have the team do the same exercise and compare your original draft with theirs.

1. Take inventory of the characteristics that your ideal members bring to the team (nouns).
2. Identify the skills, abilities, or actions that your team members can do that best serve the team's outcomes (verbs).
3. Describe the perfect workplace when the team is serving its purpose.
4. Integrate the responses into a one-sentence purpose statement for the team.

Even though we said this was a fun exercise, it is also where the hard-line questions must be considered that will ultimately link the team's purpose with the organization's vision. You must weigh business issues against available budget and potential payoff. Be prepared to answer: *What is the general purpose of the team? What are the possible desired outcomes or deliverables? Are there apparent measures or indicators that define the limits of the team's responsibility? What are the team's key areas of responsibility?*

Here is an example of a purpose statement created by the sponsor of a product development team:

> *Our purpose is to use our passion for teaching and knowledge of adult learning theory to produce and promote an innovative self-leadership product line that enables thousands of individual contributors around the world to break through their assumed constraints, celebrate their points of power, and collaborate for success with their manager.*

The following statement of purpose demonstrates the flexibility of this template and how it can be used in almost any situation—in this case, a nonsecular application:

> *The Parish Mission Advancement Committee purpose is to use our creativity and enthusiasm to envision and plan for 2010 so that all registered parishioners at St. Catherine of Siena are growing closer to Jesus Christ, are more engaged in the life and activity of the parish, and reflect Christ's love to all we encounter.*

The Type of Team Is Determined by Its Purpose

As the team's sponsor, consider how the purpose of the team should determine the type of team you are forming. The possibilities are shown in Table 14.1.

TABLE 14.1

TYPE OF TEAM BY PURPOSE

Type of Team	Part or Full Time?	Temporary or Standing?	Multi-Level or Homogeneous?
Cross-Functional Team— When purpose and outcome require members representing various departments, functions, or organizational interests.	Either part or full time	Either standing or temporary	Either multi-level or homogeneous
Work Unit Team—When purpose or outcome requires people who do the work or produce a product within a particular area or department.	Full time	Standing	Homogeneous
Management Team—When purpose or outcome requires leaders of major areas in the organization who have position power and meet frequently to discuss and solve the organization's problems and implement solutions.	Full time	Standing	Homogeneous— rarely include more than two layers of the hierarchy

Task Force Team—When a large group of people drawn from multiple functions and levels are temporarily assigned to investigate issues or problems and make recommendations to top management.	Part or full time	Temporary	Multi-level

3. GENERATE POTENTIAL TEAM VALUES

The practice of envisioning in the other contexts typically includes clarifying rank-ordered values. However, in your role as team sponsor, it is premature, unfair, and impractical to impose values to team members. Rather, envision the general guidelines and boundaries you see the team operating within, realizing that when the team is activated, it will be up to it to make the values specific, operational, and its own.

Conceive the team's boundaries by asking and having answers to questions such as: *What cost limits or considerations are there? What are the timelines for delivery of outcomes that cannot be missed? Are there restrictions concerning utilization of woman- and manpower? What organizational values cannot be violated at any cost or benefit? What sacred cows must be spared? What are the limits of authority for the team?*

As sponsor, your role is to give or secure adequate authority for the team to use appropriate resources and make choices that increase its capacity to be effective and implement agreed-upon solutions. A primary reason that teams fail is that they are not empowered to act. For example, task forces charged with disclosing improprieties or suggesting improvements often have their findings and plans passed on to the bureaucracy to little effect—except to kill the credibility of the team members and poison the concept of teams in many organizations!

The boundaries you set as a sponsor need to provide enough latitude for the future team to flex its skills and, at some point, to work autonomously—independent of your direct day-to-day influence. After you have established the general boundaries, more detailed boundaries may need to be put in place regarding obtaining permission, organizational realities that must be understood, consequences of nondelivery, and incentives.

As the sponsor, you also need to make clear if, and when, you may override team decisions you don't like; under what criteria would you find cause to overturn a team decision. It is wise to pre-establish ways for the team to let you know if you are becoming too involved in the ongoing work of the team or usurping the power and effectiveness of the team leader (assuming the ongoing team leader is someone other than you).

4. ALIGN THE TEAM'S VISION WITH THE ORGANIZATION'S VISION

It became apparent to the Regional Manager (RM) of a large pharmaceutical company that sales teams created at the district levels had floundered over the years due to their misaligned vision. The teams were composed of salespeople, each of whom represented different drugs offered by the company, but who were required to call on the same doctors within the territory. On any given day, at least two sales reps were calling on the same doctor; over the month, as many as five to seven sales reps would try to get a couple of minutes to make the case for the drug they represented.

Team meetings were usually focused on how to gain access to doctors and maximize sales. The team's vision and purpose was to maximize sales—a logical belief given their goals and reward system.

But the RM realized that if the company's vision was to improve the quality of life for their customers, then the teams' financial- and performance-based purpose was out of whack. When he visualized how things would be different if the sales teams were ideal, he realigned his vision of the teams to better reflect the organization's vision: He saw the teams as dedicated to educating and assisting doctors so they could make better decisions regarding their prescriptions and patient recommendations. As a result of his new vision, the entire district sales structure was revamped so that five to seven sales reps from the same company would no longer be calling on one harried doctor. New "pods" of sales reps began collaborating and cooperating with a focus on their end users, the patients, and their immediate customer, the doctor. Meetings became focused on how to better serve their constituents. Not only did team members' morale, passion, and energy improve—so did their sales.

TO SPONSOR OR TO LEAD, THAT MAY BECOME THE QUESTION

Your sponsorship will give the team a greater sense of its own power and more likelihood of success. In fact, your role in brokering the team in the organization may prove to be so valuable that you discover the team would be better served if you remain the sponsor and identify another as the team leader.

A team's commitment to its goals is directly connected to how well you have communicated the common purpose for which the team was created. The team's purpose is the key to the team's energy. As sponsor, you must believe so passionately in what can be accomplished that you inspire the team to create what is *in the sponsor's mind's eye*.

You will have envisioned successfully as the team's sponsor when you have imparted a purpose with meaning that transforms a team member's time from drudgery to desire—establishing the foundation from which the team will initiate its goals and produce results that make a difference.

Ultimately, you will have to let go to have something that will come back of its own character and on its own accord. When the composer frees others to make music, the music will always be something that quite unexpectedly lifts the composer as well as the players. You will have to make the choice if you are the composer, conductor, or both. Hopefully you will decide based on the team's needs and best interest—not your own.

ENDNOTES

1. Halberstam, 1999; Lazenby, 2001; Jackson and Delehanty, 1995.
2. For elaboration on the concept of Team Sponsor, see Fowler and Zigarmi, 1997.

CHAPTER 15

ENVISION IN THE ORGANIZATIONAL CONTEXT

Envision by establishing an inspiring vision for the organization that becomes a unifying force, informing strategic planning and ultimately acting as a noble guide for people's behavior and decision making.

People are *not* your organization's most important asset. People *are* your organization—everything else is an asset. If you want your organization consistently headed in the right direction with a minimum amount of misdirected energy, then the people who comprise the organization must all focus consistently in the right direction. At the same time, they must be clear about what behaviors are unacceptable—in other words, where *not* to direct their energies. This is achieved over the long term by enrolling every member of the organization in a common vision that inspires and energizes people.

Vision is the most important factor to enable long-term, sustained high performance in any organization.[1] The vision must be explicit, compelling, known, and understood by *all* members, and must serve as the primary guiding criteria for all planning and decision making.

It is not what vision *is* that is most important; it is what vision *does* that counts the most. Having a vision statement on a piece of paper gathering dust in a drawer is of no value whatsoever. The same can be said of framed vision statements that adorn the walls nicely, but fail to guide decisions and behavior. To the extent you can get everyone in the organization to understand and commit to a commonly shared vision, your organization will enjoy sustained high performance. The more people in the organization who either don't understand or don't buy into the vision, the greater the trade-off you will experience in sustaining performance.

When visions rule, otherwise debilitating deficiencies in the organization seem to take a back seat. For example, we observed one organization that baffled us, as well as most of its employees, clients, and vendors with whom we talked. Systems were nearly nonexistent; accountability measures inconsistent at best; people often murmured about bone-headed decisions or lack of decisiveness on the part of leadership. Yet turnover was almost nonexistent; people were consistently going beyond expectations to meet internal and external client needs; and leadership continued to manage growth in market share, profits, and employee benefits. What did they have that others don't? A compelling vision of an ideal to aspire to; a sense of purpose about how they contribute to the world; and values that were demonstrated through the way people were treated over time.

This intriguing organization, which will remain nameless, is a constant source of fascination for us. We have witnessed how the organization attracts values-compatible people who buy into the ideal vision and the meaningful purpose and stay year after year—even as they suffer from a lack of systems and inefficiencies. Why? Because aspiring to and living the ideal is worth more than the pain of inconvenience. It is thrilling to work in an environment where vision rules compared with working for organizations that espouse their purpose is to make money and are hell-bent on system improvement, stockholder equity, and economic measuring sticks. (We can only imagine what might happen to this organization if its leaders built upon the devotion of their people and directed their energy more efficiently through system improvement and the other leadership practices of Initiate, Assess, and Respond.)

HOW TO CREATE YOUR ORGANIZATION'S VISION

The magnitude of envisioning in the organization is far greater than in any of the other contexts. Every person, decision, and behavior will be affected by the organization's vision—whether it is a noble vision or a lame one. So even though the four steps are similar to those described in the other contexts, the process is more complicated and the implications of each word more significant:

1. Visualize the organization as if it is ideal.
2. Craft a statement of the organization's purpose.
3. Proclaim the values the organization embodies.
4. Attune people's hearts and minds with the organization's vision.

1. VISUALIZE THE ORGANIZATION AS IF IT IS IDEAL

As the leader, it will serve you and your people to have personally visualized the possibilities for the organization. Blue-sky it. If there were no limits, what could your organization do for society, how would it best serve its customers, what legacy would it leave the world? The great visionaries were able to see what others dared to dream. Don't worry about being realistic. There's plenty of opportunity for that when you get to the third leadership practice, Initiate, where you assess current opportunities and demands, and consider external constraints and internal obstacles. But this is not the time for assumed constraints or real ones.

If you have the nerve, conduct grassroots envisioning sessions and ask your employees to dream big. What you discover will not only shock and awe you, but excite and thrill you. When people dream together, the energy is palpable. The reason we say to do this if you have the nerve is because after you've generated the energy from group visualizing, you will be under greater pressure to create the structure and initiate the goals that breathe life into the vision. But as we said previously, harnessing the energy comes later; the job of envisioning is to create the energy.

2. CRAFT A STATEMENT OF THE ORGANIZATION'S PURPOSE

Again we refer you to the purpose statement template in the Appendix on the book's companion Web site and adapt the exercise—this time for the organization.

1. Take inventory of the characteristics that make the organization special and unique (nouns).
2. Identify the skills, abilities, or actions that the organization excels at doing (verbs).

3. Describe the perfect world as served by the organization.

4. Integrate the responses into a one-sentence purpose statement for the organization.

After you have written your version, ask key people or groups for theirs. When you take a grassroots approach to identifying the organization's strengths and perceived capacities, you might just learn to dream a little bigger.

Members of the Center for the Reproduction of Endangered Species (CRES), a division of the Zoological Society of San Diego, achieved this step of developing their purpose statement by collectively identifying their differentiating competencies. These are competencies that are unique to the organization and hard for someone else to emulate in the short term. CRES has numerous differentiating competencies, but the major ones include the fact that they can conduct research in three areas: 1) at the laboratory bench, where they have world-class facilities; 2) on the Zoo's collection, which is the foremost collection in the world today; and 3) in the field. Most organizations have one or the other and none have all three. Even those with exceptional collections can't match the breadth and scope of the one assembled by the Zoological Society of San Diego.

With their differentiating competencies in mind, the members of CRES compiled a motivating purpose:

Our purpose is to provide expertise, united vision, and direction for the Zoological Society of San Diego and the public so that together we can make a positive difference to biodiversity conservation worldwide and become agents for societal change.

"G" Force, a technical services company that provides inspection services to the construction industry, created a simpler and more direct purpose that reflects the culture of the organization:

Our purpose is to serve the market sectors of education, health care, transportation, water, and commercial development in the following areas: geotechnical engineering, construction inspection, materials testing, technical instruction programs, and staffing services for design and construction professionals.

3. PROCLAIM THE VALUES THE ORGANIZATION EMBODIES

It is impossible to fully energize the members of the organization without identifying the specific means values that will guide their behavior, individually and collectively, as they focus on fulfilling its purpose. A value is a belief that transcends a specific situation, object, or person, yet is applied across situations, objects, or people.[2] A means value is a value that informs the organization's members about *how* to achieve the organization's purpose. The power of the organization's vision lies in its purpose and means values.

To identify these guiding means values, you should first ask, *What are the enduring beliefs that we want to shape or guide our behavior in order that we can energize our people and fulfill our mission to the greatest extent possible?* Once these values are identified, you should rank-order them so there will be no doubt in the future about the priorities you wish to establish. Then you should identify examples of specific behaviors and behavioral guidelines you'd like to establish to demonstrate that people are acting in accordance with those beliefs and values. Categories of behavior that should be addressed include such areas as communication, decision making, responsibility, working relationships, and time management.

Examples of values might be such things as integrity, honesty, excellence, quality, and diversity. But it's not enough merely to state the values in terms of a single word. Because so many words are overworked and mean different things to different people, it's important that you define what you want these words to mean in your organization and how you expect people to act in honoring your definitions.

For example, honesty may mean simply telling the truth in all you do and making sure that whatever you do reflects reality. But it could also mean not stealing, not padding billings or trying to take advantage of customers, and not overpromising during the sales process. It's important that you spell out whatever behaviors are important to you relative to each value.

Then you should rank-order the values, stating which are more important than others. An example people often refer to when making this case is the example of Disney. Disney has numerous values, but it makes it clear that safety is the most important. So if a Disney employee is faced with a dilemma such as operating an unsafe ride or keeping productivity up, the employee will always put safety first and fix the ride to make it safe.

Over time, the values that get demonstrated on a regular basis will become your organization's norms. Norms are to organizations like habits are to people; they are recurring behaviors that members of the organization generally follow. Values and norms interact dynamically over time to shape culture.

Culture is both a cause and an effect. In its causal form, it is somewhat like each organization's unique *disease*. It's what you catch when you come to work here. It plays an important part in shaping people's behavior when they join up and psychologically commit to the cause. But it is also an effect because over time, the combined attitudes and behaviors that emerge collectively among the members of the organization shape that organization's culture.

Nothing good ever naturally evolves in organizations. This is especially true for culture. The only things that naturally evolve are friction, frustration, irritation, dissatisfaction, unhappiness, poor performance, and low morale. If you want something other than these, then you must manage culture. Culture must be managed just as diligently as every other dimension of leadership in order to sustain long-term performance.

The best way to shape a culture that will best serve the unique purposes of your organization is to identify and define a set of guiding means values. Then members of the organization should hold each other accountable for adhering to the values and demonstrating the desired behaviors. Top management has the ultimate responsibility for ensuring that everyone in the company conforms to the values and accepted norms.

4. ATTUNE PEOPLE'S HEARTS AND MINDS WITH THE ORGANIZATION'S VISION

It's the height of arrogance to think that just because you have your vision and values committed to paper that people will embrace them and take it upon themselves to breathe life into them in a meaningful way. They won't without your leadership.

Great visionary leaders throughout history have been skilled at crafting their visions, but they've been even more skilled in enrolling their followers in the vision and using vision as a powerful and dynamic leadership tool to achieve sustained high performance. In the past, we often referred to this as achieving *alignment*. This was a mistake. Alignment can be achieved in numerous ways, including coercion. A leader can force people to march in the same direction together with a collection of incentives and pressures. The problem is that eventually the alignment will disintegrate if achieved through manipulative means. It's much better to think in terms of *attunement*.

Attunement is achieved when people work together with a common focus and collaborative approach *because they eagerly and willingly choose to do so*. The basis for attunement is a vision that is shared, understood, and committed to by all members of the organization who respond to their understanding and commitment by proactively taking initiative to responsibly achieving the vision and helping others to do the same.

TENDING THE VISION

Everything you'll learn later on about creating and implementing initiatives and establishing processes and systems to support those initiatives has, as its foundation, the underlying aim of tending the vision.

The role of vision in every organization is to energize the members so each person will be inspired to commit their best efforts to achieving the organization's true focus. If you start an organization from scratch, then a fresh vision is the place to start. More often than not, however, you'll be inheriting a vision of some sort, and it usually won't be a very good one. In this case, you should also start from scratch to re-create the vision in accordance with the guidelines presented here. If you ignore this advice and start leading in the organization context with a flawed vision, everything else you do will be correspondingly weaker.

ENDNOTES

1. A large number of studies in recent years have consistently confirmed the connection between long-term success and vision. Perhaps the most substantive case is presented in *Built to Last: Successful Habits of Visionary Companies,* Collins, Jim, and Jerry I. Porras, HarperBusiness, November, 2004.

2. Zigarmi, et al., 2005, and Rokeach, 1972, 1993.

CHAPTER 16

ENVISION IN THE ALLIANCE CONTEXT

Envision by developing a stimulating vision for the alliance that capitalizes on the synergy that comes from discovering a common purpose out of the disparate and potentially conflicting agendas of alliance members.

The envisioning process for a team begins outside the team with the sponsor's plan before the actual team is formed. The same is true for alliances. The envisioning process for alliances starts outside the alliance, before the alliance is actually created. It starts with someone generating a *Big Idea* that involves collaboration between two organizations to achieve mutually aligned objectives.

GENERATE THE BIG IDEA

Here's how it usually works. Assume you run a company that makes color additives for plastics. The companies that make plastic products buy color additives from you, and they buy the resins for making plastic products from another company. Sometimes your customers encounter problems in creating their final products because your color additives don't mix properly with the other company's resins. Sometimes it's your fault, sometimes it's the resin supplier's fault, and sometimes it's the plastic manufacturer's fault.

When these problems arise, no matter whose fault it is, the customer is frustrated and it puts a strain on your relationship. So you come up with a *Big Idea* for an alliance between you and the resin supplier. It involves having your two companies work together to anticipate the total needs of the customer and deliver only products that have already been tested and proven to meet the customer's need. You telephone your counterpart in the resin supply company, explain your idea, and gain agreement that such collaboration would benefit everyone. You both agree to move forward.

Many people get fouled at this step in the process by trying to hammer out a written agreement, formal partnership, or contractual relationship. It's too early for this. Most alliances fail for the same reason most mergers and acquisitions fail: culture clash, lack of strategic focus, or faulty assumptions about the bottom-line benefits. To avoid becoming a casualty before the alliance gets up and running, you and your potential alliance partner should conduct several key considerations. *Do the two parent organizations have values alignment and cultural proximity?* The values of the two organizations won't match completely, but they should be in alignment, and the differences between the two entities should be clear. *Do the leaders from both organizations have confidence that the differences will not lead to terminal culture clash? Do both leaders have a clear plan for minimizing the differences so they don't poison the relationship?*

MAKE THE STRATEGIC CASE

Next, you should clearly spell out the strategic case for the alliance. The strategic case should be defined in nonfinancial terms. Questions to ask include: *Will this alliance help enhance our relationship with customers over the long haul? Will it enable us to better serve certain customers? Will it enhance customer share? Will it enhance market share? Will it make the alliance members more efficient? Will it give alliance members a competitive edge in the market?* Your answers to questions like these should be specific. Later on, you'll use these to evaluate the effectiveness and value of alliance.

STRIKE THE BUSINESS DEAL

Finally, you should be clear on the value of the business deal to both companies. Will both members benefit proportionately to their contribution? If not—if the deal is lopsided in benefitting one member over the other—the alliance won't last. It's not necessary that both benefit *equally*. However, it is essential that each benefits *fairly* commensurate with their contribution of resources and energy.

PICTURING THE ALLIANCE PROCESS

The alliance-building process is represented in Figure 16.1.

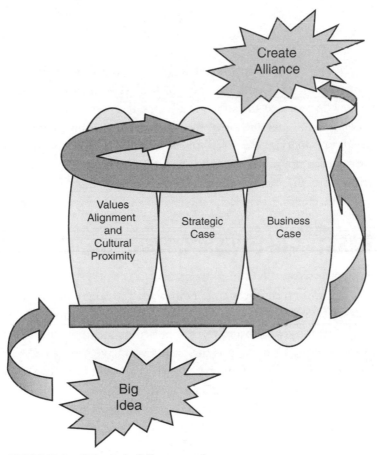

FIGURE 16.1 Alliance building process

The arrows are drawn to indicate that you will most likely conduct this assessment in several iterations, getting more specific and delving deeper with each iteration. During your first pass, you'll make a broad brush assessment of values and the culture of the two companies, articulate a fairly general strategic case, and more generally outline the business case. If you're comfortable with all three at this high level of assessment, then the next time you'll delve into substantially more detail. Again, if all three pass muster at this greater level of detail, then you might choose to make one final assessment before actually launching the alliance.

After you've completed this assessment, if the alliance still appears feasible, then you and your counterpart in the other company should create an alliance leadership team (ALT) to launch the alliance. It's important that you define the boundaries of the ALT's responsibility and the scope of its authority. Envisioning should involve leaders at the highest levels of both alliance members, and may or may not include people who will actually serve on the ALT. However, when delegating responsibility to the ALT, it is important that at least some members of the ALT must have the authority to make key decisions at the strategic alliance level without having to obtain permission from higher authority. In other words, within clearly spelled out but broad boundaries, the ALT itself must be able to function with autonomy. Once the broad vision for the alliance is defined and the proper delegations implemented by each parent company, then the ALT initiates the alliance by creating a charter, much the same way any other team should.

SUMMARY—TO ENVISION, FIRST DREAM

Carl Sandburg wrote, "Nothing happens unless first a dream."[1] When you envision, you are setting the elements in place to bring a dream to life—but you must start with the dream. In the Self Context, it is your own dream for what you want for your life and work that brings meaning and significance; in the One-to-One Context, it is the dream you have for the success of your direct reports; in the Team Context, it the dream you have for the potential of like-minded individuals dedicated to a common purpose; in the Organizational Context, it is the dream of a noble purpose that ignites the collective whole and results in the welfare of all; and in the Alliance Context, it is the dream of making a Big Idea a reality that benefits otherwise disparate entities.

Each of the leadership practices in Contextual Leadership builds upon the next. First, you Prepare by understanding, coming to terms with, and learning to adapt your disposition, values, and persona to the demands of your leadership role—no matter in which of the five contexts you find yourself leading. Second, you Envision by turning your attention outward to shape an ideal reality in each of five contexts. This brings you to the third leadership practice: You Initiate by corralling the energy generated by the vision and giving it structure with areas of key responsibilities, goals, and outcomes. As you've probably come to expect, the skills you use to Initiate in each context are similar—but as you will discover in Chapters 17–22, the complexities and form are shaped by the context.

ENDNOTES

1. *Bartlett's Familiar Quotations*, 1992, page 634:11.

CHAPTER 17

INITIATE: THE THIRD LEADERSHIP PRACTICE

Stretch a rubber band with both hands—one end over your right thumb and the other end over your left thumb. Move your thumbs apart until the rubber band is stretched taut. Feel the tension in your opposing thumbs. It requires strength to keep the rubber band stretched as tight as it will go. The natural tendency of the rubber band (and your aching forearms) is to release the tension.

Hold the tension just a bit longer and notice how the fatigue in your thumbs and forearms is suggesting you should move at least one of the thumbs toward the other. Now imagine that your right thumb represents a goal—a specific outcome you want to achieve within a specific time frame. On the other end, your left thumb represents your current reality—where you are at this moment in time in relation to the goal.

You and your rubber band have just generated a metaphor for the idea of *creative tension*—perhaps one of the most powerful concepts for activating human behavior. You prompt action by the natural tendency for tension to seek resolution. You generate creative tension when you hold a clear idea of your goal for the future and compare it to your current reality.

You prompt action by the desire or need to bring your current reality and your goal closer together.

Hopefully playing with rubber bands gave you insight as to why the third practice of leadership—to Initiate—is so crucial to achieving leadership genius.

When you initiate as a leader, you are jumpstarting the creative tension that leads to action. Whether leading in the Self or Organizational Context, when you set your own goals or the organization's initiatives, you are acknowledging polarities between the real and ideal—two polarities that generate the spark of creative tension. Using your thumbs as the metaphor once again, consider that there are two ways for you to release the tension you've created. One way is to simply let go of your goal—represented by letting the rubber band slip off your right thumb. What have you learned? If you are actually using a rubber band as you follow along, you quickly learn that letting go hurts as the rubber band snaps your left hand! But more to the point, the rubber band on your left thumb remains unmoved—your current reality remains where it started, with no movement, no progress, and no growth.

There is another, less painful way for you to release the tension—follow the path of least resistance and move your current reality toward your goal, a step at a time. Using your thumbs and the rubber band, inch the left thumb toward the right. You can feel tension releasing as it moves. Finally, the tension is released, but metaphorically, you have moved to a different reality, the one created by achieving your goal.

Initiate—it has the power of action and the hope of opportunity, no matter what the context. As a leader, you initiate in each context, but the *way* you initiate will vary, as shown in Table 17.1.

You Initiate by establishing and facilitating the goals, expectations, ground rules, operating guidelines, and steps for implementation that embody, enable, foster, and sustain a work-related vision.

If you think initiating (or goal setting) is boring, redundant, and painful, you need to trust us—capturing dreams and crafting them into reality can be stimulating, enlightening, and liberating—whether they are your own dreams, those of a direct report, a team, the organization, or an alliance. We hope to prove this to you in the upcoming chapters.

TABLE 17.1

QUICK REFERENCE GUIDE FOR HOW TO INITIATE WITHIN AND ACROSS CONTEXTS

Self Context	One-to-One Context	Team Context	Organizational Context	Alliance Context
Initiate by creating a personal performance plan that defines Key Responsibility Areas, SMART goals, and action steps for their achievement that are aligned with your work-related vision and the organization's expectations.	Initiate by establishing performance objectives based on Key Responsibility Areas, SMART goals, and a development plan for your direct report that is aligned with the direct report's work-related vision, as well as the organization's goals and vision.	Initiate by establishing a high-impact team charter that is aligned with the sponsor's vision for the team and includes team member-generated vision, goals, and operating principles.	Initiate by outlining a strategy and initiatives with action steps for their achievement, which are aligned with the organizational vision.	Initiate by establishing a charter outlining the alliance's major goals and operating principles for fulfilling the alliance's Big Idea, as well as the visions of the partners in the strategic relationship.

CHAPTER 18

INITIATE IN THE SELF CONTEXT

Initiate in the Self Context by creating a personal performance plan that defines Key Responsibility Areas, SMART goals, and action steps for their achievement that are aligned with your work-related vision and the organization's expectations.

Maybe you had an experience similar to one of the authors before she realized the importance of knowing how to initiate in the Self Context. Early in her career, Susan was so eager to break into the advertising field that she took a lower echelon job compared to what her education and experience might suggest. Initially, she was the head "gofer" in a small ad agency, running errands, fetching, and going for whatever the account executives, clients, or executives needed. Soon she was fielding telephone calls from media salespeople, dealing with impending deadlines with production companies, proofing and editing copy, and occasionally even sitting in on creative strategy meetings. It occurred to her one day that she was the glue that was keeping the agency together. She began to feel taken advantage of, underappreciated, and underpaid.

She rejoiced when the president of the firm announced that a big-time advertising consultant was being brought in to help make the agency more efficient. She gladly completed the consultant's requests; she filled out the requisite activity and time logs, accounting for every 15 minutes of time. Surely, she surmised, the consultant would recognize her contributions, value, and worth to the company and suggest a promotion and a raise.

When the day came for her performance review, Susan was excited and curious. The meeting started out as she hoped. The consultant commented on the variety and number of tasks she did each day, he lauded her commitment and sincere effort, and he acknowledged her contributions to the everyday chores that she took on. Then he said, "Susan, the fact is, you could make a much greater contribution and be much more effective if you weren't so friendly." Taken aback, she countered, "What do you mean?" The consultant went on to describe how Susan spent entirely too much time chatting with people on the phone or in the front lobby, how she seemed to be a gadfly flitting around the office, and how she wasted precious time. In her own defense, Susan explained how it was her friendly manner that kept aggressive salespeople at bay until the media buyers were ready to speak to them, how her relationships with production houses had made a difference when the art director missed a deadline, or how their clients had warmed up to her and felt welcomed when they came in for meetings.

Unimpressed, the consultant responded, "Susan, you are young. Someday you will understand. Trust me—you are too friendly; you waste too much time." Susan remembers that the meeting continued after the consultant's comment, but she can't recall any of it. She had shut down. Two months later, she was working at another agency.

Today, being older and somewhat wiser, Susan acknowledges that despite his awkward delivery, the consultant may have had a point; she realizes that by rejecting his feedback, she may have missed out on valuable information and insight that could have accelerated her career. In retrospect, she also realizes that if she had been proactive about initiating and setting goals, she could have redirected the feedback into something more meaningful. For example, what if she had responded with something like this: "Wayne, I understand that you think I'm too friendly and waste time. I need you to help me understand what I could and should be doing differently. Here are the goals we set for the past three quarters. Each quarter I have met or exceeded expectations. What is it I could be doing more of if I weren't so friendly?"

You can imagine how this response could have resulted in a much different conversation—one with the potential to positively guide her behavior and contribute to the agency. When you initiate in the Self Context, you take the lead in establishing the expectations by which you will be judged, assessed, valued, compensated, and rewarded. Your goals and outcomes are clear and provide the benchmark for your behavior and performance. You effectively remove the subjective opinion that others, particularly your boss, have of your efforts and contributions. Armed with objective data, you can justify your actions; and if you come up short, you can solicit meaningful feedback.

OVERCOMING GOAL SETTING HANG-UPS

It's interesting that almost every self-help book on bookstore shelves makes a case for setting goals as an integral part of achieving meaningful outcomes that bring you personal joy and satisfaction. It seems obvious that a dream leads to a vision; a vision leads to goals; and goals lead to action that will help you realize your dream. Yet when it comes to setting goals in the workplace, people's feelings seem to run the gamut from ambivalence (they can take goals or leave them), to a belief that goals are a waste of time, to downright fear and resentment that goals are the next worst thing to Big Brother watching over you.

Because most of the early research on goal setting was conducted to help managers and organizations maximize efficiency, performance, and productivity, it isn't surprising that people find goal setting just another form of control.[1] We are hoping that you, like Susan in the earlier story, will overcome goal setting hang-ups you might have, and come to realize that taking responsibility to initiate your own goals in the workplace is worthwhile and important for reasons in addition to clarifying expectations and justifying your behavior.

Recent studies indicate that there is not only good science behind the art and skill of goal setting—but reason for self leaders to join the bandwagon to set goals at work. The conscious intention created when you set a goal is a major factor in your motivation and sustained performance at work.[2] It is clear that goals focus your energy and activity, optimizing the hours in a day. They help you regulate your energy output, because studies indicate that people put forth effort in proportion to the difficulty of the goal.[3] You build character, because difficult, challenging goals tend to generate the energy for you to persist more than easy goals.[4]

Performance improves when your outcomes and expectations are clear and agreed upon. Over the years, the impact of goal setting on individual performance has been confirmed and reconfirmed.[5] We challenge you to notice the difference between those times when you have had important goals operating in your life and when you haven't.

It is time for self leaders to overcome their hang-ups regarding goal setting in the workplace. This is our attempt to debunk potential obstacles to goal setting. Ask yourself how many of the hang-ups to goal setting as described next resonate with you; then consider the strategies provided for overcoming the potential assumed constraint.

HANG-UP: I WAS DELEGATED A GOAL I'M NOT SURE I CAN ACHIEVE

In one study, Air Force trainees underwent the challenging goal of mastering flight simulation. If the would-be pilots wanted to prevent crashing and burning—which is a frightening prospect, even in simulations—they would have to master a number of skills. But, the simulation's competitive nature shifted their focus to "winning" and the consequences of failing *instead* of focusing on learning new skills. The result? Their performance was poor and error-prone because their attention was diverted from learning essential information and developing the skills needed to ultimately improve their performance.[6]

In the long run, one of the benefits of goal setting is that they motivate you to focus your energy, exert effort, and persist over time. *But this is only true after you possess the ability or basic skills required to achieve the goal.* If you don't have the ability demanded in order to achieve the goal, your resulting self-doubt will lead to poor performance.[7]

Strategy: When you are delegated a challenging or complex goal that requires skills you do not yet possess, you either need to renegotiate the goal or find a way to focus on learning, rather than the goal outcome. Reframe the goal so that you don't set yourself up for failure. Break the end goal into mini-learning goals with specific learning outcomes.[8]

For example, you are new to sales and are given the goal of generating $275,000 in sales per quarter for the next fiscal year. Not only have you never attained that level of sales, there are also essential skills you must master before you can hope to achieve the expected outcome. Break the goal into mini-learning goals such as *Demonstrate the four steps of the value-selling process by the end of next quarter* or *Recite product benefits and competitive advantages during a sales simulation exercise next month*. These mini-learning goals will provide stepping-stones to success that build your confidence over time and give you greater potential to meet the sales goal.

HANG-UP: GOALS ARE OUTDATED AS SOON AS THEY ARE WRITTEN

Does the focus of your organization change so rapidly that goals seem irrelevant as soon as they are written? Does your manager seem to flip-flop overnight from one priority to another? Do you subscribe to the rationale that things are moving so quickly, it's a waste of time to set goals? This way of thinking might indicate that goal setting is not the problem, but rather the way you set goals. Rule of thumb: If goals are outdated before you begin, your focus was probably on tasks instead of goals. Goals should reflect outcomes that only change incrementally if the organization continues to exist, such as a certain level of customer satisfaction, product or service quality, profitability, cost reduction, and so on. As a self leader, you may not have control over these types of goals, so the trick is to reframe your individual goals so they are personally motivating while also helping the organization to achieve its goals.

Strategy: Set goals for each of your primary areas of responsibility. Make sure these goals are stimulating, help you grow, and make the greatest contribution. If the organization's direction changes, you will still benefit from your efforts. When focused on the contributions and growth possible within a role, the changing face of the organization will not dramatically affect you or your goals.

HANG-UP: UNCLEAR OBJECTIVES

While the fact that you did not receive clear objectives might be true, in many circumstances this is more an excuse than a real obstacle.

Strategy: Take a stand. Even if your manager or organization is unclear regarding objectives, it doesn't mean you have to follow suit. Determine the contribution you want to make. Decide what will put meaning in your work-life. Then communicate with your manager and clarify the expectations you established. Most managers will be grateful that you initiated in this way and be relieved that you determined a direction for your efforts despite the organization's lack of one.

HANG-UP: UNREALISTIC ORGANIZATIONAL GOALS

Unrealistic goals are worse than no goals. When organizations ask people to aim for the stars and they work like crazy to meet the expectations but only get to the moon, they feel defeated. The organization may be thrilled with the trip to the moon, but the next time it asks people to shoot for the stars, the savvy employees respond with, *Who are you kidding?* They may not even attempt to get to the moon. But worse is the victim mentality that accompanies such unrealistic outcomes. Resentment, frustration, and inevitable failure are the most probable outcomes when people are held accountable for unrealistic goals.

Strategy: Clarify, as best you can, what you feel is realistic. If you cannot get buy-in from your manager or organization, then set goals that work for you as an individual. Even if you fail to achieve the unfair goals set for you, you will retain a sense of inner fulfillment from accomplishing the goals you set for yourself.

HANG-UP: LACK OF MANAGER INVOLVEMENT

Your primary issue is that your manager doesn't set goals with you, or doesn't allow the time to set goals with you.

Strategy: Maybe you should consider yourself lucky. You not only have the opportunity to impress your manager, but you also are more likely to be setting goals that are meaningful to you. This is your chance to create meaning in your work—it is one of the great benefits of being a self leader. Studies reveal that a majority of workers rank "interesting work" as a prime motivator.[9] It is within your control as a self leader to set goals that are interesting to you and result in a motivating environment. This is what initiating in the self context means—being proactive about setting goals and asking for help setting goals that require an expertise you don't have.

HANG-UP: I STILL DON'T SEE THE VALUE OF GOAL SETTING

We believe we have presented good reasons to set a goal. But, if none of them move you, then consider this: *A person who does not have a goal is used by someone who does.* If you ever felt used or under-appreciated by friends, family, colleagues, co-workers, or management, you can appreciate this sentiment. If self leadership is having the mindset and the skillset to take responsibility and initiative for succeeding in your work-related role, then setting goals is a strategy for lifting you from victim-mode to proactive-mode.

Getting agreement from your manager on goals can be one of the greatest benefits—it highlights your initiative, makes your contributions more obvious, and provides proof of your progress. Goals give you an objective way to measure your performance—potentially eliminating the frustrating subjective judgment of whether you deserve a four or a five on your performance review's five-point scale.

We were recently in a retail store and overheard a group of employees talking about the scoring on upcoming performance reviews. One young manager declared, "I don't believe in giving fives. It doesn't leave anything more for people to work toward." Unfortunately, we hear this lame excuse for subjective performance evaluations too often. Unable to stop ourselves, we had to intercede by asking: *What do you do when a person achieves the agreed-upon goals? Is it fair to deny someone a five in that situation?* He shot back with one of those *What are you talking about?* looks that prompted our second question: *Do you and your direct reports have specific and measurable goals that make it clear what a five looks like?* A young man who was obviously not a manager piped up, "That's the problem! We don't even know what a five means in this company, so no one is willing to give one!"

As a self leader, make it *your* business to know what a five looks like between you and your manager—even if the company doesn't have communicated standards of performance. When you and your manager have agreed upon your goals, not only are expectations clear, but as time goes on, you will have justification asking for what you need.

HANG-UP: I DON'T KNOW HOW

Finally some honesty and vulnerability! It requires skill to master the art and science of goal setting.

Strategy: Ask your manager for help—admit that you need direction and instruction on setting goals so that in the future you can be more collaborative in the process. If your manager doesn't know how to set effective goals (which may likely be the case), then we encourage you to read the next chapter, where we give leaders in the One-to-One Context a basic primer for initiating goals with their direct reports.

PUTTING GOALS IN THEIR PLACE

Don't set goals for the sake of setting goals. Your energy gets focused where goals are set, so direct your energy to something meaningful. Every goal you write should be important enough that the outcomes others are counting on you to produce are at risk of being unfulfilled if your goal is not accomplished.

That's not to say that everything needs to be turned into a goal just because it relates to something important in your life or work. One of our friends, a goal-driven person, decided to take up the martial arts. She investigated the myriad of options and finally selected Shaolin Kung Fu. Her rationale surprised us. The martial arts, especially in the West, are extremely goal-oriented—at every stage of your development, you receive a different colored belt to signify your progress. Because of this focus, martial arts schools have reduced the "art" to measurable objectives. Hence, there are specific skills and forms you must be able to demonstrate to pass the tests and move to the next level. You learn your skills and forms, pass your tests, pay your money, and receive a new colored belt as you move up the ladder of expertise. This formula has spurred widespread interest and participation in the martial arts—that's the positive perspective. But the goal focus all but eliminated the *art* from martial arts—failing to reinforce the mental and spiritual elements that truly define a master martial artist. As a result, there are ten-year-olds with black belts, the highest rank of accomplishment.

The martial art our friend chose to learn used a different approach. In the ancient Chinese tradition when you are young child, you receive a long white belt that is wrapped multiple times around your small waist. As you practice, you don't wash the belt. By the time you are an adult, the belt has turned black (and isn't wrapped nearly as many times around your waist). You only become a black belt with time, experience, and wisdom to augment your skill.

Our friend decided that she wanted to study her martial art without the pressure of an external focus of different colored belts to drive her—but as a statement of a life-long commitment to excellence. That didn't mean she wouldn't aspire to improve or learn the various forms and skills necessary to become a master. She would simply practice because she enjoyed it. You see, goal setting is a technique for increasing the probability that your performance will improve in a particular area. You set goals because there is a gap between your real and ideal; because there are skills or performance standards that you must achieve to fulfill the expectations of your role; and because objective measures help you facilitate communication (especially between you and your manager in the workplace).

We share this story of the martial artist because the job of a self leader is to recognize the areas of opportunity that will be enhanced through goal setting and those where it's simply best to let life unfold. There are some things in life that you should do for the sake of doing them—because they bring you joy or because you are in the moment. Don't be so future oriented that you drive the present out of your life.

ENDNOTES

1. Mento, et al., 1987.
2. Latham and Wexley, 1981; Locke and Latham, 1990.
3. Earley, Connolly, and Ekegren, 1989.
4. Latham and Wexley, 1981; Locke and Latham, 1990.
5. Ibid.
6. Ackerman, 1987; Ackerman, 1989; Kanfer and Ackerman, 1989.
7. Ibid.
8. Bell and Kozlowski, 1995; Brown, 2001; Clark, Dobbins and Ludd, 1993.
9. Kovach, 1976.

INITIATE IN THE ONE-TO-ONE CONTEXT

Initiate in the One-to-One Context by establishing performance objectives based on Key Responsibility Areas, SMART goals, and a development plan for your direct report that is aligned with the direct report's work-related vision as well as the organization's vision and initiatives.

Setting your own goals is one thing, but when you are a leader in the One-to-One Context, your leadership responsibility is to ensure that others have the structure they need to satisfy their work-related vision as well as the organization's vision.

HARNESS THE ENERGY OF VISION

If you've done the work of the second leadership practice and guided your direct reports through the envisioning process, good for you. The vision your direct reports have created for their work-related roles is an emotionally charged declaration of an ideal that stimulates their *motivation and energy*. Now you need to harness and direct that energy through the third leadership practice—*initiate*.

If you are a sales leader, then setting goals is nothing new for you—in fact, most sales organizations are all about the numbers. Too bad. Not that numbers aren't important as guidelines and mechanisms for feedback, but goals could and should be so much more. If you are the leader of an administrative staff, the idea of goals probably leaves you scratching your head. It's near to impossible, you must think, to set goals for the receptionist or the secretary whose jobs are to be reactive. Too bad. Because goals provide the structure to harness and direct energy—and no one needs that more than administrative staff (who are among the most stressed people in the workplace precisely because they don't have a sense of control over their environment[1]).

We propose you initiate a structure for shaping how energy gets directed—from general to specific. In other words, begin with a broad idea of the expectations you have for a direct report; from there, get specific about what you expect as measurable outcomes; and finally detail how they should/could go about accomplishing those outcomes. Here's a little test. Sort the following three statements that are related to a salesperson's role from most general to most specific:

A. Make at least seven sales calls a day by phone, five days a week, for the next two months, by referring to leads generated by the last convention exhibition.

B. Promote, solicit, and close on company products and services in order to maintain and increase corporate revenue.

C. Increase sales volume by 3.8–4.2 percent in the next twelve months while maintaining 15 percent profit before taxes.

Statement (B) is the most broad and comprehensive statement defining a functional area of a role—we call it a *key responsibility area*. Statement (C) is more specific than the key responsibility area and articulates a specific and measurable outcome to be accomplished over time that will fulfill the promise of the key responsibility area—it is a *goal statement*. Statement (A) is the most specific and describes how the goal will be achieved through discrete and often repetitive action—it is a *task statement*.

Is it really necessary to make these seemingly subtle distinctions? We think so. A lack of clarity regarding outcomes fosters miscommunication and missed expectations. Work hard to articulate what you want your direct report to achieve; your language can only be clear if your intent, purpose, and outcomes are clear. The art and skill of harnessing a vision and initiating action is doing the hard work of conceptualizing what you want as outcomes. Goal setting is an art that takes skill. Be patient: Art takes time to master; skill takes time to build.

The following sections will provide an outline for how to initiate with your direct reports:

1. Identify three to five key responsibility areas for a role (general).
2. Set goals that help fulfill the expectations of each key responsibility area (less general; more specific).
3. Generate tasks that help achieve the goals (most specific).

More specific how to's are provided in the Appendix on the book's companion Web site because we're tired of telling leaders what to do but not how to do it. If leadership is a practice, then having the skills to practice is essential to leadership success.

1. IDENTIFY KEY RESPONSIBILITY AREAS FOR A ROLE

Our clients are consistently amazed at the clarity that comes through the discussions aimed at answering the question: *What is the job and why does it matter?* The beauty of developing key responsibility areas is in going beyond a job description to focus on contribution. Please don't get hung up on the nomenclature—we use key responsibility areas, known in many organizations as KRAs—because we need a term to describe the *process* of refining the functions of a role.[2] And that's what is most important—the process. Generating a KRA requires tugging at meaning, laboring over a particular word, and struggling for agreement. In the end, the process clarifies the role your direct report plays, but also helps you and your direct report *appreciate* the role he or she plays.

For example, let's say you are a sales manager. The sales representatives that report to you may engage in four or five *functions* that could be the source of key responsibility areas, such as the following:

- Build customer relationships
- Communicate product knowledge
- Forecast sales
- Prepare bids and proposals
- Close product sales

Each of these ongoing functions could generate a key responsibility area statement. For our working example, let's take the function of *close product sales*. A statement reflecting this particular function might be . . .

> *Promote, solicit, and close on purchases of designated company products and services in order to satisfy customer needs and increase district and organizational revenue.*

Notice that this key responsibility area statement contains three elements: *Does* • *What* • *Why*. First, it synthesizes a cluster of actions that describe what your direct report *does* within this function of closing product sales (*promote, solicit, and close*). Next, it relates what those actions are connected to (*purchases of designated company products and services*). And finally, it clarifies the intent of the function and the contribution and benefits to the organization; it makes the connection between individual effort and organizational welfare (*to satisfy customer needs and increase district and organizational revenue*).

HOW MANY IS ENOUGH?

The rule of thumb is that most roles or jobs can be described by three to five key responsibility areas. Less than three key responsibility areas may spell impending boredom because the job or role doesn't have enough depth or breadth, or underutilization—given a typical work week, the person could probably be contributing more than the job is currently demanding. More than five key responsibility areas might result in a lack of focus and dissipation of energy—not giving the individual enough time to do any one aspect of his or her job well.

Taken together as a group, key responsibility areas *could* be considered a substitute for a job description, but they are not the same.[3] Key responsibility area statements are more flexible, easier to refine and re-prioritize than a formal job description, and should ultimately lead to goals with action plans.

KRA AND THE ORGANIZATION'S VISION

Individual effort and organizational vision come together when you and your direct report discuss and formulate their key responsibility area statements. The *Why* component helps both you and the follower *live* the organizational purpose and values. It helps your direct report *think organizationally*, yet act commensurate with specific role requirements and expectations. A key responsibility area for a salesperson might reinforce the organization's vision on customer satisfaction but also reinforce activities that will increase organizational revenues (and sales commissions). Both outcomes must be accomplished without harm to the other.

When you guide your direct report in formalizing key responsibility areas, you are identifying *ongoing functions* that must continually be done if the organization is to remain vital.

GET AGREEMENT

The true power of writing key responsibility areas comes through collaboration between you and your direct report. An exercise we often recommend is called the *Five on Five*. Identify the top five key areas of responsibility for a particular role or direct report and rank-order them in importance from 1 to 5, with 1 being most important. Ask your direct report to write what they believe the top five key areas of responsibility are in order of importance. Don't worry if they don't yet know how to write a formal KRA statement— their rough estimates will be enough to begin the process.

Compare your list to your direct report's list. Where are the discrepancies? What needs to be aligned? What are the implications for disagreement? For example, what if you believe the primary key responsibility area is to provide customer service, but your direct report thinks it should be factual on-time record keeping? That might explain why they can be found in the office doing paperwork instead of meeting face-to-face with clients.

If you want to dig deeper, compare estimates on what percentage of time you think should be spent on each key responsibility area on a weekly or monthly basis. The discrepancies may shed light on past squabbles and help prevent future misunderstandings and missed expectations. KRA statements are powerful tools that describe and clarify the essence of a role, the scope of the work that is required, the contribution to be made, and a rationale for why the role exists.

2. SET GOALS

What criteria will you use to determine if a key responsibility area is being fulfilled or optimized? According to research, *goal setting is the most critical skill for guiding your direct reports to expected outcomes.*[4] In fact, if your direct report doesn't have goals, no matter how much time and attention you give to providing other forms of leadership on their behalf, there's a good chance they will not meet expected outcomes, let alone sustain high performance.

Your role in the One-to-One Context is to develop the person who reports to you, but your ultimate responsibility is to the organization and its outcomes. Ironically, you may best be serving your organization by focusing on your direct report and their success. When they achieve their goals, the likely result is higher productivity and profitability for the organization. Effective goal setting could result in better (safer, less expensive) products and services or better customer service. Remember, action is stimulated through the creative tension generated when goals are set. It is crucial that you either set goals with your direct report or oversee their own efforts to set goals.

Setting goals with your direct report is also just good managerial practice. You will have more objective ways of measuring productivity. Your direct reports might discover ways to accomplish goals that lead to the improvement of systems and processes. Perhaps most importantly to you, it is simply easier to help your direct report grow, develop, and perform at high levels when you have commonly held outcomes.

No matter what level of expertise your direct report has as they set goals, it is your role to help them understand which goals will be most meaningful in the big picture to meet organizational goals and in light of their own career goals and dreams. Only you can help them understand what standards are reasonable given what others are doing in the organization or in the industry. And they will depend on you to inform them about which resources are available—or unavailable—that could impact the goal's timeline and attainability.

GOAL SETTING AND PERFORMANCE

Is there any empirical evidence that helps us understand how setting goals may impact individual or organizational performance? The answer is a resounding *YES!* Your direct report's conscious intentions or goals are a major determinant of their work motivation and performance. There are three reasons why goal setting affects performance:[5]

1. Setting goals directly affects what people think and do. Goals focus activity.
2. Goals allow for the regulation of energy. People put forth effort in proportion to the difficulty of the goal, assuming that the goal is accepted.
3. Difficult goals lead to more persistence than easy goals.

Newer studies[6] are beginning to confirm that goal setting as an organizational practice may indeed make a positive impact on businesses' bottom line.

There are some interesting qualifiers to the impact goal setting can exert on individual performance.[7] When your direct report participates in goal setting, they will often set goals higher than those you would have just assigned unilaterally. This is important, because when they accept their goals and have the ability to achieve them (or are confident they can gain the ability), the higher the goal, the higher the performance.

As influential as goal setting itself can be to performance, there must be some latitude for an individual to influence their own performance. For example, if work processes or technology rigidly determine performance—such as assembly lines, mandated or scripted sales approaches, iron-clad procedures for handling customer complaints—then goal setting may show little effect on performance.

If your direct report feels threatened in the process of goal setting, and goals are used as hammers instead of motivators, they will attempt to lower expectations whenever possible. Supportiveness leads to higher goals being set than are set in nonsupportive or hostile environments.

GOAL-SETTING TECHNIQUES

Our belief is that the *best way to lead others in goal setting is to first learn to write your own.* Leading from the inside-out is a more genuine, authentic, and usually more effective way to lead than prescribing for others what you cannot do for yourself. So feel free to apply the techniques for yourself before using them in the other four contexts with direct reports, teams, organizational initiatives, or alliances.

A goal statement should be spun out of a particular key responsibility area. Recall the statement for the salesperson described earlier?

> *To promote, solicit, and close on the purchases of designated company products and services in order to satisfy customer needs and increase district and organizational revenues.*

This key responsibility area could generate three possible goals or outcomes. A goal could be written on promotion, or solicitation, or closings. The KRA includes *built-in* priorities, with sales closure having the most impact to the bottom line. Salespeople can promote and solicit sales without closing; however, in the long run, a salesperson cannot close on a huge volume of sales without promoting and soliciting sales.

A goal statement should be central to the key responsibility area from which it stems. The following goal meets our criteria:

> *Close on $350,000–$375,000 worth of product X, and $250,000–$275,000 worth of service Y, with an average pre-tax profit of 7 percent in the next 12 months.*

This goal statement can be summed up in three words: *Achieve • Outcome • When.* A goal specifies the action necessary (*Achieve*) to reach the desired result (*Outcome*) by a certain time (*When*) in order to fulfill a key responsibility area. The goal statement does not state *how* to achieve an outcome. Instead it identifies what end results are desired by when.

MAKE GOALS SMART

For many years, the SMART[8] acronym has been used to help validate the potential effectiveness of a goal. There are a myriad of variations on SMART, but we think this version generates the most essential criteria for setting goals that not only have a chance at being achieved, but who are *worth* achieving. SMART stands for Specific and Measurable, Motivating, Attainable, Relevant, and Trackable. The specifics for how to make your goals SMART are in the Appendix on the book's companion Web site, but a sample of a SMART goal is provided next.

A SMART Goal Sample

Is our sample goal statement SMART?

> *Close on $350,000–$375,000 worth of product X, and $250,000–$275,000 worth of service Y, with an average pre-tax profit of 7 percent in the next 12 months.*

Notice how the goal is *specific and measurable*. It specifies a range of dollar amounts that must be closed. If the salesperson closes more than $375,000 in product X sales and more than $275,000 in service Y sales, it reflects above-average results. Closing less than $350,000 in product X and less than $250,000 in service Y would result in the salesperson's performance being seen as below average.

There is also a quality measure in the goal. The total dollar amount in both product and services must be sold at a 7 percent pre-tax profit. That gives the salesperson some leeway to sell product at a lower or higher margin, but the average for the total dollar volume must be at or above 7 percent. This quality measure prevents selling only quantity; it prevents volume at the expense of a reasonable margin.

Assume that product and service sales numbers are based upon the salesperson's past performance, industry averages, and other salespeople's performance. Those are good indicators that the goal is *attainable*. The goal implies that if volume is reached with only one product but not the other, then the goal was not achieved. If there is a chance of either the product or the service being substantially more difficult, then the two goals should be separated out or lower dollar standards could be set.

Because the goal was generated from a specific key responsibility area, it is *relevant*. Because a timeline is included, the goal is *trackable*. Is the goal *motivating*? That can only be determined by the person who must achieve the goal and will become clear through discussion, coming to agreement, and generating of the tasks that will lead to an action plan.

3. GENERATE TASKS

After the SMART goal is established, tasks or action items are needed that lead to the achievement of the goal.

A Task Statement can be summed up in three words: *Performs Activity • How*. Tasks are the discrete, step-by-step details that, when combined, form an action plan specifying how the goal will be achieved. But if the tasks do not yield the desired progress, then they can, and should, be altered or tweaked to accommodate the goal. An example of a task statement is:

> *To make at least seven sales calls a day by phone, five days a week, for the next two months, by referring to leads generated by the last convention exhibition.*

Notice that the task statement includes a discrete action that can be done in a short period of time and, unlike a goal statement, doesn't contain a standard. A task should also include one action verb that is directly related to accomplishing the goal, and the word *by* followed by a list of smaller discrete actions that explains how the activity will be performed.

Don't Confuse a Goal with a Task

Confusing a goal with a task can be a fatal flaw because the goal is usually lost.

Here's a common example of losing the goal because of a task-focus. You want to lose weight and get in shape, so you set a goal: *Exercise three to five times per week for the next six months.* You have the best of intentions. But due to legitimate circumstances, you can only work out twice in a particular week, or heaven forbid, only once. By definition, you already failed to achieve your goal, so you give up. This is why so many New Year's resolutions, such as *Get in shape,* fade by February—they were never goals, but tasks that when not accomplished led to abandonment of the original outcome.

A goal expresses the end result to be accomplished; a task spells out *how* the end result will be accomplished. Although a goal is not written in stone and should be reviewed and examined for continued relevance or attainability, it is usually steadfast. The tasks in the action plan, however, will shift and change to best accommodate the goal's achievement. Therefore, in the preceding New Year's resolution example, the *Achieve • Outcome • When* goal statement might be: *I will reduce* (achieve) *my body fat by 5 to 7 percent* (outcome) *by the end of the third quarter of this year* (when). A task statement for an action step to help achieve the goal might be: *I will work out three to five times per week by running at least once a week, attending the gym twice a week, and cycling whenever possible.*

There's another important reason not to confuse goals and tasks. If there is a focus on how to achieve a goal before the goal is set, the goal setter could be overwhelmed by assumed constraints and never set the goal. Instead, set the goal, and ways to accomplish the goal will reveal themselves. We once witnessed a woman who expressed a desire to return to school for a graduate degree. She immediately began deliberating over how she could do it, focusing on who would take care of the children while she was at night school, how to pay for the books and tuition, and whether her manager would be threatened. By the time she contemplated an action plan, she talked herself out of the very idea of getting a master's degree. We encouraged her to set the goal: *I will attain my master's degree by the end of next year.* By focusing on the goal—rather than the tasks to achieve the goal—she stimulated her awareness about the possibilities of how to achieve it and was able to generate a creative, flexible action plan.

LINKING KEY RESPONSIBILITY AREAS, GOALS, AND TASKS

We mapped our sales example in Table 19.1 to demonstrate how a key responsibility area begets a goal that generates tasks.

TABLE 19.1
LINKING KEY RESPONSIBILITY AREA, GOAL, AND TASK

Key Responsibility Area Statement	Goal Statement	Task Statements
Promote, solicit, and close purchases of designated company products and services in order to satisfy customer needs and increase district and organizational revenue.	Close on $350,000–$375,000 worth of product X, and $250,000–$275,000 worth of service Y, with an average pre-tax profit of 7 percent in the next 12 months.	Generate a potential customer list by sorting through leads received from two or more conferences. Make five cold calls each day to potential customers. Send out at least one information packet per day in response to a customer request.

The most important focus when leading in the One-to-One Context is the growth and development of your direct report. But their growth and development should occur as their key responsibility areas and goals are being served, as well as the organization's vision and strategic initiatives.

Your leader-follower relationship will be forged and tested in the give-and-take dialog that stems from tugging at your direct report's key responsibility areas and goals. The quality of the organization's output will also depend on your conscientious focus on these vital interactions. But your true leadership potential will be realized when key responsibility areas and goals set in motion all kinds of considerations, such as your direct report's self-concept, prior experiences, readiness to learn, and achievement motivation. You must be obsessively concerned with the application of adult learning principles if the skills and energy of your direct report are to be enhanced and sustained.

Leading your direct report through the invariable ups and downs that eventually result in the achievement of their goals and fulfillment of their key responsibility areas requires assessing their performance and responding to their needs, which just happen to be the topics of Chapters 25, "Assess in the One-to-One Context," and 29, "Respond: The Fifth Leadership Practice," respectively.

LEADERSHIP AND HIGHER ORDER THINKING

Initiating requires *higher order thinking*. It involves clearly formulating and stating the most central responsibilities that must guide the actions of your direct reports. If these central responsibilities are clearly delineated and communicated, the *ready, fire, aim* mentality is avoided. You are seen as credible because learning starts on the right foot, your direct report is focused, and both of you are free to work on *how* to accomplish the goals that yield results.

When we observe leaders immersed in the daily grind, we often hear them say they don't have time to formalize key responsibility areas, set SMART goals, and shape tasks into action plans. We get the old *alligators* excuse (hard to think about clearing out the swamp when you are surrounded by alligators). Yet they then have to find the time to deal with the consequences of failed outcomes and under-performance. We ask, plead, and cajole leaders to remember—a lack of clarity and specificity in outcomes promotes performance variance.

Think about this: The best duets start with a score or written music. The high order skill of initiating provides the needed music for the people you are developing and holding accountable for producing outcomes. Eventually, both you and your direct report will be able to improvise on the theme; but even the best jazz has the structure of a theme. As the leader-teacher, you must be thoughtfully clear about key responsibility areas, goals, and tasks—no ifs, ands, or buts.

ENDNOTES

1. *Issues in Labor Statistics*. U.S. Department of Labor. Bureau of Labor Statistics. Summary 99-10. September 1999.

Hackman, J. R. and G. R. Oldham (1976). Motivation through the design of work. *Organizational Behavior & Human Decision Processes*, Vol. 16(2), pp. 250-279.

Karasek, R. A. (1979). Job demands, job decision latitude, and mental strain: Implications for job redesign. *Administrative Science Quarterly*, Vol. 24, pp. 285-308.

2. Key responsibility area, or KRA, is the term we've chosen to use, but the name or label is not important; it is the process it represents—no matter what you call it.

3. The main difference between KRAs and job descriptions is that a job description does not contain information about either the job's specific functions or why the function is important. Job descriptions should, of course, contain a list of skills and experiences necessary for the employee to be successful. However, KRAs usually contain a comprehensive statement of the specific functions to be served, not job skill data.

    Job descriptions are usually used to form the basis of a job posting, hiring notice, or advertisement to attract suitable candidates, to orient new employees to the functional areas for which they are accountable, and to serve as a basis for job classification and the establishment of salary range. Most often, a job description will include a position title, a narrative paragraph or two describing major and minor functional areas of responsibilities, and a list of prerequisite skills needed by possible candidates. The list of skills might include educational requirements or years of experience needed in certain areas.

4. Zigarmi, et al., 1997; Latham and Wexley, 1981; Locke and Latham, 1990; Toerspstra and Rozell, 1994.

5. Locke and Latham, 1990.

6. Reber and Wallin, 1984; Terpstra and Rozell, 1994.

7. Latham and Wexley, 1981.

8. The SMART acronym has been used for many years to validate whether a goal meets the rigorous demands that give you a fighting chance to achieve it. The traditional version of SMART uses five criteria to help judge the quality of the goal: Specific, Measurable, Attainable, Relevant, and Trackable. While useful, this model misses the emotional element that makes pursuing and achieving a goal meaningful and worthwhile. We've amended the SMART model so that specific and measurable are combined into one category, and the M becomes "Motivating" to help ensure that your goal generates the energy you will need to pursue, persist, and ultimately achieve your stated outcome.

CHAPTER 20

INITIATE IN THE TEAM CONTEXT

Initiate in the Team Context by establishing a high-impact team charter that is aligned with the sponsor's vision for the team and includes team member-generated vision, goals, and operating principles.

When the kings and queens of England granted land to deserving individuals in centuries past, they granted charters, empowering individuals with the right to own, farm, and govern the land. In return, the landlords paid the royalty a percentage of the profits made from the land. In effect, a charter was an agreement granted by the king or queen.

Today, the concept of a sovereign granting favors to others may seem a bit patronizing, but some of the properties of granting a charter remain helpful in a team culture. While the organization confers certain rights, authority, and resources to the team, the team, in return, is responsible for producing certain results. The process of establishing the relationship of the team to the organization and of the team members to each other is what we call *chartering*.

Chartering is absolutely essential for the team's success. It is how the team's scope, goals, norms, and other essential elements for high levels of team performance are defined. The team sponsor envisioned a blueprint for the team (in Chapter 14, "Envision in the Team Context"); the charter is the detailed plan—with the endorsement of the sponsor, team leader and members, and the organization. As with England's royalty, a charter needs to be written down so it can be understood and agreed upon by those it affects. After the charter is created, team members will continue to refer to it to remind themselves, their sponsor, and the organization of their mutual agreements.

A TEAM WITHOUT A CHARTER . . .

No matter how skilled you are as a team sponsor or leader, you need to create a team charter. It is the single most critical success factor to a team's success. In fact, a team with a superior charter and mediocre leadership can reach superb performance; but the team will *never* reach superb performance with superior leadership and a mediocre charter.[1]

Whether you create the charter at the team's first meeting or during a specially scheduled chartering session, allow at least four hours to a full day. Before you shudder and declare it impossible, challenge your assumed constraints and consider *why* a charter is a critical success factor. You will save time in the long run, but what's more important is how much more effective your team will be because you established guidelines that govern the team and individual behavior; you created a team purpose and goals that are stronger than the interests of individual members; you determined benchmarks against which team outcomes can be measured; you established a baseline against which team member behaviors can be assessed; and you provided the team with information that will enable it to self-correct.

A charter consists of six vital components that should be developed through dialogue among the team sponsor and team members. Before we reveal these essential elements of your team's charter, you need to consider who is leading the team and who the team members will be.

WHO'S LEADING THE TEAM?

If you're reading this, then there's a good possibility you think you are a team leader—or hope to be. Maybe you sponsored a team and are now contemplating who should take the leadership role from here. The fact is—the team can function during its initiation without a formal leader (gasp!), but only if there is a *nonmember* of the team who can facilitate the chartering. (In our experience, a qualified facilitator may be better suited to guide team members through the landmines of self-interest, personality conflicts, and values differences that may exist as the team first comes together.) So there are three ways to determine team leadership:

- The sponsor becomes the leader and charters the team.
- The sponsor appoints a leader who charters the team.
- A leader emerges from the team's membership during chartering facilitated by a non-member.

The following guidelines are written as if you are a chosen leader taking your team through the chartering process for the first time. If you are currently the leader of a team in progress, it's not too late to initiate the team's charter—better late than never!

An important note: Team leadership may initially be assigned or predetermined, but in a mature team, the team leadership is fluid, constantly changing, always in recognition of technical and interpersonal skills, and above all, shared. This concept of shared leadership in a self-managed team will be more thoroughly explored in Chapter 26, "Assess in the Team Context."

WHO'S ON THE TEAM?

After you know the team's leader, it's time to populate the team based on the sponsor's vision of ideal team members. Begin with a brainstorm of team member characteristics necessary for the team to accomplish its outcomes. Consider technical expertise, diversity of experience, point of view, cultural perspectives, and organizational or political savvy. It is good to remember that technical expertise is no substitute for the interpersonal skills necessary to bring out the motivation and excitement in others. In fact, technical expertise and human understanding might be inversely correlated in some people. Ultimately you must weigh which is most helpful or detrimental to the team's output and long-term prospects.

With team member criteria in hand, take the time to brainstorm specific prospective members. Make a list of prospects, listing their occupation, area of expertise, and other known characteristics relevant to team membership (such as their DISCposition or Values Point of View). Compare your prospects to your list of criteria and compile an initial list of team members.

Great teams don't take team membership lightly. As sponsor or leader, you should give consideration to the appropriate size of the team and the requisite skill sets and personalities for ideal members. The makeup of the team members is so critical to professional sports that they allow for trades midway through the season. We're not suggesting you fashion your team blueprint by mirroring professional sports, but there are valuable lessons to be learned from the great professional team leaders.

CHOOSING MEMBERS

One of the first questions you should consider is: *How many people should I have on this team?* Having too many people on a team is unproductive; not having enough people is unproductive. Of course, the specific number you choose depends of the type of team and the scope and complexity of its outcomes or project.

For reasonable productivity, the minimum size for a team is four people; the maximum is 12.[2] Because many leaders do not possess the skills of Jesus Christ, who led a team of 12 to great effect, consider the optimum size of a values-based team to be eight to nine people. Even the legendary sports coaches in football, baseball, soccer, baseball, and cricket, with teams ranging in size between 12–45, break the team into subgroups led by assistant coaches who are responsible for the day-to-day work and skill-building for role-specific team members. The primary coach plays the role of integrating all the sub-units and reinforcing the team's purpose and goals. If you don't have that luxury, stick to eight or nine team members.

ESSENTIAL COMPONENTS OF THE CHARTER

The charter itself will guide the team as it goes about its day-to-day business, but the most beneficial aspect of chartering is the process itself. This is where the team takes the original blueprint provided by the sponsor and builds its foundation and infrastructure.

A charter consists of six components that should be developed through dialogue between the team sponsor and team members:

1. Team Vision
2. Team Outcomes
3. Team Operating Guidelines
4. Team Norms and Ground Rules
5. Team Roles and Responsibilities
6. Charter Endorsement

The significance of each of the charter components and tips for completing them are provided next.

TEAM VISION

The sponsor envisioned the team from *his or her perspective* by visualizing what the team looks like in the ideal, crafting a statement of purpose, proclaiming rank-ordered values, and aligning the team's vision with the organization's vision. (The sponsor's role is described in Chapter 14.)

The team uses the sponsor's vision as a starting point as they initiate their charter with a vision that that includes the same elements so they can be compared, contrasted, made more relevant, and improved upon.

VISUALIZE THE POSSIBILITIES

You may need to remind team members of the power of visualization. In this case, you are attempting to create an emotional notion of what the team's opportunities are. Begin with each individual's notion and then find commonalities. At the end of this exercise, you may not have an ironclad statement of what a compelling future looks like, but you will have synchronized team member's picture of the team's possibilities.

Now that members have visualized the ideal team, imagined the best-case scenario without limitations, and recognized the team's potential, they are more likely to create a purpose with passion and values with heartfelt meaning that are motivating to both team members and its constituents.

CRAFT PURPOSE STATEMENT

An important first step for crafting a purpose statement is to brainstorm the assumptions regarding purpose, responsibilities, authority, and boundaries that team members have, based on their perceptions of the sponsor's purpose. This is a critical step because it confirms or negates differing perceptions, potential areas of conflict, and misunderstandings before the team gets into the actual crafting of the purpose.

After assumptions and boundaries have been clarified, team members can try their hand at crafting a purpose statement. Our recommendation is that individuals write their own, then sub-groups combine their multiple ideas into one representative statement, and then finally the sub-groups come together to craft one statement that individuals and sub-groups can endorse.

We recommend the same template for crafting a team purpose statement as you used to Envision (Chapters 11–16 and outlined in the Appendix on the book's companion Web site). Whatever method you use, be sure that all team members feel they have contributed, that their viewpoint was honored, and that they can agree with the purpose. Don't be frustrated if the process takes longer than you thought it would—this may be the most important thing your team does to ensure its future success.

A team we were facilitating had spent hours formulating their purpose. It seemed the activity was completed and successful. But before leaving it and moving on to the next chartering step, we looked into the eyes of each team member and asked for their honest appraisal. One woman shook her head and said, "Yes, it's fine." Something in her tone did not ring true, so we pressed, "Are you sure? There seems to be a hint of hesitation. It might be helpful for us to understand what it is." The woman paused for an awkward period of time, but her teammates waited, for they too could now tell there was a potential issue. The woman finally said that she was disappointed with the purpose statement—that while it was functional, it didn't seem to capture the spirit of their visualizing or the promise of what was possible. Her emotional and eloquent description of what she felt was missing from the team's purpose statement resonated with the team. She hadn't said anything earlier because she didn't know how to fix it; she just knew it wasn't right.

We all assured her that it wasn't her job at this point to have all the answers—that a team is valuable because of the collective energy, expertise, and insights. To the credit of the team, they agreed to spend another hour tweaking and revising the statement. It was fascinating to behold. They transitioned from a group trying to formulate a technically correct statement of their purpose, to a team united in their desire to invoke passion into their purpose. Before the hour was up, they agreed on a new purpose statement, and a funny thing happened. People started high-fivin' each other, body slamming, and demonstrating other out-of-character displays of joy and excitement. The woman who had hesitated was acknowledged for her honesty—which later on in the chartering process became one of the team's most important values.

To this day, if we don't get team members explicitly expressing their satisfaction over the team's purpose statement, we do not move them to the next step. We're hooked on high-fives and body slams.

RANK ORDER VALUES

After the team has crafted its purpose statement, it needs to identify heart-felt values that will guide future decisions and actions. The team's values should answer the questions: *What does the team stand for?* and *What standards are important to the team, to the way it works, and to its products or services?*

Consider principles such as Integrity, Creativity, Excellence, Quality, Practicality, Learning, Diversity, and so on. Be sure to have team members communicate the meaning and description of values being considered. Eventually the team needs to come to agreement on three to five values, the values' definition, and behaviors that demonstrate the value that the entire team can embrace.

If values are to be useful in team decision making and guiding team member behavior, they need to be rank-ordered. As a team, agree on which value has the number-one priority, number-two priority, and so on.

We were working with a very large, progressive pharmaceutical company that prided itself on its values. Every team built their values off the organization's values. Their values included performance, teamwork, respect for people, community, and customer focus, among others. So far, so good. The problem was that there was no ranking of the values' priorities. So when a sales team faced a problem with allocating resources and was trying to determine their best course of action, they weren't sure if it was more important to guarantee their quarterly sales numbers, to save the client relationship, or to honor the needs of a team member suffering a health crisis.

On the other hand, a team we worked with had very clearly prioritized values, so when push came to shove, they knew it was best to leave money on the table if it meant violating a customer relationship in the long run, or a team member's health and loyalty. The team's values stipulate *how* the team should go about attaining its performance, outcomes, or profitability.

One more note about your team's values. Your team members will represent a variety of values points of view. Be aware of how those individual valuing systems play into the formation of the team's values. For example, Loyalty Seekers and Equality Seekers will most likely advocate values that represent social means values; Justice Seekers and Freedom Seekers will most likely voice a preference for personal means values. At the risk of seeming to promote one valuing system over another, team values need to be geared toward the welfare of the whole—that's what makes a team different from individuals acting on their own behalf, or a group of individuals who do not necessarily have allegiance to the team. Having said this, it is appropriate to guarantee selective individual rights when ground rules and operating guidelines are established later in the chartering.

In the end, the team's values should reflect three considerations:

- What standards are important to the way the team works and to its products and services?

- What unifying beliefs are important to keep in mind as the team goes about its business?

- What is the rank order of the values? Which value has priority when push comes to shove and a decision must be made?

ALIGN THE VISION

At this point in the chartering process, it is important for each team member to be aware of—and satisfied with—how the team's vision aligns with the organization's vision and their own work-related role. If the team's purpose is at odds with one's role or doesn't have the endorsement of the team member's manager, it might create a values quandary and competing ulterior motives.

For example, take the team whose purpose was to design a process for communicating and selling to third-party vendors (people or organizations that sell the company's products to their own clients). One of the team members was a regional sales manager who believed that third-party vendors in his territory were in direct competition with his sales reps. Despite the effort to create a noble purpose and rank-ordered values for the team, this member was having difficulty accepting the team's vision in comparison with the one he and his own team had crafted for his territory.

When visions don't align, you have a couple of choices. You can replace the team member, change the team's vision to accommodate the misalignment, or help the team member understand how two seemingly disparate visions complement one another. In our example, the team helped the manager realize that the bigger picture was increasing the organization's sales and getting their products to as many people as possible. But the team also tweaked the language in their purpose and values to reflect their intention to increase third-party sales without infringing on or cannibalizing direct sales efforts. As the chartering process continued, goals were set to reinforce their approach.

TEAM OUTCOMES

The team's boundaries and primary expectations have already been envisioned by the sponsor. Now the team needs to accept and confirm those expectations by establishing three to five key responsibility areas with at least one SMART goal each. (The tasks and action plans generated to achieve the goals aren't included in the team charter document, but are kept separately so they can be monitored and updated by team members who are responsible for overseeing the goal.)

Given the complex nature of a team, it is critical to formalize goals. Every member must be crystal clear about what the team's outcomes and expectations are—and their role in meeting them.

TEAM OPERATING GUIDELINES

Without operating guidelines, work may not get done, conflict is assured, and ambiguity will frustrate even the most dedicated team members.

The team needs to establish operating guidelines—*agreed-upon procedures that maximize time and output*—in at least four areas: meeting structure, problem-solving process, decision-making policies, and conflict resolution procedures. Notice how a team wastes valuable time when it doesn't have a plan for conducting team meetings. Notice how unvoiced problems undermine progress when there is no formalized way to handle problem-solving. Notice how a team alienates team members when an overpowering leader or clique makes unilateral decisions on behalf of the team because there is no agreement on how to make decisions. Notice how rival sub-groups form when conflict arises but is not dealt with straightforwardly or openly.

Your team may also want to consider additional guidelines. For example, what happens if outcomes, goals, or expectations are changed or shifted—is there a way to formalize change? Has the team defined project improvement strategies—how will the team change things that are not getting results; how will the team handle changes within or outside the team? Have evaluation strategies been defined—how will you judge the team's effectiveness?

TEAM NORMS AND GROUND RULES

Despite more than 5,000 years of civilization, when people work together, they need ground rules to deal with each other. Ground rules are guiding principles or rules that govern *interpersonal conduct* among members. They describe how people should treat each other. If things become unruly, uncomfortable, overly emotional, or dysfunctional, the team ground rules need to be evoked.

Every team has norms—even if it is the first time a team has met. Someone shows up late to the first meeting and no one says anything—that's a norm. A cellphone rings in the middle of the meeting, and it is tolerated—that's a norm. A norm is an accepted way of doing things—but it may not be *the best way* of doing things. High-impact teams observe their norms and, when necessary, establish ground rules to help form new norms.

When you are observing your own team, ask yourself questions to get a sense of its norms in use and areas for possible new ground rules: *Has the team defined ways people should behave toward one another? Is there an accepted way of sharing information? How can team members better support one another? Is there a method for monitoring team behavior? How will the team handle changes?*

Ground rules should be established in areas that affect the interpersonal dynamics of team members. For example, when most problems arise in a team, people point the finger to communication. After observing the team's norms around communication, it may want to establish ground rules to encourage active listening and discourage interrupting.

In addition to ground rules for communication, your team should consider ground rules for giving and receiving feedback, commitment and involvement, leadership, setting tone, and celebration.

As your teammates embark on their journey together, don't forget the importance of understanding the variety of DISCpositions represented on the team. By sharing this information, many of the potential conflicts and obstacles the team will face can be better understood and dealt with. For example, if you map out the primary DISCposition of each team member, you may notice that there is a preponderance of Extroverted Controllers ("D" DISCpositions) who are inclined to rush to judgment, not tolerate process, and focus on outcomes. There will be times when the D's results-orientation is helpful and needed, but it may take the balance of the lone Introverted Accepter ("S" DISCposition) to pull the team back and encourage more thoughtful analysis or decision making from time to time.

As the team leader, you need to be mindful of who is getting airtime and if the introverts are being involved and their ideas solicited, for example. Of course, it is also the responsibility of individuals to use their versatility and adapt their disposition when the team needs them to behave outside their comfort zone.

Operating guidelines ground rules are what ultimately bring the values of the team to life. For example, a team we worked with had a value of creative thinking and innovation. One of their guidelines was to not always accept the first idea out of the shoot, but to generate at least three viable alternatives before making a decision.

TEAM ROLES AND RESPONSIBILITIES

Team responsibilities are a set of roles that the whole team or individual members will be accountable for during the team's operation. Roles and responsibilities may be collective, paired, or individual. This distinction is important to ensure balance between a team approach and individual accountability.

COLLECTIVE RESPONSIBILITIES

Every member is equally and personally responsible for accomplishing collective responsibilities. For example, when everyone on the team collectively agrees to contribute to a team outcome: *All team members will contribute to the promotion and production of the annual fund-raising event with a goal of raising $30,000 after expenses.* Or, when a ground rule requires all members to participate: *All team members will assist in the resolution of conflict that may occur between two team members.*

PAIRED RESPONSIBILITIES

Paired responsibilities are shared by two team members, one acting as a support to the other. Sharing the responsibility between at least two team members is a failsafe measure to ensure the likelihood of an important job, task, or role being done. It is especially wise for parts of a project that are critical to achieving outcomes. When sharing responsibility, one member still has the lead or primary responsibility, and the other team member is given secondary responsibility to monitor and support as needed. Both are fully and equally accountable for the result. An example is: *Bill will schedule the meeting room for the team meetings, and Jan will be the backup.* Paired responsibility may be a key to creating a team in which peer pressure evolves naturally.

INDIVIDUAL RESPONSIBILITIES

Along with the obligation of team results, an individual team member will be assigned primary responsibility for pieces of work because of his or her particular expertise and interest. The primary responsibility for preparation or fulfillment of the work is individual, but the team will still review and provide input.

Some individual roles will be from the output perspective—related to achieving the team's outcomes and goals, such as: *Bob will be doing a market analysis for this prototype and will present it to the group by X date.*

Other individual roles will be assigned from a process perspective—related to *how* the team achieves its outcomes and goals. The most important *process* roles are those of the team or meeting leader, process observer, scribe or recorder, and timekeeper. It is important that these roles have clearly defined responsibilities and that the team members assigned to them are held accountable for specific team member behavior.

Team Leader or Facilitator

The function of the *team leader or facilitator* is to lead the team through its work to the outcomes and deliverables agreed upon. In general, the role means to repetitively focus the team on the goals and the processes to achieve those goals. It is also the team leader's role to help team members deal with the interpersonal dynamics that increase their sense of cohesion and honesty.

Process Observer

The function of a *process observer* is to aid the team in both its interpersonal dynamics and its group processes. This role helps the team maintain high levels of synergy in problem solving. The process observer role will also help prevent behaviors motivated by self-interest that may affect team decision making and conflict resolution.

The person in this role must be vigilant about observing team members' behavior and holding them accountable to follow the processes they agreed to. The process observer role may be a permanently assigned role, but it may be more effective to rotate it periodically.

Scribe

The function of the *scribe* is to record, in writing, the major themes expressed in meetings. Typically the team scribe has the responsibility to track team discussion during the meetings, as well as handle the logistics of minutes, agendas, and materials needed by team members. This team member is also a fully participating member. Because of the detailed nature of this role, it is better to have one individual fill the role, reassigning only periodically.

Timekeeper

An obvious, but oftentimes overlooked, role is the *timekeeper*, whose most important task may be to negotiate use of time when an agenda item requires more time.

CHARTER ENDORSEMENT

The charter endorsement is the final step in the chartering process.

TEAM ENDORSEMENT

All team members must fully and completely agree to work toward endorsement of the charter, working out any individual reservations about the various components. The team must be unified around a common purpose, outcomes, guidelines, and ground rules. Each team member must agree to commit his or her best efforts to the team outcomes. Team members, having had their chance to influence the charter, must now fully agree to support the charter or be prepared to step out of the team.

SPONSOR ENDORSEMENT

The sponsor's approval is given for the content of the charter and the commitment to support it with resources as required.

COMMUNICATION OF THE CHARTER TO THE COMMUNITY

The charter should be communicated to the people who are most affected by the team's work. By sharing the charter with primary contacts, the team can increase its credibility and probability of success with these external groups. The endorsement process should be completed by announcing the team's vision and outcomes to the general organization and community the team serves.

The chartering process results in a document that promotes the aims and principles of a united group while defining the boundaries and limitations within which the team must operate.

After the charter has been signed off by its sponsor and team members, and introduced to the community it serves, the actual work of your team begins. But your team's strong foundation and infrastructure has given it a much higher probability of success than teams that have not done the hard, but mostly satisfying, work of chartering.

ENDNOTES

1. Wageman, 1997.
2. For expanded rationale for the most effective size of a team, see Fowler and Zigarmi, 1987, pages 61-63.

CHAPTER 21

INITIATE IN THE ORGANIZATIONAL CONTEXT

You Initiate in the Organizational Context by outlining a strategy supported by initiatives with action steps for their achievement that are aligned with the organizational vision.

You might not think of a Catholic parish as a model for a business organization, and the parish certainly doesn't look to business as a model; however, we submit that both types of organizations will benefit from the same *process for taking action*—whether it's to fulfill a vision, proactively embark on a goal, or initiate a change. It doesn't matter if you are leading a church, a mom and pop company, a public sector organization, or a Fortune 500 business; you are responsible for conceptualizing, legitimizing, and supporting the implementation of initiatives that will ultimately determine your success as an organization.

Unless there's a monumental event that warrants an upheaval, such as an imposed government regulation, a merger, buy-out, or a financial disaster, your organization's overall vision will probably not change radically. It's more likely that you will be called upon as the organization's leader to initiate a strategic plan and SMART goals that will help ignite its current vision. Your challenge is to make sense of the organization and determine what's required to take it to the next level; to ensure that critical initiatives are mandated and implemented. But first you've got to stop playing organizational *Whack-a-Mole*.

BREAK THE WHACK-A-MOLE HABIT!

Think of a major, strategic-level problem in your organization that, if it were solved, would make things better. How long has the problem existed? Six months, one year, two years, three years? You are in a position of leadership, you know the problem exists—has existed for a long time—and yet you haven't solved it. Why? Because you have been busy playing the organizational version of the arcade game of Whack-a-Mole! Little insidious problems keep raising their heads and you shift your focus from big picture, strategic issues so you can whack these little pests with the mallet of the day. In fact, you have gotten very skilled at clobbering the little critters—you even feel the rush of excitement that accompanies the game as you anticipate the next head popping up.

While busy playing Whack-a-Mole, you lose sight of the big picture, the organization's strategic vision, and strategic challenges. It takes discipline to resist whacking the moles and tackling the more difficult and long-term issues facing the organization.

It is your responsibility to create initiatives to take your organization to its highest potential; to frame these initiatives in a way that focuses and inspires the people who implement them. This effort requires more complex leadership behaviors and demands greater discipline than in any other context. This responsibility also generates a couple of major concerns: Where do initiatives come from? How do you go about deciding the priorities?

SORTING THROUGH CONCERNS

When we consult organizations, we have the leader of the organization and his or her top executives work through a sorting exercise to identify and prioritize concerns. The executives sort through hundreds of so-called problems and opportunities and designate each as either Not Relevant or Legitimate Concern. It is fascinating to put executives into pairs or small teams and ask them to agree on their concerns.

In the end, a concern stems from one of the five categories that mirror the structure of organizations described earlier in Chapter 4, "The

Organizational Context: Your Role in Generating the Organization's Vitality." A concern might be related to

1. *Needs, opportunities, demands, and resources* (The basis of the organization's existence)
2. *Vision, values, and norms* (The organization's strategic drivers that provide direction)
3. *Processes, structure, and policies* (The organization's framework that provides organization)
4. *Activities, practices, and behaviors* (The organization's intervening variables that provide the link between direction and organizing framework)
5. The triple bottom line of employer of choice, provider of choice, and investment of choice (The organization's key results areas)

Each aspect of the organization's structure provides a wellspring of concerns that can be turned into opportunities for initiatives that either fulfill the organization's vision or address a problem or issue that is preventing it from reaching the next level. Sample concerns are provided next for each category. See if any of them resonate for you and your organization.

NEEDS, OPPORTUNITIES, DEMANDS, AND RESOURCES

When you scan the environment to uncover potential opportunities or problems that may lead to initiatives and goals, these are samples of the types of concerns you discover that need to be addressed:

- External changes pose a serious threat to our future.
- We are not growing, are losing momentum, or are on the decline.
- Our competitors are growing faster than we are.
- Changing market demographics are causing new challenges or problems.
- Local economic conditions will adversely affect our performance.

VISION, VALUES, AND NORMS

These are examples of revisiting your strategic drivers to see if there are potential issues you need to address:

- Not every organizational member fully understands our vision.
- We let most aspects of our culture *evolve* rather than deliberately creating an organizational culture to support our vision.
- We are not flexible enough.
- We avoid dealing with difficult or challenging issues.
- We don't have a process for dealing with breaches in values-driven behavior.

PROCESSES, STRUCTURE, AND POLICIES

These are examples of issues concerning the organization's framework—and by far the category with the most potential number of areas for improvement:

- Our structure is not right for our vision.
- Decisions don't last.
- Leaders do not set clear standards and hold people accountable to them.
- Goals in one group are out of alignment with goals of other groups— we sometimes work at cross-purposes.
- Training and development for personnel is inadequate.
- Our systems don't support the goals people are expected to achieve.
- Our board of directors isn't functional.

ACTIVITIES, PRACTICES, AND BEHAVIORS

These are examples of issues you need to recognize for dealing with implementation of current initiatives:

- We don't respond to our client's needs as quickly as we should.
- We don't do a good job of building long-term relationships with our vendors.
- We don't regularly solicit our clients for feedback on possible improvements.
- We don't regularly improve the way we do things based on internal and external feedback.
- Our technology is not state-of-the art.
- Our facilities are inadequate.

EMPLOYER, PROVIDER, AND INVESTMENT OF CHOICE

These are samples of concerns that address key responsibility areas for the organization:

- We have high turnover among staff.
- Stress levels are too high.
- We are finding it difficult to recruit the best talent.
- We have too many customer complaints.
- Customer loyalty is low.
- Productivity is low.
- Profit margins are low.

PRIORITIZING THE CONCERNS

Concerns can be organized following the cause and effect relationship, or causal flow, of the organization's structure. The highest priority concerns relate to *needs, opportunities, demands, and resources.* The next priority concerns relate to *vision, values, norms,* and so on through the structure to the *key areas of responsibility or organizational outcomes.*

For example, if you were starting a brand-new company, your highest concern would be to focus on opportunities, market demands, and resources you have available. Next you would clearly define the expected norms and values that breathe life into your vision. Then you would create the processes, structure, and policies that would support everyone's efforts. After that, you would identify necessary activities, practices, and behaviors. If all this were carried out effectively, your company would consistently produce rewarding results in the triple bottom line.

However, most leaders are not starting out anew. Therefore, many of the factors at each level of the organizational structure are already in place or have been operating for some time. This means you might focus on the issues that are causal at first, but you might also focus on issues with a lower level of causality that are more critical because of their current level of impact on performance. For example, if technology is so outdated that you can't serve your customers or track inventory effectively, that may become a priority over reacting to a competitor's recent entry into the marketplace.

When concerns have been agreed upon and prioritized, reframe them into problem statements that contain enough information so that someone reading it for the first time would understand it. For example, a concern over *turnover is too high* might be stated as: *How can we reduce our 7 percent turnover in the upcoming year?* These problem statements in the form of questions become your strategic agenda and spawn SMART goals to be achieved within a specified time period. The agenda and SMART goals comprise your organizations strategic plan.

REACTIVE VERSUS PROACTIVE AGENDAS

Your ultimate objective, whether following the preceding suggested procedure or not, is to create a strategic agenda that contains a plan to permanently solve the problems you have identified. But the agenda we have described is a *reactionary* agenda based on current concerns; it could or should also include a *proactive agenda* based on your organization's vision. Rather than only focusing on concerns, you proactively seek out opportunities to better fulfill your vision. For example, if one of your values is to be a learning organization, your proactive operational agenda might include establishing an internal university to better educate and develop your people, or the creation of a scholarship program for deserving employees.

Over time as you lead in the organizational context, you'll create initiatives that deal with all the dimensions of organizational functioning. Sometimes you'll create initiatives to breathe life into the vision. Other times, you'll scan the organization from top to bottom, identify specific concerns that exist in the various dimensions, prioritize them according importance, and begin attacking them one by one. Sometimes you'll take these issues on yourself, and other times you'll delegate the problem-solving responsibility to others. Either way, you have used problem-solving and decision-making in a strategic process to initiate goals that will help ensure the vitality of your organization over the long haul.

CHAPTER 22

INITIATE IN THE ALLIANCE CONTEXT

*Initiate in the Alliance Context by establishing a charter outlining the
alliance's major goals and operating principles for fulfilling the alliance's
Big Idea as well as the visions of the partners in the strategic relationship.*

An alliance is a special entity—the coming together of potentially disparate
organizations to form a strategic relationship. To initiate in the alliance
means forming a charter, as it did in the Team Context. In this case,
however, an alliance leadership team—a group of people from both alliance
member organizations—is responsible for doing the chartering that will
eventually influence rotating team members. If an alliance sponsor created
the initial Big Idea that spawned the alliance, then his or her vision will be
the kickoff point for the alliance leadership team. But ultimately, the
alliance leadership team will generally be held accountable for the performance and results of the alliance.

CRAFTING THE ALLIANCE CHARTER

The alliance charter should include the vision, purpose, and values; outcomes and deliverables; operating guidelines and ground rules; and roles and
responsibilities.

ALLIANCE VISION, PURPOSE, AND VALUES

In a parallel process to the process described for creating the team charter in Chapter 20, "Initiate in the Team Context," the alliance members need to individually visualize what an ideal collaborative effort looks like and then find the commonalities. The alliance can then craft a purpose statement that includes a clear definition of the alliance's long-range reason for being. It might also include a statement of what the alliance is not in order to help clarify boundaries of purpose.

Because alliance members will represent different departments within an organization or, if it's an external alliance, different organizations, it is especially important to spend the time grappling with and agreeing to mutually shared values. These values should reflect the philosophical beliefs or underlying philosophies that will guide the behaviors and decisions of the alliance members when conducting alliance business or acting on behalf of the alliance.

OPERATING GUIDELINES AND GROUND RULES

Most alliances are created with the idea of being perpetual—unlike a project team that has built-in termination based on accomplishing its goals. This is why operating guidelines and ground rules that describe how the alliance will function are so important. How often members will meet, how meetings are structured, protocols for communicating with nonalliance members within the organization or between organizations, reporting procedures, processes for making decisions and solving problems, communication guidelines for alliance members, and the like must be considered and agreed upon. In general, all processes, norms, and expected behaviors by alliance members should be spelled out in advance to avoid confusion or conflict once the alliance is operating. The charter should also answer: *How will grievances and problems be addressed? How will the performance of the alliance overall be evaluated? By whom?*

ROLES AND RESPONSIBILITIES OF ALLIANCE MEMBERS

The alliance charter should identify and define each of the critical roles necessary for effective alliance team functioning. As in a team charter, these should include such roles as meeting facilitator, scribe, and timekeeper. Regarding leadership, questions need to be answered such as: *Will there be an alliance team leader? If so, how long will the term last? How will the team leader be chosen—by the team itself or by someone outside the team? How long will alliance members serve? Is their service full time or part time? Who evaluates team member performance? How? How will new or rotating alliance team members be chosen?*

Because strategic alliances are usually formed across corporate boundaries and because there is a great deal at stake, it is probably best to have a facilitator who is *not* going to be a member of the alliance leadership team (and perhaps also isn't an employee of either parent company) to take the team through the alliance leadership team chartering. If carried out properly, this will result in faster trust building, a greater likelihood that the foundations created are truly win/win, and a higher likelihood that all the issues—especially the most sensitive ones—will be addressed more competently.

OUTCOMES AND DELIVERABLES

As in the other contexts, key responsibility areas describe the major ongoing functions of the alliance; goals are short-term and long-term statements of measurable results to be achieved that will lead the fulfillment of the key responsibility areas. All these come together in a strategic plan for the alliance. The plan should be evaluated to ensure it serves the needs of both parent organizations and their respective visions and strategic plans. The plan should also describe how performance compared to the plan will be reported (most likely quarterly) and for revising and updating it in the future (most likely annually).

SUMMARY—INITIATING IS SMART

Initiating is not the most glamorous leadership practice; indeed, it may be the most difficult. It requires more time, analysis, discipline, and adherence to process than any of the other leadership practices. But we also hope you can appreciate how key responsibility areas and subsequent goals and tasks create a bridge between a vision and action that enlivens the vision.

Think about the SMART goals that are the cornerstone of an individual performance plan or organizational strategic plan, or a team's or alliance's charter. With goals that are specific and measurable, motivating, attainable, relevant, and trackable, the people you lead are set up to win. They will be able to deal with obstacles that inevitably arise during the pursuit of a goal and impede progress. Badly conceived and constructed goals set up you and those you lead to fail. Over time, energy will diminish and performance will be deterred. When goals are not part of a mutual process, people will feel controlled—which may lead to compliance, but rarely to autonomy.

Initiating shouldn't be considered something one *must* do; it is done because it works. Initiating results in more energy, passion, and commitment; it provides a way to perceive growth and garner satisfaction. When you master the art and science of initiating, you give people a sense of anticipation, hope, and opportunity. Hopefully you find those by-products worthy of your time, effort, and expertise.

CHAPTER 23
ASSESS: THE FOURTH LEADERSHIP PRACTICE

Imagine two little old ladies standing in front of the mall directory at a large shopping center. They are trying to locate a particular store but are struggling to figure out how to get there. Finally, they sight the little red dot: *You are here.* One of the ladies shakes her head in amazement and says to her friend, "I don't understand it! How do they always know where we are?"

As a leader, you need that little red dot, as well. The store the little old ladies were trying to reach represents your goal. Think of the dot as representing where you are in terms of achieving the goal—your current reality. As with the little old ladies at the mall, you need to know where you *are* before you can figure out *how to get* where you are going.

The fourth leadership practice, Assess, means knowing how to find the red dot—or current reality—in relation to a goal that needs to be achieved. After the current reality has been assessed, a plan can be mapped out to reach the desired destination. What do we mean by current reality? It is a combination of your current ability and energy to pursue and achieve a particular goal.

As with the other leadership practices, you assess in all five contexts; but *what* and *how* you assess varies from context to context, as shown in Table 23.1. For example, you will assess the ability and energy of a direct report to achieve his or her goal differently than you will assess the ability and energy of a team involved in an interdependent team goal.

TABLE 23.1

QUICK REFERENCE GUIDE FOR HOW TO ASSESS WITHIN AND ACROSS CONTEXTS

Self Context	One-to-One Context	Team Context	Organizational Context	Alliance Context
Assess your own phase of performance by looking at indicators of Ability and Energy on a work-related goal.	Assess your direct report's phase of performance by looking at indicators of Ability and Energy related to an agreed-upon goal or task.	Assess the team's phase of performance by looking at indicators of Ability and Energy related to goals and outcomes identified in the team charter.	Assess the organization's phase of performance by looking at indicators of Ability and Energy of the people in the organization as they implement an organizational initiative.	Assess the alliance's phase of performance by looking at indicators of Energy and Ability related to the goals and outcomes identified in the alliance charter.

You Assess by appraising the Ability and Energy of an individual, team, organization, or alliance to achieve a specific outcome.

Notice in Table 23.1 that the indicators of ability and energy in a given situation reveal what we call the *Phase of Performance*. It turns out that on the journey to achieving a goal, there are predictable ebbs and flows of ability and energy. If you aren't aware of these predictable phases, you can lose your way and never reach your destination.

PREDICTABLE PHASES OF PERFORMANCE

Research, learning theory, and anecdotal evidence suggests that when your goal is challenging or complex, there's a high probability you will falter in its pursuit.[1] Why? Because there are predictable patterns that will derail you if you're not aware of them and know how to cope with them.

We have integrated the research and organized the predictable patterns into five phases of performance. It is important to note that these five phases merely *describe* your current reality on a particular goal in an instance in time—they do not *explain why* you are in a particular phase. However, by observing the indicators of ability and energy, you will most likely be able to determine the causes yourself.

We have labeled the five phases Curious, Confronting, Cautious, Achieving, and Discerning. The research validating the phenomenon of the five phases is interesting, relevant, and helpful, but perhaps not as convincing as your own experience.[2] So we will begin with an example you can hopefully relate to—driving a car.

DRIVING THROUGH THE FIVE PHASES

Think about your own experience learning to drive a car, and as you read the following scenarios, pay particular attention to the two primary indicators of your phase of performance: Ability (either high or low) and Energy (either high or low).

CURIOUS PHASE

Remember when you were a teen and your goal was to get (and keep) your driver's license? Did your parents need to coax you behind the wheel? Did they need to spend time convincing you that you could do it if you'd only try? Probably not. Like most teens, you could hardly wait for the freedom and independence that driving offered. In fact, your parents' (and the driver ed teacher's) greatest challenge was to channel your enthusiasm and energy into productive driving lessons that would teach you everything from how to adjust the mirrors to the rules of the road. This is a great example of the Curious Phase of Performance, where your Ability is low but your Energy is high—a potentially dangerous combination. Ability, in this goal situation, is determined by the skill necessary to pass your written and practical driving tests. Because you had no prior driving experience, you would most likely have failed the driving test, but you would have done it with great enthusiasm and naïve confidence.

It is said that knowledge without enthusiasm is boring, but enthusiasm without knowledge is chaos. The trick in the Curious Phase is to minimize the chaos, curb your enthusiasm, and take the time and effort to learn what you need to learn.

CONFRONTING PHASE

Your parents gave you a couple of lessons and allowed you to drive in traffic a few times. At this point, you were probably feeling one of two things. Either you were getting impatient and irritated with having an adult in the car to monitor your every move, or you realized that driving wasn't as easy as you thought and therefore felt a sense of trepidation as you turned the key. While you still desperately wanted the license to drive by yourself, you were discouraged at the time it was taking to master the finer points of maneuvering in traffic, parallel parking, and backing into a parking space.

In the Confronting Phase of Performance, your Ability only slightly increased, but your Energy dropped. The trick in the Confronting Phase is to overcome your low Energy and continue learning.

CAUTIOUS PHASE

Finally you were of age and it was time for the big driving test. For the most part, you were ready, but despite the new knowledge and skill, there was hesitation when in heavy traffic, heart pounding as you took a steep hill (especially if driving a stick shift), or mild panic during a snowstorm or driving on ice. You studied the rules booklet, memorized all the sign symbols and their meaning, and practiced parallel parking until the tires on the right side of the car were nearly worn. When the day finally arrived and the examiner with the clipboard told you to get behind the wheel of the car, you weren't as confident as you were with mom and dad in the car.

In the Cautious Phase of Performance, your Ability is moderately high, but your Energy fluctuates. The trick in the Cautious Phase is to trust your Ability and rebuild your Energy.

ACHIEVING PHASE

Now, years after receiving your license, you can drive on automatic, even if you use a standard shift. Sometimes you arrive at a destination and don't remember the details of driving there. Renewing or keeping your license is not an issue. In fact, you are planning a cross-country road trip because you enjoy being behind the wheel.

You are at the Achieving Phase of Performance, when Ability and Energy are both high. The trick in the Achieving phase is to sustain the passion that gives you the high Energy to continue doing what you have been doing.

DISCERNING PHASE

Depending on circumstances, you may get to the Discerning Phase of Performance, where you wonder if you want to sustain the Ability and Energy to retain your high performance. Maybe you live in New York City and realize that public transportation is more efficient than maintaining a car and the skills to renew a license. Maybe you lost your night vision and are afraid to drive in the dark. Maybe you reached the age where you don't trust your reflexes and your Ability to drive safely.

In the Discerning Phase of Performance, you question whether it is worth the continuing effort to be a high achiever on a particular goal.

ASSESSING BY CONTEXT

Your leadership role is to identify indicators of performance in the context in which you are leading. As is often the case, if you begin by understanding how to assess your *own* performance, you will have a head start in assessing the performance of *others*. The next five chapters are designed to help you do just that.

ENDNOTES

1. Pratt, 1988; Grow, 1991; and Knowles, Holton, and Swanson, 1998.

2. For basic information regarding how to assess the five phases of performance, see Part Two, "The Five Practices of Contextual Leadership," in this book. For more information on the research associated with assessing phases of performance, see the Appendix on the book's companion Web site.

CHAPTER 24

ASSESS IN THE SELF CONTEXT

Assess your own phase of performance by looking at indicators of Ability and Energy on a work-related goal.

Did you ever start a diet and then give up? Begin an exercise program and then quit? Been in a relationship that failed? Most of us can answer *Yes* to at least one of these questions.

Learning to assess your phase of performance won't guarantee success in all your endeavors. It will, however, help you understand why you failed to achieve goals in the past, and how you can achieve them in the future. If you study the goals you did *not* achieve, you will probably discover that you gave up, quit, or abandoned these goals in fairly predictable circumstances. Typically, you start off on a new goal as curious, and then flounder as you confront realities that don't meet your expectations—this is often when you give up on the diet, quit the exercise program, or go into disillusionment in a relationship. If you don't quit, but progress, you become cautious or hesitant before achieving your goal. After you have mastered or achieved the goal, there comes a time of discernment—questioning if the goal is still meaningful, if it still requires your conscious or conscientious effort, or if it is something you can let go.

Assessing the current level of Ability and Energy you have to pursue and achieve your goal will ultimately help you determine what you need in order to progress from one phase of performance to the next.

ASSESS ABILITY

You possess Ability when you *know how to achieve the goal and have the skill to do it*. In the driving example used in Chapter 23, "Assess: The Fourth Leadership Practice," Ability was initially demonstrated by passing both the written and road tests. It's one thing to know how to drive a car and another to be able to do it to the standards required by law. Ability is not a frame of mind or belief in yourself. Ability is having the skill you need to achieve the goal you are working on. Ability can be demonstrated and repeated over time.

To assess your Ability on a goal, ask yourself this question:

Can I demonstrate the behaviors necessary to achieve the standards for this goal and repeat it, when necessary?

If your answer is *No*, then you have low Ability on the goal; if *Yes*, then you have high Ability.

ASSESS ENERGY

Energy is the *psychological impetus to do what is needed to achieve the goal*. Energy is reflected by your motivation, desire, self-confidence, enthusiasm, and willingness to pursue the goal and sustain achievement over time.

Ability to achieve a goal typically increases over time (unless the goal is skill-based, and after a period of inactivity, the skill is lost—as with a golf swing!), but Energy fluctuates.

To assess your Energy on a goal, ask yourself this question:

Do I have the self-assuredness and inner desire necessary to initiate, be persistent, take risks, and overcome emotional roadblocks to achieve this goal?

If your answer is *No*, then you have low Energy on the goal; if *Yes*, then you have high Energy.

ABILITY, ENERGY, AND YOUR PHASE OF PERFORMANCE

Table 24.1 reflects how combinations of Ability and Energy comprise the five phases of performance, from the beginning stages of taking on a goal, to the final stages of achieving and discernment.

TABLE 24.1

COMBINATIONS OF ABILITY AND ENERGY IN THE PHASES OF PERFORMANCE

Phase of Performance	Level of Ability	Level of Energy
Curious Phase	Low	High
Confronting Phase	Low to Some	Low
Cautious Phase	Moderate to High	Low (Fluctuating)
Achieving Phase	High	High
Discerning Phase	High	Low (Questioning)

You usually begin at the Curious Phase with a combination of low Ability and high Energy. (You *could* start out at the Confronting Phase with low Ability and low Energy if you agreed to a goal where you are not internally motivated and are only pursuing it, for example, out of fear of losing your job.)

Assess your phase of performance on a goal by asking two questions related to Ability and Energy:

1. Can I demonstrate the behaviors necessary to achieve the standards of this goal and repeat it, if necessary? (Ability)

2. Do I have the self-assuredness and inner desire necessary to initiate, be persistent, take risks, and overcome emotional roadblocks to achieve this goal? (Energy)

Assessment is an ongoing process. The answers to the two questions determine which phase of performance is *currently* being experienced. As your Ability increases and Energy fluctuates over time, your phase of performance will also change.

HOW TO GAUGE ABILITY AND ENERGY

Imagine you are on a road trip and run out of gas. Some of us don't need to imagine it—we've been there. As your car sputters to the side of the road, you chastise yourself for forgetting to check the gas gauge or tempting fate by running on fumes. It is just as foolhardy to ignore your levels of Ability and Energy during your journey toward your goal as it is to ignore the gas, oil, and heat gauges in your car on a road trip.

What gauges do you check for Ability? What do you look for to determine if your Ability to achieve a goal is low (Curious and Confronting Phases), moderate to high (Cautious Phase), or high (Achieving and Discerning Phases)?

Your Ability is low if you cannot currently demonstrate the skills required to master the goal. Your Ability is high when you have mastered the skills, procedures, and strategies necessary for achieving your goal—to the point where you don't need to think about them consciously. In fact, when your Ability is high, it's a waste of cognitive energy to think about how to do what you're doing. So after you mastered driving, it is a waste to use your mind consciously thinking about the dozens of little actions required to drive to and from work. When you were first learning, it was essential to maintain that kind of focus.

Is your Ability transportable? Some skills, such as planning skills, writing skills, or speaking skills, can be used or applied to several different work outcomes. Let's say you have worked for several years as a sales clerk for the retailer Banana Republic. Customer service and general knowledge of retailing, fashion, and restocking might be considered transportable skills. Now you are moving to a different retailer, T.J. Maxx. If you assume that the Achieving Phase of Performance you had reached on your major goals at Banana Republic will transfer to your new job at T.J. Maxx—even though you may have similar goals and outcomes—be prepared to fall flat on your face.

Regardless of previous retail experience and transportable skills, you still begin at the Curious Phase on goals in your new situation; you need to learn a new approach in a different culture. Banana Republic's marketing and retailing approach is quality, trend-setting clothing. Customers need and expect a high-involvement with a sales clerk who knows the merchandise. T.J. Maxx considers itself the leader in off-price brand-name clothing and home goods procured by savvy buyers who get great deals on overstock items, last year's fashions and models, and manufacturer's overruns. T.J. Maxx customers enjoy the thrill of the hunt; they neither need nor want extensive sales clerk involvement. While your retail experience is admirable, you cannot claim the Ability it takes to be a high achiever when you move to a totally different retail environment.

But what if the retailers were similar; even owned by the same parent company—say Banana Republic and the Gap? You would still need to get up to speed on subtle, but critical, cultural differences, as well as procedural and product variations.

But don't despair! Your transportable skills will likely help you move more quickly to the Achieving Phase than someone with little or no retail experience. So, transportable skills will not determine your initial assessment of your phase of performance, but they may affect how quickly you move through the five phases of performance on similar goals.

When you face a complex or challenging goal, it is especially important to continually gauge your Ability and your level of Energy to pursue the goal. Over time, your mindset will be as important, if not more so, than your skill set. Your self-assuredness or confidence may flag in the pursuit of a complex and challenging goal—that is when your enthusiasm, desire, and motivation are most challenged.

THE CAVEATS OF SELF-ASSESSMENT

A caveat is a warning or caution. The word was chosen purposefully to reflect things that you should be aware of when self-assessing, but they are not necessarily negative.

For example, moving from one phase to the next is not a bad thing—in fact, it is a natural progression of learning and performing. However, if you are not aware when it is happening, then you may not be aware that your needs changed. For example, when you move from the Curious Phase to the Confronting Phase, you need to address not only low Ability, but also your wavering Energy on the goal. When you move from the Achieving Phase to the Discerning Phase, you need to address Energy questions that weren't an issue in the past.

In most cases, the caveats of self-assessing lead you to deeper, more meaningful insights that help make self leadership worth the effort.

CAVEAT 1: HONESTY FACTOR

Because no phase of performance is *bad*, there's no reason to fear an honest assessment.

We worked with a nuclear power plant that will remain anonymous where there was a decidedly macho-like culture among the primarily male workforce. We discovered young workers who felt it was not acceptable to admit a lack of Ability. Frightening to imagine, but workers were refusing to ask for help when they needed it! The culture placed such high value on competence that the young man feared admitting they didn't have it. Ironically, such a culture almost ensures they'll never get it! We cannot emphasize this enough: Your phase of performance merely reflects where you are on a natural path to accomplishing your goal. If you are not honest about your current reality, you will not get what you need to progress, and you will stall, quit, or worse yet, bluff your way through—to your detriment and, in the case of the nuclear power plant workers, to the potential determinant of others.

CAVEAT 2: MANAGER'S PERCEPTIONS

When you discuss your phase of performance with your manager, you may be surprised when he or she doesn't share the same perception of your Ability and Energy on a goal. Your phase of performance may appear different on the outside than it does on the inside. For example, your manager may look at your past experience and training to date and assess that you are in the Achieving Phase. However, because you lack confidence and feel tremendous self-doubt, you may actually be in the Cautious Phase.

If your manager is unaware of your actual phase of performance, it is likely you won't get your needs met, at least not from your manager. This is especially problematic if your output or productivity declines or doesn't increase. If that's the case, don't fault your manager. It is your responsibility to convey your level of Ability and Energy and ultimately get your needs met.

Another likely scenario is when you think your Ability is high, but your manager thinks it's low. You will both need to explore the discrepancy. It could be that your manager made a legitimate assessment because he or she has never seen you demonstrate the desired behaviors. The burden of proof resides with you. It could be that you over-assessed your Ability due to over-confidence. In this case, you need to be honest about your Ability to do the goal to the standards required.

During the discussion of your phase of performance, you and your manager may discover that the goal initiated was not as SMART as it needs to be and the standards are not clear or realistic. Think of a discrepancy between you and your manager on your phase of performance as an opportunity to partner and clarify your goal, your Ability, your Energy, and your needs.

CAVEAT 3: BIG GOAL SYNDROME

Sometimes even a SMART goal can be too complex to assess. It's possible that no one phase of performance can fairly reflect your Ability and Energy on the myriad of sub-goals required to accomplish the overall goal. In such a case, narrow the focus of the goal or break it down into major tasks and assess the parts. For example, if you have a new goal to increase sales in your territory by 10 percent by the end of the next quarter, you may need to break it down to sub-goals such as product knowledge, communication or writing skills, price negotiations, closing skills, and so on. When you assess your Ability and Energy on each component needed to increase sales by 10 percent, you will realize you are at different phases of performance on each.

CAVEAT 4: OUTSIDE INFLUENCES

A bad hair day can affect the amount of Energy available for a particular goal. While the example may seem trivial, the point is not. There are many factors that affect your self-assuredness, outlook, confidence, motivation, and thus your Energy on a goal. Even if emotional factors are not goal-related, they can affect the way you approach the goal. This is one of the reasons that, despite a hesitance to go there, it is sometimes appropriate and important to discuss personal life matters at work. If outside events diminish your Energy and affect your productivity, they need to be discussed. One of the skills of a self leader is being able to face your emotional nature and respond in a way that keeps you moving through the five phases of performance to complete a goal.

CAVEAT 5: CURSE OF THE CONFRONTING PHASE

When your Ability and Energy are both low, you may question whether the effort required is worth the payoff your future performance might bring. As you contemplate abandoning your goal, the Confronting Phase of Performance may feel like a curse. But consider it a blessing. This is the phase where you now have enough information to consciously decide whether your goal is worth pursuing. This is where you realize there is a gap between your idealized expectations and the sometimes-harsh reality; this is where you learn to either cope with reality or change it. This is where you discover your character; where you build the empathy that will help you coach and lead others in the future. This is the time you will remember with a sense of satisfaction and appreciation for how far you've come when, and if, you finally arrive at the Achieving and Discerning Phases.

ASSESSMENT IS ONGOING

Assessing your Ability and Energy is not a one-time proposition. It is an on-going challenge to notice how—or if—your Ability progresses and how your Energy fluctuates as you pursue your goal. The practice of assessing is also ongoing because you will always have a variety of goals going on at any one time that demand attention to your Ability and Energy.

Of course, assessing your Ability and Energy is just the beginning—how you respond to your assessment is the topic of Chapter 29, "Respond: The Fifth Leadership Practice." This is where the myriad of skills for being a self leader come into play. If you don't have the skill to get your needs met at each phase of performance, you simply won't progress from the Curious Phase to the Achieving/Discerning Phases of Performance.

CHAPTER 25

ASSESS IN THE ONE-TO-ONE CONTEXT

Assess your direct report's phase of performance by looking at indicators of Ability and Energy related to an agreed-upon goal or task.

We are willing to bet that you've had this managerial experience: You diligently give your direct report instructions on what you want done and how you want it done. Satisfied that you've done your job, you expect him to do his. Days later, you find that the job is *not* done. You express your concern. Days later, the job *is* done, but it isn't anything like you had asked. You are frustrated, even a little angry; but mostly you are mystified. What happened?

There is a good chance that you need to look in the mirror. Often, when a direct report doesn't live up to your expectations on a work-related goal, it's because you have incorrectly assessed their phase of performance on that goal. Learning how to drive a car helped you understand the phases of your *own* performance; now you need to become skillful in assessing *other* people's Ability and Energy. When you can assess your direct report's phase of performance on a particular goal, you will be more likely to respond to their needs appropriately.

Take the time to assess the Ability and Energy of a direct report to accomplish a particular outcome, and you save time because you're not misapplying your leadership efforts and you focus on what he or she needs to eventually become self-sufficient and sustain high performance.

Sometimes you may miss the clues that can help you understand someone's Ability and Energy, especially if you are in a rush or make unwarranted assumptions. As a teacher and facilitator of your direct report's development, you must be aware of how people acquire skills. It means appreciating how a person develops and maintains confidence in their own abilities; it means appreciating how a person develops and maintains their motivation over the long-term.

HOW YOUR DIRECT REPORT LEARNS AND ACQUIRES SKILL

A funny thing happened on the way to studying and understanding human learning and development. Early researchers studied animals first and then made suppositions about how humans learned.[1] Much of managerial thinking today is still being unjustifiably influenced by Pavlovian theory and thinking.

If you examine the literature on human development, not animal learning theory applied to humans, you will find the writing is split into a body of work on child development[2] and a body of work on adult development.[3] Adult development is further divided into adult learning theory and adult life-span development.[4] What is more relevant to you as a leader is the research concerned with adult learning at *work*.[5]

The study of adult skill development in the work setting is a recent phenomenon.[6] Contextual Leadership is based on a synthesis of this emerging research, as well as adult learning theory, in light of our leadership focus.

WHAT TO LOOK FOR WHEN ASSESSING

Assessing your direct report's phase of performance will always be dynamic because their Ability and Energy on any particular goal will change depending on the circumstances. The path your direct report follows as he or she pursues a goal or learns to master a skill requires you to be watchful and patient. It also requires you to develop the habit of asking one important question each and every time you work with someone: *What is this person's Ability and Energy to achieve this outcome?* When asking this question, there are indicators you need to observe and recognize.

INDICATORS OF ABILITY

The most obvious indicator of the Ability individuals have on the goal or outcome being assessed is their past history or performance record. But it's important to remember that you must have seen a demonstration of that ability before assuming it exists!

You need to observe a person's technical knowledge, their understanding of the goal's requirements, its importance, and the stakes involved. Notice their appreciation of the complexities involved and their grasp of the action steps necessary to accomplish the goal.

If you realize a person has no or little capacity for these indicators, then you must conclude that this person has little or no Ability, at the present time, to accomplish this particular goal. If you are uncertain or admit you don't know, then you must make a judgment call regarding their Ability. Better to assume a person does *not* have the Ability and err in favor of underestimating than the other way around. Your assessment of the person's Ability is what will determine the way you respond to their need for supervision, guidance, and direction. Better to have to loosen up the reins and acknowledge their Ability was higher than you realized than to have to tighten up your reins and express disappointment.

An indicator that can influence your assessment of a person's ability is their transportable skill—abilities that are general in nature, garnered from past experience, that could be brought to bear in completion of this assignment or goal. Maybe this person possesses the problem-solving, planning, interpersonal, or time-management skills that you feel are necessary to accomplish the assignment or goal. These transportable skills are truly an asset; however, you are assessing the person's Ability to apply those transportable skills to this particular assignment. Ultimately, what you are assessing is the demonstrable Ability to accomplish a particular goal or task. Even with high transportable skills, the person may have Ability below what is needed for optimum performance. The transportable skills will be helpful to the person in the long run as they develop over time—in fact they will develop more quickly as a result of them.

For example, you hire two young men from outside your company to handle incoming customer-service calls. One of your new hires is fresh out of college; the other held a similar customer-service job for another company. You have assigned each of them a goal to produce a report at the end of every quarter to synthesize customer comments that will be used as data in the company's quality improvement efforts. When assessing the Ability of each employee to produce the report, you have to assess them both with low Ability because neither of them has ever produced the particular report in the specific way you are asking them to create it. However, you may find that the new employee develops Ability on this assignment more rapidly than the college grad because of his transportable skills from his former job, including handling customer complaints and questions, recognizing new-product opportunities, producing Excel spreadsheets, and so on.

INDICATORS OF ENERGY

To gauge the Energy individuals have to achieve a defined goal or outcome, consider their interest in the goal. How would you know if someone is interested or motivated to pursue a goal or accomplish an assignment? What are indicators of interest or motivation? Look for the person's initiative, willingness to take appropriate risks, eagerness, persistence in the face of difficulty, desire to work independently, an appropriate air of confidence, and alignment of the goal to relevant aspirations, as examples.

Have you ever heard yourself complaining about a person's "attitude?" Two major perspectives have emerged from research concerning the attitudinal aspects of learning and performance: self-confidence and motivation.[7]

The self-confidence perspective suggests that people self-monitor and self-evaluate their performance in light of desired outcomes. So when there is a large discrepancy between a person's desired outcomes and their performance, it may cause them to feel discouragement, negativity, and loss of faith in their competencies. The result? Their loss of confidence usually lowers their attention and effort on the goal or assignment.

The motivation perspective asserts that Energy comes from what the person expects to gain as a result of accomplishing their goal. The person expects to derive benefit from their goal accomplishment. Researchers assert that a person loses motivation on outcomes when the accomplishment of the outcome doesn't, or no longer, satisfies their need or motive.

You have probably experienced a loss of confidence or loss of motivation yourself as you've worked to achieve a goal. Everyone has at one time or another. The challenge is for you to acknowledge this byproduct of the human condition, recognize it as a normal phase in the learning process, and have compassionate understanding so you can help others move through it.

VARIATIONS OF ABILITY AND ENERGY

The combinations of Ability and Energy will lead you to one of the phases of performance, as revealed in Chapter 23, "Assess: The Fourth Leadership Practice." For convenience, we are providing the chart again in Table 25.1.

TABLE 25.1

COMBINATIONS OF ABILITY AND ENERGY IN THE PHASES OF PERFORMANCE

Phase of Performance	Level of Ability	Level of Energy
Curious Phase	Low	High
Confronting Phase	Low to Some	Low
Cautious Phase	Moderate to High	Low (Fluctuating)
Achieving Phase	High	High
Discerning Phase	High	Low (Questioning)

CAVEATS TO ASSESSING OTHERS

There are four important qualifications to be considered when attempting to confirm someone's phase of performance.

1. DON'T CONFUSE PERFORMANCE WITH *PHASE OF* PERFORMANCE

When a person is not performing well on a given outcome, it might be an important sign for you to look into the issue, but beware: Poor performance does not signify root cause. Lack of performance may stem from several sources. It could be a sign that your direct report is in the Cautious Phase with high Ability but fluctuating Energy that's causing a temporary performance slump. In other words, a lack of performance could be low Ability or low Energy or *both*.

2. A DROP IN PERFORMANCE MAY BE A DROP IN MOTIVATION

If someone has been performing quite well on a given goal but is not doing so now, it is fair to assume that this person has moved from the Achieving Phase to the Discerning Phase. It is not an Ability question because past performance would suggest ability has been high. Unless the technology or laws governing the achievement of assigned outcomes changed drastically, the root cause for the drop in performance is most probably a change in the person's motivation. Remember, in instances where an individual was performing quite well and is no longer doing so, your leadership instincts should be to try to understand the reasons, not punish the person.

3. IT COULD GET PERSONAL

In cases where the issue is a drop in Energy, the reason could be caused by either on- or off-the-job factors. In either case, seek to understand the underlying reasons before doing or saying much else to the performer.

Off-the-job factors—such as an emotional event of death, divorce, separation, and such—are not the responsibility of the leader to *fix*. Time and skillful counseling can help. But it is the obligation of the leader to uncover and understand the reasons for the change in Energy in order to help the person find resources that will restore balance to the nonwork-related factor that influences on-the-job energy and focus.

With on-the-job factors—such as disenchantment that comes with perceived broken promises, passed-over promotions, loss of status, reaching a plateau, pay issues, and career development concerns—it is the leader's obligation not only to understand these factors but also, if possible, to help the individual resolve the issues. The ultimate end is to help the person you lead so their Energy for performance can be fully restored.

4. OPPORTUNITIES FOR PARTNERING

Sharing and negotiating your assessment of a person report's phase of performance is a great tool to open up two-way communication. The person can ask for what they need, and you can get what you need because issues are clear. If there is an irreconcilable difference in how you and the person you lead perceive their Ability and Energy on a low-stakes goal or outcome, then give them the benefit of the doubt by adhering to their assessment and resulting steps for improvement. If the stakes are high and timelines are short, then you should use your prerogative and ask the person to adhere to your assessment and the resulting steps for improvement.

LOGICAL STEPS FOR LEADING IN THE ONE-TO-ONE CONTEXT

There is a flow or sequence to leading in a One-to-One Context that demands a great deal of mental preparation if you want to increase the probability of success in a leadership interaction with the person you lead. Consider Figure 25.1.

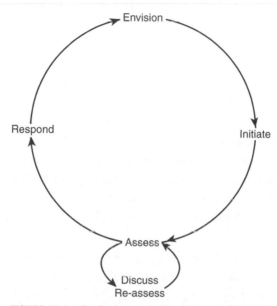

FIGURE 25.1   Logical steps of leading in a One-to-One Context

The Envision and Initiate practices are hard for most leaders to do because they often become ensnared in the *activity trap* of a time-starved, fragmented, short-term, alligator-infested, daily routine. To Envision and Initiate requires *alone* time to be reflective and think about big-picture outcomes. Then you must reflect on the needs and motives of the person who must accomplish the vision and goals.

After envisioning and initiating, you assess by meeting with the individual and confirming (or redefining) your assessment of their Ability and Energy on the various goals they are expected to achieve. This is important because you will base your future leadership responses on your assessment of their phase of performance.

If you serve people in order that they serve the organization, you must involve them in *give and take* decisions that reveal what you can do to help them become independent, excellent performers. When all the assessing is accomplished, then what remains to be done is to respond to their needs through your appropriate leadership behavior—which just happens to be the topic covered in Chapter 29, "Respond: The Fifth Leadership Practice."

ENDNOTES

1. For examples, see Skinner, 1953, 1968; Thorndike, 1913; and Watson, 1924. In modern-day leadership, see Daniels and Rosen, 1986; Connellen, 1978, 1988; and Blanchard, et al., 2002.

2. For examples, see Bruner, 1966; Kohlberg, 1965; and Piaget, 1968, 1970.

3. For examples, see Kohlberg, 1973; Loevinger, 1976; Brookfield, 1986; Candy, 1991; Knowles, et al., 1998; and Gesell, 1946.

4. For examples of adult-learning literature, see Brookfield, 1986; Pratt, 1988; Candy, 1991; and Knowles, et al., 1998. For examples of life-span literature, see Erickson, 1959; Kohlberg, 1973; Sheehy, 1977; Loevinger, 1976; Levinson, 1978; Brim and Kagen, 1980; Sheehy, 1995; Levinson, 1996; and Demetriou, Doise, and Van Lieshout, 1998.

5. For examples of adult-learning and leadership at work, see Argyris, 1957, 1962; Vroom, 1964; Terborg, 1979; Blanchard, Zigarmi, and Zigarmi, 1985; Kanfer and Ackerman, 1989; Hersey, Blanchard, and Johnson, 1996; Winters and Latham, 1996; Bandura, 1997; and Zigarmi, et al., 2005.

6. Dweck, 1986; Wood, Mento, and Locke, 1987; Nissen and Bullermer, 1987; Kanfer and Ackerman, 1989; Locke and Latham, 1990; Winters and Latham, 1996; Bandura, 1997.

7. Kanfer and Ackerman 1989.

CHAPTER 26

ASSESS IN THE TEAM CONTEXT

Assess the team's phase of performance by looking at indicators of Ability and Energy related to goals and outcomes identified in the team charter.

Several years ago, an NBA championship basketball team was asked to play volleyball in a charity event. The team's members were some of the best athletes in the world—well-conditioned, professional athletes, who were tall! For the past year, they had played together better than any other basketball team in the U.S., finishing the year playing at the Achieving Phase of Performance. Even though volleyball was obviously not their sport, everyone expected they would make it a good contest. To put it bluntly, they sucked. Same team; different goal; different phase of performance.

Fast-forward to the 2004 Summer Olympics in Greece. America has fielded a young team of its best and brightest young professional basketball stars. They will be coached by the man who led his team to the NBA championship in his first year with the team. The U.S. men's basketball team, gold medalists in 12 of the 14 Olympics in which it has participated, own a remarkable 109–2 win-loss record in Olympic play for a .982 winning percentage. Since the 1992 Olympic rule change that allowed professional NBA athletes to play on their country's team, and America fielded the

Dream Team with the likes of Michael Jordan and Magic Johnson, basketball has been a slam dunk for the U.S. Olympic team with a 24–0 record.

But, in Greece, a strange thing happened—the team lost its first game and went on to win what felt like a disappointing bronze medal. What happened? Different team; same goal; different phase of performance. Just because a team has done well in the past doesn't ensure its success given an influx of new members and different circumstances. The 2004 team only had two returning players from the previous Olympic team; its new players, while multi-million dollar professionals, had never played together, let alone at the Olympics representing their country.

A unique entity is created when people come together in a team. The entity takes on a life of its own, a strange mixture of the Ability and Energy of each team member that results in the team's own phase of performance. When you assess the team, you are appraising the collective Ability and Energy for the team to achieve a particular goal or initiative.

While it is your responsibility as the team leader to assess the team's Ability and Energy as it goes about achieving its goals, it also falls to the team members to play the dual role of participant/observer and notice the indicators that give rise to the team's phase of performance.

SIGNIFICANCE OF ASSESSING THE TEAM

When you and your team members accurately assess the team's phase of performance, you can determine if the team needs skill training, resource management, or process improvement. You can acknowledge emerging leadership and changing perceptions; you can recognize the onset of *group think* that occurs when team members fear destroying hard-won harmony; and gauge the team's inclination to embrace diversity, challenge each other in constructive ways, and use differing opinions to enhance innovative thinking. There is a hidden challenge in the preceding paragraph; maybe you caught it. Notice that the first set of benefits derived by assessing the team's phase of performance relates to the team's Ability and Energy to achieve a goal or initiative—they are outcome-oriented. The second group of benefits relates to the team's Ability and Energy to work together cohesively; they describe *how* the team goes about achieving its goals and outcomes—they are process-oriented.

You may recall the discussion in Chapter 3, "The Team Context: Your Role in Facilitating High Impact Teams," on the dual perspective of teams—outcome and process. The significance of assessing in the Team Context is that as a leader, you will gain the insight needed to respond to what the team most needs from you—either help with *what* they are trying to achieve (outcome perspective), or help with *how* they are going about working together as they achieve it (process perspective), or both.

INDICATORS OF TEAM PHASE OF PERFORMANCE

Research validates how typical it is for teams to evolve through stages—in fact, over the years a number of authors have written about the phases of team evolution. Although there might be slight differences among various models, if you examine them you will see the similarities that appear in the literature on the phases of team evolution.[1]

As the team's leader, you must learn to distinguish the well-researched indicators that reflect a team's phase of performance. The team experiences the same five phases of performance as individuals, organizations, and alliances—but the indicators at each phase are decidedly different. Remember that some of the indicators may be reflecting outcome-oriented needs; others will be process-oriented needs. Yes, your leadership role grows exponentially more complex in the Team Context!

ASSESSING THE TEAM'S CURIOUS PHASE

This startup phase is usually filled with optimism and anticipation for most team members whose attitudes rest on their expectations of team purpose and possible organizational impact. Most people want to be helpful and productive when coming to a team assignment. There may be some anxiety about how to fit in and lack of clarity of purpose and outcomes—but enthusiasm and hopefulness overcome the concerns at this phase. Ability may be low, but Energy is high.

When you hear team members asking certain types of questions, there's a good probability your team hasn't left the Curious Phase of Performance. Notice how team members wonder about both outcome and process issues, including their individual role and how other members fit into the big picture, who is in charge, and who has power. Basically the team has legitimate start-up concerns questioning expectations, outcomes, the nature of their commitment, and the team's purpose.

ASSESSING THE TEAM'S CONFRONTING PHASE

This let-down phase is characterized by team member disenchantment, frustration, and dissatisfaction resulting from what is happening in team meetings compared to what team members think ideally should be happening. Team member expectations are not being met by other members or by the team leader. It may also be that expectations for interpersonal conduct have not been stated or agreed upon. Oftentimes this is where power struggles begin to emerge among members as they continue to search for their identity within the team. Ability is still low and Energy has dropped.

Notice the balance of outcome-oriented questions and process-oriented questions that reflects both low Ability and Energy for the outcomes that need to be achieved and the processes being used to reach them. Team members are wondering how the team might realign expectations and work processes, how to confront a disruptive team member, how to build greater expertise and increase productivity, and how to cope with the dissatisfaction that certain team members seem to feel. In the Confronting Phase, people are teetering in their commitment, which has fallen, and are concerned about their tension, which is high.

ASSESSING THE TEAM'S CAUTIOUS PHASE

This uplifting phase should see a lessening of tension among team members and an increase in the use of processes and procedures that facilitate how work gets accomplished. Guidelines and ground rules have become clearer and received more group support. Unspoken interpersonal issues between team members are being put to rest either by agreed-upon processes or by direct feedback. During this stage, it is important to observe team norms and refine ground rules. Ability is high, and Energy is on the upswing, but continues to fluctuate. The Energy deficit can be overcome by developing conviction in the collective power of the team.

Notice how many of the issues that team members express are outcome-oriented (few) and how many are process-oriented (most). That should give you some insight into the nature of the Cautious Phase. Team members are wondering how they can help the team attain a sense of harmony and appreciation for one another; how they can resolve rather than simply avoid conflict; and how do they avoid group think. In this phase, team members want to help the team realize its potential and possibilities.

ASSESSING THE TEAM'S ACHIEVING PHASE

This productive phase is marked by team performance and deepening positive team member relationships. Team member exchanges are authentically confrontive and yet collaborative. Team outcomes are being met. Ideas are sorted and used based on their contribution to a common vision. The team has a history of productive conflict that has built solid trust among team members. The team members share a common language, a set of common experiences, and a passion for shared vision that is extraordinary. Ability and Energy are both high.

Notice how there is a positive tone of the few process-oriented questions the team asks; the team's process is clicking on all cylinders. Enjoy the moment, but beware of the inevitable Discerning Phase that will follow, for as the line goes, "All good things must come to an end." That's not to say that if you respond appropriately, there won't be more good things in the form of new goals, new challenges, and greater opportunity

ASSESSING THE TEAM'S DISCERNING PHASE

This close-down phase is differentiated by team member withdrawal and closure. Team members' Energy diminishes as the work comes to an end and task issues have been creatively solved. Abatement of desire and focus comes with goal achievement. Honorable closure is appropriate, but the team must guard against closure that is premature. Ability is high, but Energy has waned.

When your team is in the Discerning Phase of Performance, notice that some of the questions that team members ask reflect both outcome and process perspectives   some of what the team is working through is related to specific goals and initiatives; some of what the team is working through is its options as a team going forward. Team members are wondering how the team is going to reach honorable closure; how the learning, data, and information can be passed on; and how team members can positively exploit their experience and growth.

ARE TEAMS WORTH IT?

When you consider the complexity of teams and the skill required by both the leader and the team members to reach the Achieving Phase on meaningful goals, it is natural to question if it's worth it. Perhaps a better, and more legitimate, question is: *What are the alternatives?* Frankly, if individuals acting on their own accord can accomplish the same outcomes as a team, then a team approach is probably not worth it. We've been called in to consult a number of teams only to discover that their purpose was essentially the job description of the individuals on the team. Their feelings of frustration for what they felt was time wasted in meetings were legitimate—the team approach was superfluous and a waste of their time.

On the other hand, we've been involved in literally dozens of teams over the years where business models were created that changed the way the organization operated, where the combined talents and skills of individuals came together to create an extraordinary product that no individual could have accomplished if acting independently. We imagine that you, too, have experienced the satisfaction from people uniting for a common purpose to create something special. It doesn't mean there weren't difficult times, but because the team leader and members responded to the needs of the team and its purpose, rather to their individual needs, the team was able to move from Curious to Achieving. There's nothing like it. That's why winners give such boring acceptance speeches on awards shows, naming every person who was involved with their movie, album, or TV show—they realize they have been singled out for what was often a team effort and feel the need to acknowledge that.

In fact, studying team leadership in unexpected milieus is a wonderful way to appreciate the power of teams and the meaning of leadership. Read the credits after any movie these days—especially costume movies with special effects—and appreciate the effort and skill of a Steven Spielberg, Peter Jackson, Ridley Scott, or Akira Kurosawa. Watch an alternative sporting event, such as cycling, that most people think is an individual sport, and you'll discover the subtle (to those new to the sport) team component that lifts the experience to another level. In the Tour de France, Lance Armstrong proved not only to be an exceptional athlete, but a great team leader.

The answer to the question, "Are teams worth the effort it takes to envision, initiate, and assess, let alone develop the leadership skills necessary to respond," is *It depends*. If there is an opportunity for alchemy to happen when people of diverse skills, talents, and passions come together for a common purpose to create something greater than an individual or group of individuals might accomplish, the answer is undeniably *Yes!* If you agree, then Chapter 29, "Respond: The Fifth Leadership Practice," will outline the skills you need to lead a HIT—high impact team.

ENDNOTES

1. For classic writings on team phases, see Blanchard, Carew, and Parisi-Carew, 1990; Chang, 1994; Katzenback, 1993; Lacoursiere, 1980; and Tuckman, 1965.

CHAPTER 27

ASSESS IN THE ORGANIZATIONAL CONTEXT

Assess the organization's phase of performance by looking at indicators of Ability and Energy of the people in the organization as they implement an organizational initiative.

A recent article in *Fortune* magazine, entitled "Why CEO's Fail," drew the conclusion that the primary reason for most failures in the executive ranks occur because of a failure to implement. Unsuccessful leaders seem not to follow through to ensure their initiatives achieve the desired goal.[1] As often as not, the failure can be attributed to the fact that the executive misjudged the Ability and Energy of the people in the organization relative to the specific initiatives attempted.

For years, Hughes Aircraft Company was a high-technology engineering and development company that supplied highly complicated technical systems such as satellite communication systems to a very limited number of customers, such as governments or very large companies. A few years back, while developing the components for one of these systems, Hughes scientists developed the first microchip that could be used to make a digital watch. Excited about their discovery, Hughes executives decided to go into the watch-making business—they would sell digital wristwatches designed around the chip and make a fortune. Their watch initiative failed miserably for a number of reasons: Their marketing department was savvy about selling to one big customer, not millions of consumers; they knew nothing about mass market distribution systems; and their manufacturing operations were designed around low-quantity, custom products more than high-volume, mass-production techniques. Because they didn't accurately assess the organization's phase of performance in these key areas, they took a bath before they decided to sell their chips to traditional watch-making companies.

When you assess in the Organizational Context, you must discern the organization's phase of performance relative to specific proactive initiatives or desired changes.

HOW TO ASSESS THE ORGANIZATION'S PHASE OF PERFORMANCE

There are two reasons for assessing in the organization context. First is to determine the task-focused Energy and task-related Ability of the people required to carry out the initiatives so the leaders can provide the appropriate focusing or inspiring behaviors to take the followers to the next level. Second is to determine the specific information needs of the followers in order to provide the right information to guide their actions.

Assessing in the organization context should lead to an understanding of the type of information people need in each phase of performance and the type of leader behavior necessary to respond to their Ability and Energy relative to the initiative. These are outlined in Table 27.1.

TABLE 27.1
NEEDS AND RESPONSES FOR ASSESSING IN THE ORGANIZATION CONTEXT

Phase of Performance	Information Need	Ability/Energy	
Curious	What is the initiative?	Low A	High E
Confronting	How will it affect me?	Low A	Low E
Cautious	What do I need to do?	High A	Low E
Achieving	What is the impact?	High A	High E
Discerning	What's next?	High A	Low E

Each phase of performance is characterized by the type of information people need, as spelled out next.

ASSESSING THE ORGANIZATION'S CURIOUS PHASE

In the Curious Phase, people need information that explains the initiative, its purpose, breadth, and scope. They want to know what it is. They do *not* want to be sold. They have low Ability to deal with the initiative, but they'll have a high degree of Energy to focus on learning about the initiative and the leader's expectations.

ASSESSING THE ORGANIZATION'S CONFRONTING PHASE

At the Confronting Phase, followers' concerns shift more to the personal level. They want to know how they will be affected by the initiative and its outcomes. In particular, they want to know whether they will win or lose as a result of the initiative.

This is the phase of performance most often misdiagnosed and most inappropriately responded to. Followers say, *We need to know more*, meaning, *We want to know how we'll be affected by this*. Leaders too often respond with, *What more do you need to know? We've already told you all about the initiative.* Frustration ensues because information of one type is asked for and another is given.

ASSESSING THE ORGANIZATION'S CAUTIOUS PHASE

During the Cautious Phase, the followers' concerns turn more to issues regarding implementation. They want to know where they can go for help, and what to do to be able to refine their performance in order to sustain it. They still aren't completely convinced that this is achievable and worthwhile, but because they are seeing some results, they keep moving ahead. People are asking for more assurances, evidence that the initiative is worth their effort, and proof that progress is being made.

ASSESSING THE ORGANIZATION'S ACHIEVING PHASE

During the Achieving Phase, followers develop a great of self-confidence and confidence in the organization, accompanied by a desire to expand their impact outward and make a larger difference. They are concerned with learning about the impact they are creating and also with information that will help them expand their impact outward. They need ideas on how to celebrate successes and get others involved in the good work that is being done.

ASSESSING THE ORGANIZATION'S DISCERNING PHASE

The Discerning Phase of the Organizational Context is mismanaged more than any of the others. This is largely because many leaders assume that sustained achievement is a place and not the result of an ongoing process. Over time, followers begin to challenge existing processes and procedures and want to do things different, even though the past has proven successful. They are often bored or unchallenged by their high level of performance and want to discover ways to either improve current methods or scrap them. If not led properly at this level, the overall performance will deteriorate. It is either time to inject a booster shot into the initiative or realize that the original initiative needs updating, revising, or overhauling—which could imply starting a new change initiative and beginning the phases of performance over again.

KNOW WHAT PEOPLE NEED

When people in an organization face an initiative that spells a change in a system, process, or behavior, they react in predictable and sequential concerns. Most leaders, impervious to the concerns people have, end up trying to "sell" their initiative, and then wonder why no one is buying.

The five phases of performance reflect the shifting needs, questions, and challenges that people have as they cope with an organizational initiative—from the Curious Phase, where they initially need basic information about the change; to the Confronting Phase, where they are concerned over how it affects them personally; to the Cautious Phase, where they begin to ask for the how-to's of implementation; to the Achieving Phase, where they have questions about the impact the initiative is having; and finally to the Discerning Phase, where they wonder about issues of refinement and continuous improvement.

Too many worthwhile organizational initiatives have failed because leaders were not aware of their people's changing needs. Of course, awareness is one thing, but so is your ability to respond appropriately and give them what they need. Your options for responding in the Organizational Context are covered in Chapter 29, "Respond: The Fifth Leadership Practice."

ENDNOTES

1. "Why CEOs Fail," *Fortune*.

CHAPTER 28
ASSESS IN THE ALLIANCE CONTEXT

Assess the alliance's phase of performance by looking at indicators of Energy and Ability related to the goals and outcomes identified in the alliance charter.

To assess in the Alliance Context is almost identical to what you learned in the Team Context, including the dual outcome and process perspective that both the leader and alliance members must be aware of and respond to. There *is* one important caveat—assessing an alliance is more difficult than assessing a team. Alliances can be uneasy because team members come from different departments within the organization, or most often, from different organizations with their own visions, values, and goals—or, agendas. Hopefully the alliance was made between or among compatible organizations, but even so, differences will exist. At times, the only thing holding the alliance together will be the Big Idea that brought them together in the first place.

HOW TO ASSESS AN ALLIANCE'S PHASE OF PERFORMANCE

When you lead an alliance, you must continually assess its Ability and Energy to do what needs to be done from an outcome perspective as well as process perspective to achieve the outcomes of the Big Idea. Here are the indicators to be mindful of as you lead your alliance.

ASSESSING THE ALLIANCE'S CURIOUS PHASE

When the alliance is at the Curious Phase with low Ability and high Energy, most of the issues concerning the alliance members will be outcome-oriented, with a few process-oriented questions reflecting the curious nature of the alliance at this stage of the game. Notice how members are curious about how their agendas will mesh, where the power resides, why they need each other, and how individual agendas will be met by the alliance's agenda.

ASSESSING THE ALLIANCE'S CONFRONTING PHASE

Every alliance enters the Confronting Phase at some time or another on a goal. With leadership that is responsive to the questions of alliance members, this time can be used to realign expectations and procedures, ground rules, and norms to deal with the issues inherent with the alliance's low Ability and low Energy. Notice how members wonder about issues such as authority, realistic goals and action plans, veto power, resources, decision-making, and conflict resolution.

ASSESSING THE ALLIANCE'S CAUTIOUS PHASE

The Cautious Phase is where your understanding of disposition, values, and persona comes to your aid. Your preparation for leadership will help you understand and respond appropriately to interpersonal, motivational, and efficacy issues (team members' *belief* in the alliance's ability to achieve its goal) that result from high Ability and fluctuating Energy.

Notice how alliance members have concerns about process. They wonder how to deal with political problems that may be brewing, small interest groups that are forming, and the fact that some agendas are being met and not others. They voice concerns over ways to keep interpersonal problems from boiling over, to manage disagreements, and to validate the alliance's contributions to the member organizations. Ultimately, they question if their output is worth the effort.

ASSESSING THE ALLIANCE'S ACHIEVING PHASE

In the Achieving Phase, when the alliance has high Ability and high Energy on a goal, you will probably welcome the types of questions and concerns you hear. The process issues that remain are more positive and celebratory in nature; the outcome issues are more opportunistic. Alliance members are wondering how to enhance their efforts, refine the processes for greater efficiency, deepen member relationships, and reward members for the contributions and effort. Basically the members want to be sure the alliance is doing its best work.

ASSESSING THE ALLIANCE'S DISCERNING PHASE

When the alliance is high achieving, at some point members must determine what it takes to sustain that performance—and if it is worth the effort. Maybe there are other goals that are more important to fulfilling the alliance's Big Idea. If not, then the alliance must discern the future of the actual alliance itself.

Notice that alliance members will start to question if it's time to terminate the alliance, or at least modify the charter to revive enthusiasm and relevance.

YOUR DUAL ROLE AS ALLIANCE LEADER

It is worth reminding you that as the leader of an alliance, you are also a functioning member. One of the most difficult aspects of leading a team of any type is that dual perspective. You not only need to be actively involved, but you also need to be able to impartially observe, listen, question, and feel what is happening with the alliance's phase of performance on each of its primary goals. Not easy. Given the potentially disparate agendas of the members representing different organizations in the alliance, assessing its phase of performance can be complex.

It's easy to see how your responsibility to assess the alliance's phase of performance takes on great importance. But what may be even more challenging is to respond appropriately to the needs you have assessed for the alliance to thrive. This is why Chapter 29, "Respond: The Fifth Leadership Practice," is dedicated to how to respond in the Alliance Context.

SUMMARY—ASSESS BEFORE YOU ACT

To assess means having the skill to *identify the indicators* that tell you how much Ability and Energy those you lead have when it comes to pursuing a particular goal or initiative. The *combination* of Ability and Energy tells you what *phase of performance* an individual, direct report, team, organization, or alliance is currently experiencing on a specific goal or initiative. Your assessment of the phase of performance will ultimately guide your leadership response. If you act before you assess, then even your best intentions may be off the mark. The next six chapters provide a reference so you can use the appropriate skills given your assessment of the leadership situation.

CHAPTER 29

RESPOND: THE FIFTH LEADERSHIP PRACTICE

You have the opportunity of your career—the most highly regarded journal in your field has asked you to write an article. The deadline is imminent, and the article just hasn't come together yet. What do you do? You have assessed your Ability and Energy on the project and have determined that you are at the Confronting Phase of Performance. How you *respond* as a self leader will determine if you make it to the Achieving Phase and get the article submitted in time and to the standards of excellence that you dreamed about and others expect.

You have accompanied your direct report as she makes calls to physicians detailing the latest clinical studies for your company's breakthrough drug. As her manager, you need to be sure she is following strict procedures set down by your organization and the FDA *and* that she meets her sales goals. Sometimes she performs at expected standards; sometimes you wonder if she's even paying attention to what she's doing. Your assessment: She's at the Cautious Phase on her sales goal. How do you *respond* as her manager?

Your team is firing on all cylinders; people are working well together, and productivity is high. The team has been in the Achieving Phase, and you wonder if it can last—is it about to enter the Discerning Phase? What leadership *response* is appropriate?

People in the organization have just gotten wind of a major initiative to launch products and services globally. What is your leadership plan of action—how do you *respond* to the needs of your people who are in the Curious Phase on this initiative?

An alliance that started off great with a mutually agreed-upon Big Idea now seems to be rife with mistrust and accusations of nonperformance between the principals of the two organizations. The alliance is in the Confronting Phase of Performance. As its appointed leader, how do you *respond*?

To answer these types of questions you need to master the last, but far from least, leadership practice: Respond.

LEADERSHIP RESPONSES—YOU'VE GOT OPTIONS

Some leadership skills enable you to *Focus* those you lead; other skills help you *Inspire* those you lead.

When your leadership intent is to Focus, you need to provide guidance, structure, and detailed direction that will help increase a person's Ability. If you are leading in the One-to-One Context, for example, focusing would include setting the goal, generating an action plan, teaching step-by-step how-to's, problem solving, establishing timelines, clarifying priorities, delinating roles, monitoring performance, and giving pure informational feedback.

When your leadership intent is to Inspire, you need to find ways to build mutual trust, create a motivating environment, and enhance people's self-concept in relation to their goal—in other words, you need to help them increase or stabilize their Energy. If you are leading in the One-to-One Context, for example, inspiring would include listening, facilitating problem solving of others, sharing information, providing rationale, encouraging, and involving people in two-way communication and decision making.

To Respond appropriately means you either Focus, Inspire, do both, or do little of either—it depends on the phase of performance of the individual, team, or organization you are leading, as demonstrated in Table 29.1.

TABLE 29.1

HOW TO RESPOND TO EACH PHASE OF PERFORMANCE

Phase of Performance	Ability Level	Energy Level	Leadership Response: Focus	Leadership Response: Inspire
Curious	Low	High	High	Low
Confronting	Low to Some	Low	High	High
Cautious	Moderate to High	Fluctuating	Low	High
Achieving	High	High	Low	Low
Discerning	High	Low	Low	High

You can see how each phase of performance with its combination of Ability and Energy calls for a particular leadership response. We've chosen a personal example from two of the authors of this book to demonstrate how these responses can play out in the Self Context—hope you enjoy our little life lesson.

CYCLES AND PHASES

Our goal was to dip the rear tires of our bicycles in the Pacific Ocean and 4,200 miles and nine weeks later, dip our front tires in the Atlantic Ocean. This seemingly SMART goal came as a result of envisioning ourselves at major turning points life—our 50th and 60th years. We decided a personal key responsibility area for being healthy senior citizens was in order.

CURIOUS

It was easy to assess our phase of performance: We were typical beginners at the Curious Phase of Performance. To say we had low Ability is an understatement; we had never tackled a long-distance cycling ride before. Six months before the trip, we didn't even own bikes. To say we had high Energy was true; we were excited for a mid-life adventure. Ignorance is bliss.

Our goal to ride across America was a complex one, with a variety of mini-goals and skills—many of which we couldn't even imagine at the start. We didn't know what we didn't know. The key to our success would be in knowing how to respond to our particular needs at each phase of performance on the various trials we would face: Using the clip-on bike shoes, climbing mountain passes in the Rockies, riding 80 miles per day into headwinds for almost a week in the Black Hills, enduring lightning and thunderstorms with pouring rain, and so on. Each challenge found us at a phase of performance that required a different response that corresponded to our Ability and Energy in the moment.

Refering to Table 29.1, our Curious Phase, with low Ability and high Energy, meant we needed high focusing and low inspiring. For example, we needed experts to help Focus us on the purchase of the right bikes for the trip, select appropriate camping gear, and create a training schedule. We didn't need anyone to Inspire us—we were just excited to take a sabbatical from many years of hard work and be in the open air for nine weeks. That was before we actually experienced the clip-on bike shoes.

CONFRONTING

The old adage *You never forget how to ride a bicycle* was said before the days of clip-on bike shoes. These absolutely frightening contraptions lock your shoes onto the pedals so you maintain power on the up-stroke as well as the down—very critical for long-distance and up-hill riding. They are a very practical invention, until you need to stop, fail to twist out of the locks, and fall over as if you are one with the bike.

It only took a couple of hours before we were face-to-face with the Confronting Phase on the skill of riding with our shoes locked into the pedals. The thought of riding in traffic and having to stop at a stoplight, unclip, and not fall was enough to keep us on the high school's track for practice. Referring to Table 29.1, we now needed to be both focused and inspired because of our low Ability and low Energy. We not only needed guidance on how to clip in while getting the bike in motion and unclipping before pulling on the brakes, but we also needed stories of encouragement, acknowledgment of progress, and empathy for our bumps and bruises.

For most people over 40 years old, much of the new-fangled bike gear can be intimidating, to say the least. If we hadn't known how to respond to our many and shifting needs, we would never have embarked, let alone made it, from the West Coast to the East Coast. We asked for and received focusing by tapping the resources at the neighborhood bicycle shop, reading anything Lance Armstrong wrote, and subscribing to cycling magazines. We received the inspiration we needed by talking and riding with empathetic friends who also happened to be expert cyclists and joining a local bike club (where amazingly compassionate experts took us under wing).

CAUTIOUS

Fortified by our practice efforts, we began our cross-country adventure. But it became painfully obvious during the first evening that our phase of performance on almost every aspect of the tour was different from our fellow riders. Most were either young (just out of college) or long-time cyclists who had dreamt about this trip and prepared for years. Within days, we realigned our goal. Instead of being in the EFI group (people whose goal was to ride Every Flipping Inch from coast to coast), we decided to join the *If you're totally wiped out, ride in the support van group*. We acknowledged that we were learners and would have to build our strength and skill on the road.

We found ways to respond to our needs through our own inner willpower or through the kindness and generosity of others. Interesting, when you know how to ask for what you need, people want to help. We needed leadership and discovered that a leader is anyone who can Focus and Inspire you. One day in June, we found ourselves facing our greatest challenge yet, Teton Pass in Wyoming. We had mastered clip-on bike shoes; we had ridden almost 1,000 miles in two weeks; and on this particular day, we had ridden 40 miles to the lunch stop. With another 31 miles and the 8,429 foot climb up Teton Pass left to go, we became disheartened.

Referring to Table 29.1, we were clearly at the Cautious Phase when it came to Teton Pass. We had moderate-to-high Ability, but were experiencing low Energy. Could we make it? Did we want to? The heat was intense. There was no pressure from the group. In fact, a number of people decided to call it a day and ride to Jackson Hole, Wyoming in the support van. We talked it out with our biking buddies and two of them offered their services: They would Inspire us; we didn't need the Focus. They would ride with us, empathize with us, cheer us on, and push us up the steep mountain pass in spirit, if not literally. Without their inspiration, there's a good chance we wouldn't have made it to the top of the pass; we certainly wouldn't have had the crazy exhilaration of the 60 mph descent.

ACHIEVING

There were definitely moments when we were in the Achieving Phase on certain aspects of the ride. There were 100-mile days when the weather was glorious, the scenery breathtaking, and the terrain's rolling hills not too demanding or grueling, and we had high Ability and high Energy to ride. In those circumstances, we didn't need someone to Focus or Inspire. It took us awhile, but we finally reached the Achieving Phase on drafting each other (riding close behind a bike to take advantage of the vortex that's created, enabling the rider to use less effort).

DISCERNING

There were some aspects of our goal where we passed from the Achieving Phase to the Discerning Phase, and we questioned if we should continue or quit. For example, even though we could set up our camp each night with military precision, the sleeping conditions made it difficult to sleep soundly. We would awake exhausted, unable to fully recover from the previous day's grueling mileage. Those were the times we acknowledged our high Ability, but heeded our low Energy and headed for a hotel for the night instead of pitching the tent.

Despite being in the Discerning Phase on some aspects of our goal, we made a conscious decision to keep going. But others quit. They just couldn't face more of the 4-Hs: Heat, Hills, Humidity, and Horseflies. One strong, European rider whose high Ability made it easy for him to handle the physical rigors of the riding, quit after deciding he no longer wanted to deal with large expanses of empty countryside or American drivers who had no regard for cyclists. He could no longer cope with his low questioning Energy.

LESSONS LEARNED

We heeded the lesson learned about low Ability and needing high Focus: When leading in the Self Context and you need focusing, take the initiative to get the direction, structure, and skill-building help you need to increase your Ability to achieve your goal. If your learning stagnates, so will your progress, and you will move quickly from the Curious Phase to the Confronting Phase. You will either quit or languish in the Confronting Phase if you don't get the Focus you need.

Our lesson on having low Energy and the need for someone to help Inspire us: When leading in the Self Context and you need inspiration, take the initiative to ask for or find the encouragement, faith, and self-reliance necessary to build the Energy to continue pursuing your goal. Inspiration can be found within yourself or by knowing what to ask for from others. If you get to the Confronting or Cautious Phases and can't generate the Energy needed to continue, *it's okay* to make a conscious decision to quit or give up on the goal. What is sad and debilitating is to be unaware of the Energy shifts that are a natural aspect of learning, and to give up, without the opportunity to get the inspiration you need to continue.

THE GRATIFICATION RESPONSE

It was gratifying to realize that a potentially bone-headed bicycling goal was achieved as a result of understanding how to *respond* to the cycles—um, phases of performance we experienced along the way.

You can experience the exhilaration of achieving your own goals, but perhaps even better, you can experience the gratification response—helping those you lead achieve *their* goals by knowing how to best respond to their phase of performance.

RESPONDING IN EACH CONTEXT

Responding demands great versatility on your part, as shown in Table 29.2, which outlines the most critical skills for responding in each context.

You Respond by taking the appropriate leadership action with individuals, teams, organizations, or alliances to develop their abilities and energies to achieve specific outcomes.

To respond effectively, you need to be aware of your leadership options and develop the different skills demanded by each context.

As a self leader, you are responsible for responding to your own needs—whether it means providing it yourself or asking others to Focus and Inspire you. The five skills for responding in the Self Context were chosen because they give you the focus and inspiration to empower yourself to achieve your goals.

It's not what you say; it's what you do. Let's face it. When all is said and done, your leadership is an impression in the mind of the follower, based on your consistent, frequent, patterned behavior demonstrated over time. Responding in the One-to-One Context is *what you do* as a leader of an individual.

TABLE 29.2

QUICK REFERENCE GUIDE FOR HOW TO RESPOND ACROSS ALL FIVE CONTEXTS

Self Context	One-to-One Context	Team Context	Organizational Context	Alliance Context
Respond by using these skills to get the focusing and inspiring you need based on your phase of performance for a particular goal: Sustain Self Motivation, DISCover Time, Solicit and Receive Feedback, Promote Your Solutions, and Practice Menteeship.	Respond by using the skills to give your direct report the focusing and inspiring needed based on his or her current phase of performance on a particular goal: Show How, Proactively Listen, Facilitate Problem Solving, Give Effective Feedback, and DISCover Others.	Respond by using the skills to give your team the focusing and inspiring needed based on its current phase of performance on a particular goal: Structure Meetings, Facilitate Group Problem Solving, Assess Team Process, DISCover Group Dynamics, and Resolve Conflict.	Respond by using the skills to provide people in the organization with the focusing and inspiring needed based on their collective phase of performance on an organizational initiative: Scan the Environment, Frame a Compelling Message, Manage Organizational Problem Solving, Promote Justice, and Celebrate Success.	Respond by using the skills to give the alliance the focusing and inspiring needed based on its current phase of performance on a particular goal: Conceptualize and Form the Alliance, Facilitate Non-Adversarial Problem Solving, and Prepare for Win-Win Negotiations.

We have chosen the five skills that are the most important focusing and inspiring behaviors you can provide to an individual for his or her development.

As a team leader, your intention should be to gradually develop each team member's faith in the team's power and possibilities. When a group becomes a team, a transformation occurs in each member's frame of mind as they become convinced that they can accomplish more through a collective, coordinated effort than they can through their own single, individual actions. In high-impact teams, the members revel in the power of that collective action.

You know you have succeeded as a leader when *being* the leader is no longer possible—leadership has become each team member's responsibility as they follow *and* lead as expertise and energy dictate. Your leadership legacy is a team comprised of team members who are concerned with the welfare of the whole, who are concerned with the quality of their output, who want to contribute their abilities and energies to those ends.

Remember that team leadership is complex. To respond to the needs of your team requires an advanced knowledge of how to focus and inspire. But realize that team leadership ultimately requires you to give up certain power and prerogatives to the team as their feelings and behaviors of *being a team* gather momentum. It requires a sensitivity to know when to shift from being a team leader to becoming a regular team member. It requires helping team members focus on the processes needed to accomplish outcomes. The skills for responding in the Team Context were chosen with these requirements in mind.

As the leader in the Organizational Context, your *primary* responsibility lies in shaping the environment for those who think, feel, and work in the organization—creating an environment that is conducive to the development of your employee's Ability and Energy so they can achieve the organization's outcomes. Ironically, the more senior your level of leadership is, the more indirect it becomes. Others leading in the One-to-One Context have more direct opportunity to influence your people day to day. Your influence comes through the vision, values, policies, and structure that you shape indirectly. Your leadership must be more sophisticated than in other contexts because there are signals competing for the mindshare of those you seek to influence.

You also have an equally important responsibility to foster the economic health and effectiveness of the organization. Again, you most frequently do this through the indirect methods of vision, values, policies, and structure. Strategic thinking and established processes and policies are your stock in trade. You must learn to shape individual organizational work patterns *and* organizational economic health through *long-distance* policies, procedures, systems, and structures.

The five skills chosen for responding in the Organizational Context will help you and all your employees become independent, competent performers and contributors of organizational outcomes by coordinating and consistently maintaining a work environment that is conducive to the dignity, passion, and intrinsic motivation of all employees, and finally, organizational output and success.

If ever there is a time and a place for a focus on *we* versus *we/they*, it is when you are leading in the Alliance Context. The skills you need when leading an alliance will be put to good use as you practice collaboration, integrate efforts, and create synergy between entities that might otherwise be at odds with each other. Executives at IBM even coined a word to describe many of their 90,000+ alliance partners. They call them *frienemies—former enemies* (competitors, in some cases) *who are now our friends.* The skills chosen for responding in the Alliance Context will help you create this type of dynamic strategic relationship.

We encourage you to take the initiative to learn these skills, and to this end we have created a companion Web site that gives you a brief overview of each of these skills plus resources to help you master them.

PART THREE

THE PROMISE AND CHALLENGE OF CONTEXTUAL LEADERSHIP

The next time someone says, "I don't think leadership can be taught," ask them how they define leadership. Notice how they go a bit cross-eyed before spewing out laudable and intangible traits such as *acts with integrity, leads from the heart, is persistent in the face of unthinkable odds*—you get the idea. All of these traits may be what it takes to be a great leader—and indeed it would be hard to figure out how to teach or train them. But research can't and doesn't support a connection between such character traits and effective leadership. In fact, the only character trait that the great leaders seem to have had in common is a proclivity to travel and understand cultures other than their own.[1]

What *can* be proven is that when leaders *do* certain behaviors at appropriate times, they develop trust with those they lead and produce measurable results over time.[2] So while we embrace the intangibles of great leadership, we are advocating an emphasis on your leadership behavior that we know leads to leadership effectiveness. As we have demonstrated throughout this book, Contextual Leadership does three things that make it a behaviorally-based, not just a conceptually-based, model for the practice of leadership:

1. Addresses five different leadership contexts (advocating different approaches depending on whether you are leading in the self, one-to-one, team, organizational, or alliance context).

2. Provides five leadership practices that are consistent across all five contexts (normative theory—a generalized leadership strategy that enables linkages across the five contexts).

3. Describes the different tactics and skills required to deal with the circumstances and variations within each context (contingency theory—allowing that even the generalized practice of envisioning, for example, requires a different level of skill when practiced in the Self Context as in the Organizational Context).

There are two final things we'd like to present to help you grasp and ultimately master Contextual Leadership. First, we present a practical *graphic* approach that puts all the pieces together for your future reference. The Contextual Leadership graphic helps you visualize how the five leadership practices and five contexts are integrated. Secondly, we introduce you to the Leadership Imperatives—underlying assumptions and beliefs that we hope will guide your use of Contextual Leadership.

Here's hoping that the next time someone asks you, "Do you think leadership can be taught?" you will have the insight, information, and experience to answer not only through your words, but through your actions with an unqualified *Yes I do!*

ENDNOTES

1. Bass, 1990; Burns, 1978; Tett, Jackson and Rothstein, 1991.
2. For examples on trust building, see Zigarmi, et al., 2005; Zigarmi, Blanchard and Edeburn, 1997; Colquitt, et al., 2002; Dirks and Ferrin, 2002; Bass, 1990. For examples of output, see Schmit and Alscheid, 1995; Connellan, 1988; Daniels and Rosen, 1988; Locke and Latham, 1990.

CHAPTER 30

A NEW VIEW OF LEADERSHIP

Imagine you're on a journey back from outer space. You passed the moon awhile ago and are some 50,000 miles away from Earth. The jewel that glows in the thickness of night is the planet you call home—a small blue ball surrounded by blackness. As your spacecraft hurls through space, you begin to see the great divisions of blue oceans and taupe-colored land masses through the cover of clouds and atmosphere.

Now consider your journey as a leader. The first thing you begin to notice are the great divisions of the contexts—SOTOA, as seen in Figure 30.1.

Obviously, you may not lead in all five contexts all the time. If you are a frontline supervisor, for example, you may have little opportunity to lead in the Organizational Context. But you should be able to discern the context in which you *are* leading, understand how your context affects or is affected by the others, and adapt your leadership behavior appropriately.

THE 1,000-MILE VIEW

As you travel closer to the Earth from outer space, you notice something remarkable. From hundreds of miles away, you can start to make out details such as the Great Wall of China.

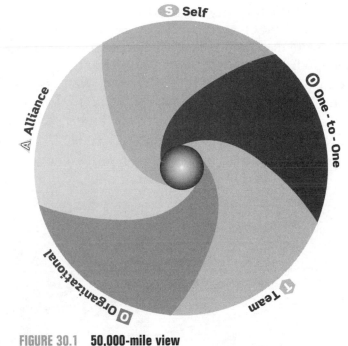

FIGURE 30.1   50,000-mile view
SOTOA: The five contexts of leadership

So too, in your leadership journey, you become aware of more detail. You can now see five layers of rings that circumvent all the contexts. These rings represent five leadership practices that are relevant regardless of the context you are leading and are shown in Figure 30.2. These are the practices that define what you *do* as a leader.

Leadership practices help you in two ways. First, you don't have to reinvent the wheel every time you move from one context to another. The process to Prepare, Envision, Initiate, Assess, and Respond is the same for each context.

Second, the five practices provide you with a consistent process that *links* the contexts so they don't exist in isolation. Let's say that you and your organization have adapted Contextual Leadership. After you Prepare for leadership by understanding how your personality influences your leadership behavior, you then Envision. If you begin in the Self Context, you envision by creating an individual vision for your work-related role. That vision gets reinforced when you and your manager envision in the One-to-One Context—integrating your individual vision into the expectations of your role and job description. In the Team and Alliance Contexts, your team and the alliance envision by creating a charter that integrates your work-related vision with those of team and alliance members to form a common sense of purpose. In the Organizational Context, envisioning is a top-down and bottom-up effort, where your vision becomes of a greater whole—making the organization's vision that much stronger. No matter how grand an organization's vision sounds, it is only as strong as the individual visions that support it. The power of a vision increases exponentially when you envision in all five contexts—especially when the energy from the vision is then harnessed through goals that are supported contextually.

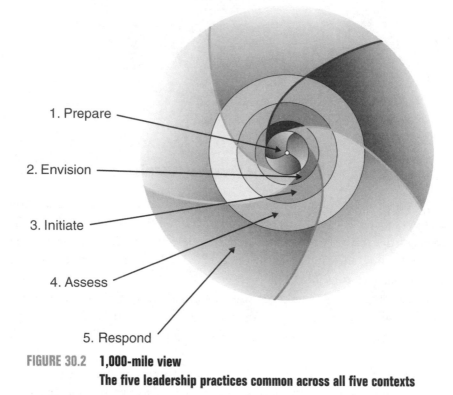

1. Prepare
2. Envision
3. Initiate
4. Assess
5. Respond

FIGURE 30.2   **1,000-mile view**
The five leadership practices common across all five contexts

TOUCHDOWN: PRACTICING LEADERSHIP WITHIN EACH CONTEXT

In your journey toward Earth, the closer you get, the more detail you see. Each continent has its own appearance and distinctive qualities. In your leadership journey, the more hands-on you become, the more you recognize the distinctive characteristics and demands of each context. So while the process to practicing leadership is the same for all five contexts, you begin to realize that the *application* of those practices is *different* in each context, as shown in Figure 30.3.

Notice the added detail to the model—in the Assess ring, you see the chevrons that represent the five phases of performance; in the Respond ring, you see the shadings that represent the skills pertinent in each context.

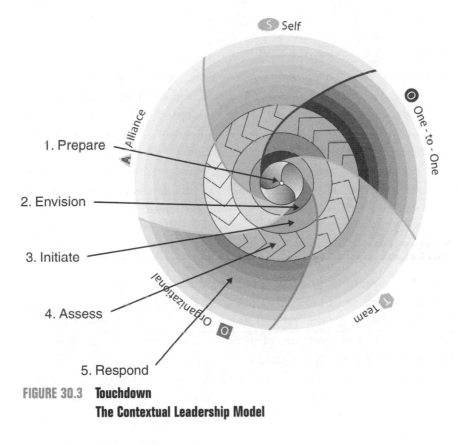

1. Prepare
2. Envision
3. Initiate
4. Assess
5. Respond

FIGURE 30.3   Touchdown
The Contextual Leadership Model

A FINAL METAPHOR

As you are about to touch down from your remarkable journey, imagine the abrupt shock as you transition from zero gravity to the pull of gravity as you enter the Earth's atmosphere. Things are happening fast and furious when suddenly you realize that instead of landing in the ocean and bobbing up to be rescued as planned, your spacecraft just keeps going. You find yourself being hurled through the murky depths of the ocean, hitting land, and entering the Earth's core in a shocking, bumpy, and uncomfortable ride. Sometimes it's darker than night, and sometimes it's so bright you can see every detail hidden in the strata of past ages. At the Earth's core, you discover molten lava, unformed, raw, and boiling to the point of pressure, which if not sufficiently released, will explode uncontrollably into the Earth's atmosphere.

Understanding your personality, acknowledging your dispositional patterns, exploring your values, and investigating your persona as you Prepare for leadership can be as rough as the journey to the center of the Earth; it can be an arduous, frightening, and painstaking experience. It can also be a satisfying and fruitful experience. As you explore your inner space, there will be times where you face dark places—afraid to look beyond the surface; there will be times of enlightening clarity. The journey to mastering contextual leadership truly begins with that exploration of your personality and how your disposition, values, and persona affect your leadership behavior. *He who knows others is wise; He who knows himself is enlightened.*[1]

This is why Prepare is the practice at the center of the Contextual Leadership Model. Your leadership begins with who you are as a person and emanates from there to everyone you lead in each of the five contexts.

CONTEXTUAL LEADERSHIP GRID

We have created a grid that encapsulates the details of Contextual Leadership, shown in Table 30.1. There is a column for each of the five contexts, beginning from the left with the Self Context. Each row defines how the five leadership practices of Prepare, Envision, Initiate, Assess, and Respond play out in each context.

Contextual Leadership is how you arouse, engage, and satisfy the values and needs of the people you lead in an arena of conflict, competition, or achievement that results in them taking action through a mutually shared vision to sustained high performance.

ENDNOTES

1.   Lao-tzu, *Bartlett's Familiar Quotations*, 1992, page 57.

TABLE 30.1

CONTEXTUAL LEADERSHIP GRID

	SELF CONTEXT	ONE-TO-ONE CONTEXT	TEAM CONTEXT	ORGANIZATIONAL CONTEXT	ALLIANCE CONTEXT
	Self Context: Having the skillset and the mindset to accept responsibility and take the initiative for succeeding in your work-related role.	One-to-One Context: Developing the abilities and focusing the energy of your direct reports so they can attain and sustain independent achievement in their work-related roles.	Team Context: Gathering, structuring, and developing the collective abilities and energies of a team of people with a common purpose, and guiding them to the achievement of interdependent goals and sustained high performance.	Organizational Context: Directly and indirectly influencing and aligning individual and team efforts toward fulfilment of the organization's purpose through systems, processes, and structures.	Alliance Context: Using networks and bilateral relationships to create a third entity that extends beyond corporate boundaries, and achieves the goals and serves the mutual interests of all the members of the alliance.
PREPARE Recognize, control, and adapt your disposition-driven behavior; develop personal values; and investigate your persona, so your leadership behavior does not predispose you to act in ways that may sabotage your effectiveness.	Prepare by reconciling your disposition-driven and values-motivated behavior with the expectations of your work-related role, vision, and goals.	Prepare by reconciling your disposition-driven and values-motivated behavior as a means of leading your direct reports as they fulfill their work-related visions and organizational initiatives.	Prepare by reconciling your disposition-driven and values-motivated behavior as a means of leading your team as it fulfills its charter.	Prepare by reconciling your disposition-driven and values-motivated behavior as a means of leading your organization as it fulfills its vision and achieves its initiatives.	Prepare by reconciling your disposition-driven and values-motivated behavior as a means of leading your alliance to fulfill its Big Idea.

continues

ENVISION	SELF CONTEXT	ONE-TO-ONE CONTEXT	TEAM CONTEXT	ORGANIZATIONAL CONTEXT	ALLIANCE CONTEXT
Visualize an inspirational ideal one can aspire to, craft a statement of purpose one can be dedicated to, proclaim rank-ordered values that act as a noble guide for behavior and decision making, and align the vision across contexts.	Envision by creating a motivating vision for your work-related role that integrates with your personal vision, helps you sustain enthusiasm for your role, and aligns with both your manager's expectations and the organization's vision.	Envision by guiding direct reports to generate a compelling vision of their work-related role that imbues their role with meaning and gives life to the organization's vision.	Envision by designing a blueprint for the team that will inspire and mobilize the team members as they initiate their charter, and that aligns with the organization's vision and expectations.	Envision by establishing an inspiring vision for the organization that becomes a unifying force, informing strategic planning, and ultimately acting as a noble guide for people's behavior and decision making.	Envision by developing a stimulating vision for the alliance that capitalizes on the synergy that comes from discovering a common purpose out of the disparate and potentially conflicting agendas of alliance members.

INITIATE	SELF CONTEXT	ONE-TO-ONE CONTEXT	TEAM CONTEXT	ORGANIZATIONAL CONTEXT	ALLIANCE CONTEXT
Establishing and facilitating the goals, expectations, ground rules, operating guidelines, and steps for implementation that embody, enable, foster, and sustain a work-related vision.	Initiate by creating a personal performance plan that defines Key Responsibility Areas, SMART goals, and action steps for their achievement that are aligned with your work-related vision and the organization's.	Initiate by establishing performance objectives based on Key Responsibility Areas, SMART goals, and a development plan for your direct report that is aligned with the direct report's work-related vision, as well as the organization's goals and vision.	Initiate by establishing a high-impact team charter that is aligned with the sponsor's vision for the team and includes team member-generated vision, purpose, values, goals, and operating principles.	Initiate by outlining a strategy supported by initiatives with action steps for their achievement that are aligned with the organizational vision.	Initiate by establishing a charter outlining the alliance's major goals and operating principles for fulfilling the alliance's Big Idea, as well as the visions of the partners in the strategic relationship.

	SELF CONTEXT	ONE-TO-ONE CONTEXT	TEAM CONTEXT	ORGANIZATIONAL CONTEXT	ALLIANCE CONTEXT
ASSESS Appraise the Ability and Energy of an individual, team, organization, or alliance to achieve a specific outcome.	Assess your own phase of performance by looking at indicators of Ability and Energy on a work-related goal.	Assess your direct report's phase of performance by looking at indicators of Ability and Energy related to an agreed-upon goal or task.	Assess the team's phase of performance by looking at indicators of Ability and Energy related to goals and outcomes identified in the team charter.	Assess the organization's phase of performance by looking at indicators of Ability and Energy of the people in the organization as they implement an organizational initiative.	Assess the alliance's phase of performance by looking at indicators of Energy and Ability related to the goals and outcomes identified in the alliance charter.
RESPOND Take the appropriate leadership action with individuals, teams, organizations, or alliances to develop their abilities and energies to achieve specific outcomes.	Respond by using the skills to: Sustain Self Motivation, DISCover Time, Solicit and Receive Feedback, Promote Your Solutions, and Practice Menteeship to get the focusing and inspiring you need based on your phase of performance for a particular goal.	Respond by using the skills to: Show How, Proactively Listen, Facilitate Problem Solving, Give Effective Feedback, and DISCover Others to give your direct report the focusing and inspiring needed based on his or her current phase of performance on a particular goal.	Respond by using the skills to give your team the focusing and inspiring needed based on its current phase of performance on a particular goal: Structure Meetings, Facilitate Group Problem Solving, Assess Team Process, DISCover Group Dynamics, and Resolve Conflict.	Respond by using the skills to: Scan the Environment, Frame a Compelling Message, Manage Organizational Problem Solving, Promote Justice, and Celebrate Success to provide people in the organization the focusing and inspiring needed based on their collective phase of performance on an organizational initiative.	Respond by using the skills to: Conceptualize and Form the Alliance, Facilitate Non-Adversarial Problem Solving, and Prepare for Win-Win Negotiations to give the alliance the focusing and inspiring needed based on its current phase of performance on a particular goal.

CHAPTER 31

LEADERSHIP IMPERATIVES

There are underlying beliefs and assumptions that are so important for being a contextual leader that we present them here as imperatives—meaning they should be seen as binding guidelines, rules, or requirements for the effective implementation of the Contextual Leadership model.

IMPERATIVE 1: INTEGRATE

A key strength of Contextual Leadership is that the combination of the SOTOA framework of contexts and five Leadership Practices provides a structure for integration on several levels, all of which are critical for leadership success.

Leaders must integrate by demonstrating a consistency of intent (overall strategy and direction) across all five contexts. The more each person, team, organizational unit, and alliance maintains attunement with the other, the more synergy will be created, the more efficient the organization will be, and the greater will be its impact. Fragmented approaches toward leadership that fail to provide this level of integration will suffer trade-offs proportional to the amount of fragmentation.

MANAGE THE RIPPLE EFFECT

Leaders must understand and maintain a strong personal conviction that leader actions are multi-dimensional. A ripple effect exists between contexts; when you act in one context, those actions affect what happens in other contexts, *whether or not you intended those effects*. Good leaders will be sensitive to this ripple effect and choose to act in ways that create positive and synergistic results across all contexts.

The best way for leaders to manage this ripple effect through all five contexts is by first ensuring that visions at all levels are aligned with each other, and then seeking to align initiatives, goals, systems (including incentive and reward systems), and processes at every level throughout the organization. An individual's role description should clearly define linkages between any teams or alliances to which that person belongs and to the organization as a whole. The same is true for teams. Every team charter should clearly define a relationship with the organization, as well as the roles of individual members.

IMPERATIVE 2: LEADERSHIP ISN'T TERMINAL

Leaders will never achieve a terminal, static end state. In many ways, it's a shame we can't see leadership as a verb rather than a noun. To emphasize a point we made early in this book: Leadership isn't something you achieve—it's something you do. A popular phrase in recent years is that excellence isn't a place; it's a never-ending process. The same is true for leadership. After you achieve yesterday's standard, you need to raise the bar. Those seeking to achieve the highest possible standard always embark on another quest as soon as the most recent challenge is met. When one becomes a leader, it should be looked at less as an achievement than as a calling. In this regard, you should understand that by accepting a leadership role, you are embarking on an ongoing journey. Even though your journey will be punctuated with successes and achievements (as well as setbacks) along the way, these milestones should merely serve as reminders that the leader's journey never ends.

IMPERATIVE 3: PROGRESS OFTEN APPEARS TO BE A SETBACK

When leaders take action, they often disrupt the *status quo*. At other times, leaders' actions force to the surface negative issues that were being ignored. Because these issues bring negative energy, many people are inclined to think, even if only temporarily, that surfacing these issues is more of a detriment than a benefit. Almost always, when individuals and groups progress from the Curious to the Confronting Phases of Performance, their progress gives the sensation of moving backward rather than forward.

The trap leaders often fall into is to respond to these sensations of backward movement by backing off from the correct leadership actions for that circumstance. Disrupting the status quo is beneficial, if the disruption leads to better outcomes in the future. If negative issues boil beneath the surface, it's almost always better to confront them before they cause an even more disruptive and dysfunctional eruption in the future. And when followers progress from the Curious to the Confronting Phases of Performance, even though the progress may be more challenging and the situation less comfortable to the leader, the leader should celebrate the progress, embrace it, and use leader behaviors that will reinforce and continue the progress. This is the only path to sustained high performance.

The key in all these circumstances is for the leader to be able to recognize progress, even though it may sometimes give the appearance of backsliding, and then to take the most appropriate leadership actions for both short- and long-term outcomes, without backing off.

IMPERATIVE 4: DON'T TAKE IT PERSONALLY

Leaders should not personalize the actions of followers. When followers question the actions of leaders, the worst way you can respond is to take those questions personally. More often than not, such questions, regardless of how they may be raised or stated, are statements about the followers' mindset—particularly their needs, motives, and concerns. To a leader who is listening carefully, these confrontations provide reliable clues about the followers' phases of performance, as well as their underlying issues and concerns that might seriously affect their performance. The leader might also pick up clues about missed communication, misunderstandings, and misinterpretation of previously sent messages. Critical confrontations give astute leaders a chance to clear up understandings that may have somehow become confused.

The less defensive behavior a leader demonstrates, the more effective that leader will be across the board, which leads us to the next imperative.

IMPERATIVE 5: LEADERS ARE NOT PERFECT

You may wish to challenge the preceding statement; the truth hurts, but not as bad as the outdated belief that leaders need to be seen as invincible, omnipotent, or above critique. The days of the *perceived* infallible leader are over. Leaders have never been infallible, even though in the past, many followers wanted them to be and many leaders actually believed it was essential that they be seen as such. Leaders are human beings. As such, occasionally they will make mistakes, exercise errors in judgment, and sometimes fail to meet the expectations of others. Does this make them failures? No, it makes them human.

One question to ask is: *How do I respond to my missteps?* If the missteps are responded to openly, honestly, and with a sincere desire to learn, then you will be seen as a responsible, and still-developing, role model. If you respond with an attitude of denial, avoidance of responsibility, and an imperviousness to reality, then you will lose credibility and trust among the followers and will eventually be denied the opportunity to lead. This is why self leadership is important for *every leader* and provides the foundation for success in every context.

IMPERATIVE 6: ACTIONS SPEAK LOUDER THAN WORDS

Leaders should take into account the symbolic nature of their actions. When you act, your actions communicate your values, true intent, and character, in a symbolic manner. In this regard, actions do speak louder than words, which is why it is important for you to *walk your talk* if you are to maintain trust, respect, and credibility of those you lead.

Different leaders might initiate similar leadership acts differently, depending on their personal beliefs, values, DISCposition, and persona. The symbolism conveyed in these differences, over time, will shape long-term outcomes almost as much as the actions themselves; over time, they will convey to followers the broader-based value and belief system held by the leader.

All of this leads to our concluding imperative.

IMPERATIVE 7: OUR ULTIMATE IMPERATIVE

To write a book about leadership in the 21st century and not address the issues of character, ethics, and responsibility would be like writing a book about the universe, solar systems, and galaxies and not addressing the issue of gravity.

The greatest threat to free enterprise, and the tremendous benefits of economic democracy and capitalism as we know it in the world today, is not terrorism. Nor is it competition from communism or fascist dictatorships. The past several decades proved that political systems rooted in those philosophies don't and won't work. *The greatest threat we face today is a breakdown in character and ethics among those who hold leadership positions in the organizations that form the fabric of our society.*

The first two parts of this book presented concepts and leadership methodology that, if properly applied, will allow a person to become effective as a leader and produce results in the Self and One-to-One Leadership Contexts. But results are not enough unless they are the right results and benefit humankind on a number of levels. Leadership methodologies can be used to achieve either good or harmful results. It is up to the leaders themselves to ensure the methods are used to achieve beneficial outcomes.

To help put this judgment in perspective, it is better to think in terms of outcomes rather than results. Results imply the organization is producing a certain number of widgets at a profit. Outcomes implies that results are being achieved, *but in addition* the organization is also socially responsible, nurturing its people, and making a contribution to the common good in a way that doesn't destroy the world in which we live.

It is imperative that: (1) your intentions as a leader is noble; and (2) you serve motives other than those of mere profit and capital formulation. Our definition of leadership implies that you must also be a servant. You simply must serve *both* the people who comprise your organization *and* society as a whole. You and the leaders of this generation must work to eliminate those bad, unhealthy, and derogatory practices inherited from our predecessors.

THE CHALLENGE AND THE PROMISE OF CONTEXTUAL LEADERSHIP

Our generation occupies an interesting niche in history. We are a generation that has lived most, if not all, of our lives in a world possessing the technology capable of completely abolishing the human race. The *good* news is we never saw this horrific power used to its full potential.

But we are also a generation born and raised with the know-how and understanding to completely wipe out discrimination, bigotry, incivility, and disrespect for human beings in all its forms. The *bad* news is we never saw this power used to its fullest potential, either.

Now we can also say we possess the understanding to lead in ways that touch peoples' lives and the world in a positive, nurturing, and sustaining way, day in and day out. Because corporations are the fundamental structure of society today, responsible corporate leadership is ultimately the most viable avenue to peace and harmony in a physically and psychologically healthy world.

Traditionally, we were content to define peace as the condition that exists when two or more nations are not at war or engaged in hostile conflict. This is no longer enough. Our generation must raise the standard. *True peace will only exist when people everywhere live and work in complete harmony.*

Work is an essential condition of life. Most of us will spend a third of our lives—more than half of our waking hours—in some kind of work setting. We need to shift our thinking so that instead of viewing work as a necessary evil, we see it as an opportunity to influence the world in such a way as to make it a better place—a better place for human beings. *Better* needs to be defined in terms other than mere output of goods and services. Again, *leaders must learn to understand the difference between output and outcomes.* Then we must discipline ourselves to assess all the outcomes of our leadership practices and ensure that *all* we do contributes to the common good on every level.

We also need to define our contribution to the common good in terms of the way we act. This includes the way we live our lives, as well as the manner in which we impact others while in our leadership roles.

If we are responsible in our actions, we can make the world of work a better place. Organizations can and should be a source of nurturing, fulfillment, character building, and collective human growth. Work should not be something that we, as individuals, survive. It should be a response to a calling that gives each of us an honored place and role to play in the world. Work should not be something that saps our strength and wears us out in a negative sense. Rather, it should be something that connects us with others in a way that advances our common good and allows each of us to respond to our calling while nurturing others to do the same.

This is the greatest challenge of our generation. Our greatest challenge is *not* to see how fast we can solve the technological problems of the world. It is also *not* to see how quickly we can sort out the intricacies of the complex world that surrounds us. Nor is it to see how much material wealth we can amass or equity we can create—either as individuals or as corporate entities. We're not saying that these don't have importance. They do. But they pale in comparison to the accomplishment we could boast in conquering the challenges of optimizing the full potential of the human race.

On the other side of this challenge is a new world—a new world characterized by harmony, respect, fulfillment, and enlightenment. Now that the opportunity has been created and the means placed in our laps, it's up to us to respond. It's our responsibility to chart the course to this new world. Each of us must take the initiative to instill this leadership imperative into every level of our essence. It won't come from one, or two, or even a handful of exemplary role models to whom we will all turn to for guidance. Rather, it will come from all of us doing our part. Therefore, our ultimate imperative is to accept the responsibility to create an enduring legacy from our generation and do everything in our power to ensure that the world will forever be a better place.

BIBLIOGRAPHY

Ackerman, P. L. "Individual differences in skill learning: An integration of psychometric and information processing perspectives." *Psychological Bulletin*, 102 (1987): 3–27.

———. "Individual Differences in Skill Acquisition." In *Learning and Individual Differences: Advances in Theory and Research*, edited by P. L. Ackerman, R. J. Sternberg, and R. Glaser. New York: Freeman, 1989.

Adams, J. A. "Historical review and appraisal of research on learning, retention, and transfer of human motor skills." *Psychological Bulletin*, 101 (1987): 41–74.

Adams, J. S. "Toward an Understanding of Inequity." *Journal of Abnormal and Social Psychology*, 67 (November 1963): 422–436.

Adizes, I. *Corporate Life Cycles: How and Why Corporations Grow and Die and What to Do About It.* Englewood Cliffs, NJ: Prentice Hall, 1988.

Aldenfer, C. P. *Existence, Relatedness and Growth: Human Needs in Organizational Settings.* New York: Free Press, 1972.

Alexandra, S., and M. Ruderman. "The Role of Procedural Justice and Distributive Justice in Organizational Behavior." *Social Science Research*, Vol. 1 (1987): 117–198.

Alleman, E. J. *Effects of Mentoring Summary of Information on Mentoring Relationships*. Mentor, Ohio: Leadership Development Consultants, Inc., 1982.

————. *Managing Mentoring Relationships in Organizations: 1991 College Industry Education Conference Proceedings*. Mentor, Ohio: Leadership Development Consultants, Inc., 1991.

Alleman, E., J. Cochrane, J. Doverspike, and I. Newman. "Enriching Mentoring Relationships." *Personnel and Guidance Journal*, February (1984): 329–332.

Allen, D. *Getting Things Done: The Art of Stress-Free Productivity*. New York: Penguin Putnam, Inc., 2001.

Allessandra, T., and M. J. O'Connor. *The Platinum Rule*. New York: Warner Books, 1996.

American Society for Training and Development. *Design Productive Mentoring Programs*. Alexandria, VA: Info-Line, September 1986.

Ancarlo, L. *Implementing Self-Directed Work Teams*. (Video) Boulder, CO: Career Track Publications, 1995.

Anderson, J. R. "Acquisition of Cognitive Skill." *Psychological Review*, 89 (1982): 369–406.

————. *Cognitive Psychology and Its Implications*. (2nd ed.) New York: Freeman, 1988.

Argyris, C. *Interpersonal Competence and Organizational Effectiveness*. Homewood, IL: Irwin Dorsey Press, 1962.

————. *Personality and Organization*. New York: Harper and Row, 1957.

Arino, A., and J. de la Torres. "Learning from Failure: Toward an Evolutionary Model of Collaborative Ventures." *Organizational Science*, 9, No. 3 (May–June 1998): 306–325.

Atwater, L. E., and F. J. Yammarino. "Does Self-Other Agreement on Leadership Perceptions Moderate the Validity of Leadership and Performance Predictions?" *Personal Psychology: A Journal of Applied Research*, 45, No. 1 (Spring 1992): 141–164.

————. "Self-Other Rating Agreement: A Review and Model." *Research in Personnel and Human Resource Management*, 15 (1997): 121–124.

Atwater, L. E., C. Ostroff, F. J. Yammarino, and J. W. Fleenor. "Self-Other Agreement: Does It Really Matter?" *Personnel Psychology: A Journal of Applied Research*, 51, No. 3 (Autumn 1998): 577–598.

Atwater, L. E., P. Roush, and A. Fischthal. "The Influence of Upward Feedback on Self and Follower Ratings of Leadership." *Personnel Psychology: A Journal of Applied Research*, 48, number 1 (Spring 1995): 35–60.

Axelrod, R. *The Evolution of Cooperation*. New York: Basic Books, 1984.

Baker, L., and K. Watson. *Listen Up: How to Improve Relationships, Reduce Stress and Be More Productive by Using the Power of Listening*. New York: St. Martin Press, 2000.

Baldwin, T. T., R. J. Magjuka, and B. T. Lohen. "The Perils of Participation: Effects of Choice of Training on Trainee Motivation and Learning." *Personnel Psychology: A Journal of Applied Research*, 44, number 1 (Spring 1991): 51–66.

Bandura, A. "Self-Efficacy Mechanisms of Anticipated Fears and Calamities." *Journal of Personality and Social Psychology*, 45 (1983): 464–469.

———. *Self-Efficacy: The Exercise of Control*. New York: W.H. Freeman and Company, 1997.

———. "Self-Regulation of Motivations Through Anticipatory and Self-Regulatory Mechanisms." In *Nebraska Symposium on Motivation: Perspective on Motivation*, edited by R. A. Dienstbier. Vol. 38. Lincoln, NE: University of Nebraska Press, 1993.

———. *Social Foundations of Thought and Actions*. Englewood, NJ: Prentice Hall, 1986.

Bandura, A., and D. Cervone. "Differential engagement of self-reactive influences in cognitive motivation." *Organizational Behavior and Human Decision Processes*, 38 (1986): 92–113.

———. "Self Evaluation and Self-Efficacy Mechanisms Governing the Motivational Effects of Goal Systems." *Journal of Personality and Social Psychology*, 45 (1983): 1017–1028.

Barrick, M.R., G.L. Stewart, M.J. Neubert, and M.K. Mount. "Delegating Member Ability and Personality to Work-Team Processes and Team Effectiveness." *Journal of Applied Psychology*, 83, No. 3 (1998): 377–391.

Bartlett, J. *Bartlett's Familiar Quotations, Sixteenth Edition*. Boston, MA: Little, Brown and Company, 1992.

Bass, B. M. *Bass and Stogdills Handbook of Leadership, Third Edition*. New York: Free Press, Macmillan Co., 1990.

Beggs, J., D. C. Doolittle, and D. Garsombke. "Work Value Orientations and Patterns: A Comparison of Future Managers with Managers and Non-Manager Groups." *International Journal of Value-Based Management*, 8, Vol. 3 (1995): 289–300.

Bell, B. S., and S. W. Kozlowski. "Adaptive Guidance: Enhancing Self-Regulation, Knowledge and Performance in Technology-Based Training." *Personnel Psychology: A Journal of Applied Research*, 55, number 2 (Summer 2002): 267–306.

Bennis, W. *On Becoming a Leader, Second Edition*. Cambridge, MA: Perseus Book Group, 2003.

Bennis, W., and B. Nanus. *Leaders: Strategies for Taking Charge*. New York: Harper and Row, 1985.

Bennis, W., and P.W. Brederman. *Organizing Genius: The Secrets of Creative Collaboration*. Reading, MA: Addison-Wesley, 1997.

Benson, H. *Beyond the Relaxation Response*. New York: Berkley Publishing Group, 1985.

———. *The Relaxation Response*. New York: HarperTorch, 1976.

Benson, H., and M. Stark. *Timeless Healing: The Power and Biology of Belief*. New York: Scribner, 1986.

Benson, H., and E. Stuart. *Wellness Book*. New York: Scribner, 1993.

Blake, R. R., and J. S. Mouton. *The Managerial Grid*. Houston, TX: Gulf Publishing, 1964.

Blanchard, K. H., and R. L. Lorber. *Putting the One Minute Manager to Work: How to Turn the Three Secrets into Skills*. New York: William Morrow and Company, 1984.

Blanchard, K. H., and S. Fowler. *Empowerment: How to Sustain Peak Performance Through Self Leadership*. Successories Libraries, Inc., 1998.

Blanchard, K. H., D. Carew, and E. Parsi-Carew. *The One Minute Manager Builds High Performing Teams*. New York: William Morrow, 1990.

Blanchard, K. H., J. Carlos, and A. Randolph. *Empowerment Takes More Than a Minute*. San Francisco, CA: Berrett-Koehler Publishers, 1996.

Blanchard, K. H., S. Fowler, and L. Hawkins. *Self Leadership and the One Minute Manager*. New York: William Morrow, 2005.

Blanchard, K. H., T. Laciwak, C. Tompkins, and J. Ballard. *Whale Done!* New York: Free Press, 2002.

Blanchard, K. H., and J. Stoner. *Full Steam Ahead: Unleash the Power of Vision in Your Company and Your Life*. San Francisco, CA: Barrett-Koehler Publications, Inc., 2003.

Blanchard, K. H., and S. Bowles. *Raving Fans: A Revolutionary Approach to Customer Service*. New York: William Morrow and Company, Inc., 1993.

————. *Gung Ho!* New York: William Morrow and Company, Inc., 1998.

Blanchard, K. H., P. Zigarmi, and D. Zigarmi. *Leadership and the One Minute Manager*. New York: Morrow Publishers, 1985.

Bliss, E. C. *Doing It Now*. New York: Charles Scribner's Sons, 1983.

————. *Getting Things Done*. Boulder, CO: CareerTrack Publications, 1985 (audio) and 1989 (video).

Bloom, H. Genius: *A Mosaic of One Hundred Exemplary Creative Minds*. New York: Warner Books, Inc., 2002.

Bluestone, B., and I. Bluestone. *Negotiating the Future: A Labor Perspective on American Business*. New York: Basic Books, 1990.

Boettinger, H. M. *The Telephone Book: Bell, Watson, Vail and American Life, 1876–1976*. New York: E.P. Dutton, 1976.

Bouchard, T.J., D.T. Lykken, M. McGue, N.L. Segal, and A. Tellegen. "Sources of Human Psychological Differences: The Minnesota Study of Twins Reared Apart." *Science*, 250, No. 497 (Oct. 12, 1990): 223.

Brim, O. G., and J. Kagan, eds. *Constancy and Change in Human Development*. Cambridge, MA: Harvard University Press, 1980.

Brookfield, S. D. *Understanding and Facilitating Adult Learning*. San Francisco, CA: Jossey-Bass, 1986.

Brown, K. G. "Using Computers to Deliver Training: Which Employees Learn and Why." *Personnel Psychology: A Journal of Applied Research*, 54, number 1 (Spring 2001): 271–296.

Bruner, J. S. *Toward a Theory of Instruction*. Cambridge, MA: Harvard University Press, 1966.

Buckingham, M., and D. Cliffton. *Now Discover All Your Strengths*. New York: Simon & Schuster, 2001.

Buckingham, M., and C. Coffman. *First Break All the Rules: What the World's Greatest Managers Do Differently*. New York: Simon & Schuster, 1999.

Burke, W. W., E. A. Richley, and A. S. DeAngelis. "Changing Leadership and Planning Process at the Lewis Research Center, National Aeronautics and Space Administration." *Human Resource Management*, 24 (1985): 81–90.

Burns, J. M. *Leadership*. New York: Harper and Row, 1978.

Byrum, S.C., and L. Kaiser. *Spirit for Greatness: Spiritual Dimensions of Organizations and Their Leadership*. Littleton, MA: Tapestry Press, Ltd., 2004.

Callister, R. R., and J. A. Wall Jr. "Conflict Across Organizational Boundaries: Managed Care Organizations Versus Health Care Providers." *Journal of Applied Psychology*, 2001, Vol. 86, No. 4: 754–763.

Calzon, J. *Moment of Truth*. Cambridge, MA: Ballinger Publishing Company, 1987.

Candy, P.C. *Self Direction for Lifelong Learning*. San Francisco, CA: Jossey-Bass, 1991.

Canfield, J., and J. Switzer. *The Success Principles: How to Get from Where You Are to Where You Want to Be*. New York: HarperCollins, 2005.

Capra, F. *The Tao of Physics*. Boston, MA: Shambala, 1985.

Carruthers, J. "The Principles and Practice of Mentoring." In *The Return of the Mentor: Strategies for Workplace Learning*. Caldwell, B. J. and E. M. Carter, eds. Bristol, PA: Falmer, 1993.

Cashman, K. *Leadership from the Inside Out*. Provo, UT: Executive Excellence Publishing, 1998.

Chang, R. Y. *Building a Dynamic Team: A Practical Guide to Maximizing Team Performance*. Irving, CA: Richard Chang Associates, 1995.

Church, A. H., A. Margiloff, and C.A. Coruzzi. "Using Surveys for Change: An Applied Example in a Pharmaceuticals Organization." *Leadership and Organizational Development Journal*, 16, No. 4 (1995): 3–11.

Church, A. H., M. Javitch, and W. W. Burke. "Enhancing Professional Service Quality: Feedback Is The Way To Go." *Managing Service Quality*, 5, No. 3 (1985): 29–33.

Church, A. H., S. G. Rogelberg, and J. Waclawski. "Since When Is No News? The Relationship Between Performance and Response Rates in Multirater Feedback." *Personnel Psychology: A Journal of Applied Research*, 33, No. 2 (Summer 2000): 435–452.

Clark, C. S., G. H. Dobbins, and R. I. Ladd. "Exploratory Field Study of Training Motivation." *Group and Organization Management*, 18 (1993): 292–307.

Clark, S. M., and M. Cocoran. "Perspectives on the Professional Socialization of Women Faculty." *Journal of Higher Education*, 57, No. 1 (1986): 20–43.

Cohen-Chorash, Y., and P. E. Spector. "The Role of Justice in Organizations: A Meta-Analysis." *Organizational Behavior and Human Decision Process*, Vol. 86 (2001): 278–321.

Cohen, S.G., and D.F. Bailey. "What Makes Teams Work: Group Effectiveness Research from the Shop Floor to the Executive Suite." *Journal of Management*, 23, No. 3 (1997): 239–290.

Collins, J. *Good to Great: Why Some Companies Make the Leap...and Others Don't.* New York: Harper Collins Publishers, Inc., 2001.

Collins, J. C., and J. I. Porras. *Built to Last.* New York: Harper Business Book, 1994.

Colquitt, J. A., D. E. Conlon, C. Wesson, C. Porter, and K.Y. Ng. "Justice at the Millennium: A Meta-Analytic Review of 25 Years of Organizational Justice Research." *Journal of Applied Psychology*, Vol. 86, No. 3 (2002): 425–445.

Connellan, T. K. *How to Grow People into Self Starters.* Ann Arbor, MI: The Achievement Institute, Inc., 1988.

———. *How to Improve Human Performance: Behaviorism in Business and Industry.* New York: Harper and Row, 1978.

Connolly, T., L. M. Jessup, and J. Valacich. "Effects of anonymity and evaluation tone on idea generation in computer mediated groups." *Managerial Science*, 36 (1990): 689–703.

Cook, C. W., and P. L. Hunsacker. *Management and Organizational Behavior.* (3rd ed.) Boston, MA: McGraw-Hill Irwin, 2001.

Cover, S. R. *Principle-Central Leadership.* New York: Summit Books, 1991.

Covey, S.R. *The Seven Habits of Highly Effective People: Restoring the Character Ethic.* New York: Simon and Schuster, 1989.

Covey, S. R., R. A. Merrill, and R. R. Merrill. *First Things First.* New York: Simon and Schuster, 1994.

Cropanzano, R. *Justice in the Workplace: Approaching Fairness in Human Resource Management.* Hillsdale, NJ: Lawrence Erlbaum Associates, 1993.

Cropanzano, R., and J. Greenberg. "Progress in Organizational Justice: Tunneling Through the Maza." In C. Cooper and I. Robertson (eds.). *International Review of Industrial and Organizational Psychology* (pp. 317–372). New York: Wiley, 1997.

Cropanzano, R., C. A. Prehar, and P. Y. Chen. "Using Social Exchange Theory to Distinguish Procedural From Interactive Justice." *Group and Organization Management,* Vol. 27, No. 3 (2002): 324–351.

Csikszentmihalyi, M. *Creativity: Flow and the Psychology of Discovery and Invention.* New York: Harper Collins, 1996.

———. *The Evolving Self.* New York: Harper Collins, 1993.

———. *Flow: The Psychology of Optimal Experience.* New York: Harper Collins Publishers, 1991.

Dalton, M. "Multirater Feedback and Conditions for Change." *Consulting Psychology Journal: Practice and Research,* 48, No. 1 (1996): 12–16.

Daniels, A. C., and T. A. Rosen. *Performance Management: Improving Quality and Productivity Through Positive Reinforcement.* Tucker, GA: Performance Management Publications, 1986.

Deci, E. *Why We Do What We Do: The Dynamics of Personal Autonomy.* New York: Grossett/Putnam Book, 1995.

Deci, E., R. Koestner, and R. M. Ryan. "A meta-analytic review of experiments examining the effects of extrinsic rewards on intrinsic motivation." *Psychological Bulletin,* 125 (1999): 627–668.

Deci, E., and R. M. Ryan. *Handbook of Self-Determination Research.* Rochester, NY: The University of Rochester Press, 2002.

———. *Intrinsic Motivation and Self-Determination in Human Behavior.* New York: Plenum Press, 1985.

Demetrious, A., W. Doise, and C. Van Lieshout, eds. *Life-Span Developmental Psychology.* West Sussex, England: John Wiley and Sons, Ltd., 1998.

Demming, W. E. *Quality Productivity and Competitive Position*. Boston, MA: Massachusetts Institute of Technology Press, 1982.

Despain, J., and J.B. Converse. *And Dignity for All: Unlocking Greatness with Values-Based Leadership*. Upper Saddle River, NJ: Financial Times Press, 2003.

DiClemente, C.C. "Self-Efficacy and Addictive Behaviors." *Journal of Social and Clinical Psychology*, 4 (1986): 302–315.

Dirks, K. T., and D. L. Ferrin. "Trust in Leadership: Meta-Analytic Findings and Implications for Research and Practice." *Journal of Applied Psychology*, Vol. 87, No. 4 (2002): 611–628.

Doz, Y.L. "The Evolution of Cooperation in Strategic Alliances: Initial Conditions or Learning Processes?" *Strategic Management Journal*, 17, No. 3 (May–June 1996): 55–83.

Drucker, P. F. *The Essential Drucker: The Best of Sixty Years of Peter Drucker's Essential Writings on Management*. New York: Harper Business Press, 2003.

Duarte, D.L., and N.T. Snyder. *Mastering Virtual Teams: Strategies, Tools and Techniques that Succeed, Second Edition*. San Francisco, CA: Jossey-Bass, A Wiley Company, 2001.

Dweck, C. S. "Motivational Processes Affecting Learning." *American Psychologist*, 41 (1986): 1040–1048.

Earley, P. C., T. Connolly, and C. Ekegren. "Goals, Strategy Development and Task Performance: Some Limits on the Efficacy of Goal Setting." *Journal of Applied Psychology*, 74 (1989): 24–33.

Eden, D., and G. Ravid. "Pygmalion versus self-expectancy: Effects of instructor and self-expectancy on trainee performance." *Organizational Behavior and Human Performance*, 30 (1982): 351–364.

Egan, G. *Working the Shadow Side: A Guide to Positive Behind the Scenes Management*. San Francisco: Jossey-Bass Publishers, 1994.

Eisenberger, R., P. Fasolo, and V. Davis-LaMastro. "Perceived Organizational Support and Employee Diligence, Commitment and Innovation." *Journal of Applied Psychology*, Vol. 75 (1990): 51–57.

Endegon, B. M., M. L. Kraimer, and R. C. Liden. "Procedural Justice As a Two-Dimensional Construct: An Examination in the Performance Appraisal Context." *Journal of Applied Behavioral Science*, Vol. 37, No. 2 (2001): 205–222.

England, G. W. "Personal Value Systems of American Managers." *Academy of Management Journal*, 10 (1967): 53–68.

Erhart, M. G. "Leadership and Procedural Justice: Climates as Antecedents of Unit Level Organizational Citizenship Behavior." *Personnel Psychology*, Vol. 57, No. 1 (2004): 61–94.

Erickson, E. H. *Gandhi's Truth*. New York: W. W. Norton, 1969.

———. *Identity and the Life Cycle*. New York: International Universities Press, 1959.

Eysenck, H. J., and M. W. Eysenck. *Personality and Individual Differences: A Natural Science Approach*. New York: Plenum Press, 1985.

Fairhurst, G.T., and R.A. Sarr. *The Art of Framing: Managing the Language of Leadership*. San Francisco, CA: Jossey-Bass, Inc., 1996.

Faust, G. W., R. I. Lyles, and W. Phillips. *Responsible Managers Get Results: How the Best Find Solutions—No Excuses*. New York: American Management Association, 1998.

Ferguson, M. *PragMagic*. New York: Pocket Books, 1990.

Fiore, N. *The NOW Habit*. Los Angeles, CA: Jeremy Tarcher, 1989.

Fischer, L. *The Life of Mahatma Gandhi*. New York: Harper and Row, Publishers, 1950.

Fisk, A. D., and W. Schneider. "Category and Word Search: Generalizing Search Principles to Complex Processing." *Journal of Experimental Psychology: Learning, Memory, and Cognition* 10 (1983): 181–197.

Fittz, P., and M. I. Posner. *Human Performance*. Belmont, CA: Brooks/Cole, 1967.

Flade, P. "Great Britain's Work Force Lacks Inspiration." *Gallup Management Journal* (Dec. 11, 2003).

Folger, R., and D. Lewis. "Self-Appraisal and Fairness in Evaluations." In *Justice in the Workplace: Approaching Fairness in Human Resources Management*. R. Cropanzano (ed.). Hillsdale, NJ: Lawrence Erlbaum Associates, 1993.

Ford, G.A., and G.L. Lippett. *A Guide to Personal Goal Setting*. San Diego, CA: University Associates, Inc., 1988.

Ford, J.K., M.A. Quinones, D.J. Sego, and J.S. Sopra. "Factors Affecting the Opportunity to Perform Trained Tasks on the Job." *Personnel Psychology*, 45, No. 3 (Autumn 1992): 511–528.

Ford, M. E. *Motivating Humans: Goals, Emotions and Personal Agency Beliefs*. Newbury Park, CA: Sage, 1992.

Fowler-Woodring, S. *Mentoring: How to Foster Your Career's Most Crucial Relationships*. (Audio-cassette.) Boulder, CO: CareerTrack Publications, 1992.

Fowler-Woodring, S., and D. Zigarmi. *The Team Leader's Idea-A-Day Guide*. Chicago: Dartnell Press, 1997.

————. *Overcoming Procrastination*. Boulder, CO: CareerTrack Publications, 1990 (audio).

Frayne, C., and G.P. Latham. "Application of Social Learning Theory to Employee Self-Management of Attendance." *Journal of Applied Psychology*, 72 (1987): 387–392.

Fritz, R. *The Path of Least Resistance*. Salem, MA: DMA, Inc., 1984.

Gardner, H. *Frames of Mind: The Theory of Multiple Intelligences*. New York: Basic Books, 1993.

————. *Creating Minds: An Anatomy of Creativity Seen through the Lives of Freud, Einstein, Picasso, Stravinsky, Eliot, Graham and Gandhi*. New York: Basic Books, 1993.

Gardner, H., and E. Laskin. *Leading Minds: An Anatomy of Leadership*. New York: Basic Books, a Division of Harper Collins, 1995.

Garfield, C. *Peak Performers: The New Heroes of American Business*. New York: William Morrow and Company, 1996.

Gawain, S. *Creative Visualization*. New York: MJF Books, 1978.

Gesell, A. "The ontogenesis of infant behavior." In *Manual of Child Psychology*, edited by L. Carmichael. New York: Wiley, 1943.

Gharajedaghi, J. *Systems Thinking: Managing Chaos and Complexity: A Platform for Designing Business Architecture*. Burlington, MA: Butterworth Heinemann, an imprint of Elsevier, 1999.

Gibson, C. B., A. E. Randel, and P. C. Earley. "Understanding Group Efficacy: An Empirical Test of Multiple Assessment Methods." *Group and Organization Management*, March 2000, Vol. 25, No. 1: 67–97.

Gist, M. E., C. Schwoerer, and B. Rosen. "Effects of alternative training methods on self-efficacy and performance in computer software training." *Journal of Applied Psychology*, 74 (1989): 884–891.

Gist, M. E., C. K. Stevens, and A. G. Bavetta. "Effects of self-efficacy and post-training intervention in the acquisition and maintenance of complex interpersonal skills." *Personnel Psychology*, 44, No. 4 (Winter 1991): 837–862.

Goldratt, E.M., and J. Cox. *The Goal Croft Road*. Aldershot, England: Gower Publishing Company, Limited, 1984.

Goldsmith, H. H. "Genetic Influences on Personality from Infancy to Adulthood." *Child Development*, 54 (1983): 331–355.

Goleman, D. *Emotional Intelligence*. New York: Bantam Books, 1995.

Green, R. "Social Motivation." *Annual Review of Psychology*, 42 (1991):377–399.

Greenberg, J. "Determinants of Perceived Fairness of Performance Evaluations." *Journal of Applied Psychology*, Vol. 71 (1986): 340–342.

———. "Reactions to Procedural Justice in Payment Distributions: Do the Ends Justify the Means?" *Journal of Applied Psychology*, Vol. 72 (1987): 55–61.

———. *The Quest for Justice in the Workplace: Essays and Experiments*. Thousand Oaks, CA: Sage Publications, 1996.

Greene, B. *The Elegant Universe*. New York: W.W. Norton & Company, Inc., 1999.

Gregg, R. B., and J. T. Wood, J.T., eds. *Toward the Twenty-First Century: The Future of Speech Communication*. Carmel, CA: Hampton Press, 1995.

Greiner, L. E. "Commentary and Revision of HBR Classic Evolution and Revolution as Organizations Grow." *Harvard Business Review*, May-June, 1998.

Greiner, L.E. "Evolution and Revolution as Organizations Grow." *Harvard Business Review*, 5, No. 4 (July–August 1972): 37–46.

Griffin, R. W., A. O'Leary-Kelly, and J. M. Collins. *Dysfunctional Behavior in Organizations: Violent and Deviant Behavior*. Stamford, CT: JAI Press, Inc., 1998.

Grove, R. *The Disney Touch*. Chicago, IL: Irwin Professional Publishing, 1997.

Grow, G. O. "Teaching Learners to Be Self-Directed." *Adult Education Quarterly*, 41 (1991): 125–149.

Gully, S. M., K. A. Incalcattena, A. Joshi, and J. M. Beaubien. "A Meta-Analysis of Team Efficacy, Potency and Performance: Interdependence and Level of Analysis as Moderators of Observed Relationship." *Journal of Applied Psychology*, 2002, Vol. 87, No. 5: 819–832.

Halberstam, D. *Playing for Keeps: Michael Jordan and the World He Made.* New York: Random House, 1997.

Halfhill, T., E. Sundstrom, J. Lahner, W. Calderone, and T.M. Nielsen. "Group Personality Composition and Group Effectiveness: An Integrative Review of Empirical Research." *Small Group Research*, 36, No. 1 (2005): 83–105.

Hall, G. E., A. A. George, and W. L. Rutherford. "Measuring Stages of Concern About Innovation: A Manual for Use of the SOL Questionnaire." Rand Center for Teacher Education: University of Texas at Austin, 1977.

Hall, G. E., and S. Hord. *Change in Schools: Facilitating the Process.* New York: State University of New York Press, 1987.

Hall, G., and S. Locucks. "Using Teacher Concerns as a Basis for Facilitating and Personalizing Skill Development." Teachers College Record, 1979.

Hammer, M., and J. Champy. *Reengineering the Corporation.* New York: Harper Collins, 1993.

Hawking, S. *A Brief History of Time.* New York: Bantam Book, 1988.

Hersey, P., and K. H. Blanchard. "LifeCycle Theory of Leadership." *Training and Development Journal*, May (1969): 26–33.

Hersey, P., K. H. Blanchard, and D. E. Johnson. *Management of Organizational Behavior: Utilizing Human Resources.* (7th ed.) Upper Saddle River, NJ: Prentice Hall, 1996.

Herzberg, F., B. Mausner, and B. B. Snyderman. *The Motivation to Work.* New York: John Wiley and Sons, Inc., 1959.

Hicks, W. D., and R. J. Klimoski. "Entry Into Training Programs and Its Effects on Training Outcomes: A Field Experiment." *Academy of Management Journal*, 3 (1987): 542–552.

High Gain, Inc. *http://www.highgain.org/*.

His Holiness The Dalai Lama and H. C. Cutler. *The Art of Happiness at Work.* New York: Riverhead Books, 2003.

Hornblower, M. "Society Great X." *Time Magazine* (June 9, 1997): 58–69.

House, R. J., and G. Dessler. "The Goal Path Theory of Leadership: Some Post Hoc and A Priori Tests." In *Contingency Approaches to Leadership*, edited by J. G. Hunt and L. L. Larson. Carbondale, IL: Southern Illinois University Press, 1974.

Howe, N., and W. Strauss. *13th Gen: Abort, Retry, Ignore, Fail?* New York: Vintage Books, 1993.

Hudson Institute and Walker Information. "The 1999 National Business Ethics Study." *http://www.walkerinfo.com*, 1999.

Humphreys, L. G. "The Construct of General Intelligence." *Intelligence*, 3 (1979): 105–120.

International Listing Association. *http://www.listen.org/*.

Izraeli, D., and E. D. Jaffe. "Predicting Whistle Blowing: A Theory of Reasoned Action Approach." *International Journal of Value-Based Management*, Vol. 11, No. 1 (1998): 19–34.

Jackson, P., and H. Delehanty. *Sacred Hoops: Spiritual Lessons of Hardwood Warriors*. New York: Hyperion, 1995.

Johnson, J. W. "Linking Employee Perceptions of Service Climate to Customer Satisfaction." *Personnel Psychology: A Journal of Applied Research*, 49, No. 4 (Winter 1996): 831–852.

Johnson, R. A. *Owning Your Own Shadow*. San Francisco: Harper, 1991.

Jonassen, D. H., and B. L. Grabowski. *Handbook of Individual Differences, Learning and Instruction*. Hillsdale, NJ: Lawrence Erlbaum, 1993.

Jung, C. G. *Man and His Symbols*. Garden City, NY: Doubleday and Company, 1964.

———. *Memories, Dreams and Reflections*. A. Jaffe, ed. New York: Vintage Books, 1961.

———. *Psychological Types*. New York: Harcourt and Brace, 1923.

———. "The Philosophical Tree." *Alchemical Studies*, Vol. 13 of the *Collected Works* (Princeton: Princeton University Press, 1976): 265–266.

Kahai, S. S., J. J. Sosik, and B. J. Avolio. "Effects of Leadership Style and Problem Structure on Work Group Process and Outcomes in an Electronic Meeting System Environment." *Personnel Psychology*, 50, No. 1 (Spring 1997): 126–146.

Kahn, R. L., D. M. Wolfe, R. P. Quinn, and J. D. Snock. *Organizational Stress: Studies in Role Conflict and Ambiguity*. New York: John Wiley and Sons, Inc., 1964.

Kanfer, R., and P. L. Ackerman. "Motivation and Cognitive Abilities: An Integrative/Aptitude—Treatment Interaction Approach to Skill Acquisition." *Journal of Applied Psychology*, No. 4 (1989): 657–690.

Kanfer, R., P.L. Ackerman, and R. Cudeck. *Abilities, Motivation and Methodology: The Minnesota Symposium on Learning and Individual Differences*. Hillsdale, NJ: Lawrence Erlbaum Associates, Publishers, 1989.

Kaplan, R. E. *Beyond Ambition: How Driven Managers Can Lead Better and Live Better*. San Francisco: Jossey-Bass Publishers, 1991.

Katie, B. *Loving What Is*. New York: Harmony Books, 2002.

Katzenback, J. R., and D. K. Smith. *The Wisdom of Teams*. Cambridge, MA: Harvard Business School Press, 1993.

Keirsey, D., and M. Bates. *Please Understand Me: Character and Temperament Types*. Del Mar, CA: Prometheus Nemesis Books, 1978.

Keleman, S. *Emotional Anatomy: The Structure of Experience*. Berkeley, CA: Center Press, 1985.

Keller, L. M., T. J. Bouchard, R. D. Arvey, N. L. Segal, and R. V. Davis. "Work Values: Genetic and Environmental Influences." *Journal of Applied Psychology*, 77, No. 1 (January 1992): 79–88.

Ket de Vries, M. F. R. *Prisoners of Leadership*. New York: John Wiley and Sons, Inc., 1989.

Khanna, T. "The Scope of Alliances." *Organization Science*, May-June 1998, Vol. 9, No. 3: 340–355.

Kleiman, C. *Women's Networks*. Chicago, IL: Ballentine Books, 1981.

Kleinbeck, U., H. H. Quast, H. Thierry, and H. Hacker, eds. *Work Motivation*. Hillsdale, NJ: Lawrence Erlbaum Associates, Inc., 1990.

Kluger, A. N., and A. S. DeNisi. "The Effects of Feedback Interventions on Performance: A Historical Review, a Meta-Analysis and a Preliminary Feedback Theory." *Psychological Bulletin*, 119 (1996): 254–284.

Knowles, E. (ed.) *The Oxford Dictionary of Phrase, Saying and Quotation*. Oxford, England: Oxford University Press, 1997.

Knowles, M. S., E. F. Holton, and R. A. Swanson. *The Adult Learner: The Definitive Classic in Adult Education and Human Resource Development.* 5th edition. Woburn, MA: Butterworth-Heinemann, 1998.

Kogut, B. "Joint Ventures: Theoretical and Empirical Perspectives." *Strategic Management Journal*, 1988, Vol. 9: 319–332.

Kohlberg. L. "Continuities in Childhood and Adult Moral Development Revisited." In *Life-Span Developmental Psychology: Personality and Socialization*, edited by Balters, P. B., and K. W. Schaie. New York: Academic Press, 1973.

———. *Stages in the Development of Moral Thought and Action.* New York: Holt, Rinehart & Winston, 1965.

Kolb, D. A. *Experiential Learning: Experience as a Source of Learning and Development.* Englewood Cliffs, NJ: Prentice Hall, 1984.

Konovsky, M.A. "Understanding Procedural Justice and Its Impact on Business Organization." *Journal of Management*, Vol. 26 (2000): 489–511.

Konovsky, M.A., R. Folger, and R. Cropanzano. "Relative Effects of Procedural and Distributive Justice on Employee Attitudes." *Representative Research in Social Psychology*, Vol. 17 (1987): 15–24.

Korsgaard, M.A., L. Roberson, and D. Rymph. "Promoting Fairness Through Subordinate Training: The Impact of Manager Effectiveness." In *Paper Presented at the Annual Meeting of the Society for Industrial and Organizational Psychology.* San Diego, CA, 1991.

Kotter, J. P. *Leading Change.* Boston, MA: Harvard Business Press, 1996.

Kouzes, J. M., and B. Z. Posner. *The Leadership Challenge: How to Keep Getting Extraordinary Things Done in Organizations.* San Francisco, CA: Jossey-Bass, 1985.

———. *Encouraging the Heart: A Leader's Guide to Rewarding and Recognizing Others.* San Francisco, CA: Jossey-Bass: A Wiley Company, 1999.

Kovach, K. A. "Improving Employee Motivation in Today's Business Environment." *MSU Business Topics*, 24, No. 24 (Autumn 1976): 5–12.

Koza, M.P., and A.Y. Lewin. "The Co-Evolution of Strategic Alliances." *Organization Science*, 9, No. 3 (May–June 1998): 255–264.

Kram, K. E., and M. C. Bragar. "Career Development Through Mentoring: A Strategic Approach for the 1990s—Part 1." *Mentoring International,* 5, Nos. 1–2 (1991): 3–13.

Kraut, A. I., ed. *Organizational Surveys: Tools for Assessment and Change.* San Francisco, CA: Jossey-Bass, 1996.

Kroeger, O., and T. M. Thuesen. *Type Talk: Or How to Determine Your Personality Type and Change Your Life.* New York: Bantam Doubleday Dell Publishing Group, Inc., 1988.

Kyllonen, P. C., and V. J. Shute, "A Taxonomy of Leaning Skills." In *Learning and Individual Differences: Advances in Theory and Research,* edited by Ackerman, P. L., R. J. Sternberg, and R. Glaser. New York: Freeman, 1989.

Lacoursiere, R. B. *The Life Cycle of Groups: Group Development Stage Theory.* New York: Human Service Press, 1980.

Landy, P. C. *Self-Direction for Lifelong Learning.* San Francisco, CA: Jossey-Bass, 1991.

Lapham, G., and K. Wexley. *Increasing Productivity Through Performance Appraisal.* Reading, MA: Addison-Wesley, 1981.

Latham, G.P., and C. Frayne. "Self Management Training for Increasing Job Attendance: Follow-up and a Replication." *The Journal of Applied Psychology* 74, No. 3 (June 1989): 411–416.

Latham, G. P., and K. Wexley. *Increasing Productivity Through Performance Appraisals.* Reading, MA: Addison-Wesley, 1981.

Lawler, E. E. *Motivation in Work Organizations.* San Francisco: Jossey-Bass, 1994.

Lazenby, R. *Blood on the Horns: The Long, Strange Ride of Michael Jordan's Chicago Bulls.* Lenexa, KS: Addax Publishing Group, 1998.

Lee, K., and N. J. Allen. "Organizational Citizenship Behavior and Workplace Defiance: The Role of Affect and Cognitions." *Journal of Applied Psychology,* Vol. 87, No.1 (2002): 131–142.

Leichtman, R., and C. Japiske. *Active Meditation.* Columbus, OH: Ariel Press, 1982.

Lencioni, P. *The Five Dysfunctions of a Team: A Leadership Fable.* San Francisco, CA: Jossey Bass: A Wiley Company, 2002.

LePine, J. A., A. Ercz, and D. E Johnson. "The Nature and Dimensionality of Organizational Citizenship Behavior: A Cultural Review and Meta-Analysis." *Journal of Applied Psychology*, Vol. 87, No. 1 (2002): 52–65.

Levinson, D. J. *The Seasons of a Woman's Life*. New York: Ballantine Books, 1996.

Levinson, D. J., with C. N. Darrow, E. B. Klein, M. H. Levinson, and B. McKee. *The Seasons of a Man's Life*. New York: Alfred A. Knopf, 1978.

Locke, E. A. and D. M Schweger. "Participation in Decision-Making: One More Look." *Research in Organization Behavior*, Vol. 1 (1979): 265–339.

Locke, E. A., and G. P. Latham. *A Theory of Goal Setting and Task Performance*. Englewood Cliffs, NJ: Prentice Hall, 1990.

Loevinger, J. *Ego Development: Concepts and Theories*. San Francisco, CA: Jossey-Bass, 1976.

Lombardo, M. *Value in Action: The Meaning of Executive Vignettes Technical Report #28*. Greensboro, NC: Center for Creative Leadership, 1986.

London, M., and R. W. Beatty. "360-Degree Feedback as a Competitive Advantage." *Human Resource Management*, 32 (1993): 353–372.

Lorenz, K. *On Aggression*. New York: Harcourt Brace, 1966.

Loucks-Horsley, S. and S. Stiegelbauer. "Using Knowledge of Change to Guide Staff Development." *Staff Development for Education in the 90's*. Teachers College Press, 1991.

Lundin, S.C., H. Paul, and J. Christensen. *Fish*. New York: Hyperion, 2000.

Luthans, F., and R. Kreitner. *Organizational Behavior Modification*. Glenview, IL: Scott Foreman and Company, 1975.

———. *Organizational Behavior Modification and Beyond: An Operant and Social Learning Approach*. Glenview, IL: Scott Foreman and Company, 1985.

Lyles, R. I. *Practical Management Problem Solving and Decision Making*. New York: Van Nostrand Reinhold Company, 1992.

———. *Winning Ways: 4 Secrets for Getting Results by Working with People*. New York: Berkley Publishing Group, 2001.

———. *Winning Habits: 4 Secrets That Will Change the Rest of Your Life*. Upper Saddle River, NJ: Pearson Education Inc., 2004.

Lyles, R.I., T. Flannigan, S. Fowler, and D. Zigarmi. *Good Leader, Good Shepherd*. In press, 2006.

Macy, G. "The Role of Values in Implementing Progressive Organizational Practices." *International Journal of Value-Based Management*, 8, No. 1 (1995): 39–52.

Manchester, W. *The Last Lion: Winston Spencer Churchill—Visions of Glory: 1874–1932*. New York: Laurel Trade Paperback, 1983.

Maney, K. *The Maverick and His Machine: Thomas Watson, Sr. and the Making of IBM*. New York: Wiley, 2003.

Manz, C.C., and H.P. Sims. *Super Leadership: Leading Others to Lead Themselves*. New York: Berkley Book, 1990.

Marston, W. M. *Emotions of Normal People*. Minneapolis, MN: Persona Press, Inc, 1979.

Maslow, A. H. *Motivation and Personality*. New York: Harper, 1954.

Massey, M. *The People Puzzle: Understanding Yourself and Others*. Reston, VA: Reston Publishing Company, Inc., A Prentice Hall Company, 1979.

Massey, M., and M. O'Connor. *The Values Analysis Profile*. Minneapolis, MN: Performax Systems International, 1981.

Mathieu, J. E., J. W. Martineau, and S. I. Tannenbaum. "Individual and Situational Influences in the Development of Self-Efficacy: Implications for Training Effectiveness." *Personnel Psychology*, 46 (Spring 1993): 125–148.

McClelland. D. C. *The Achieving Society*. New York: Free Press, 1961.

———. *Human Motivation*. Cambridge, UK: Cambridge University Press, 1987.

McGregor, D. *The Human Side of Enterprise*. New York: McGraw-Hill Book Company, 1960.

Mento, A. J., R. S. Steel, and R. J. Karren. "A Meta-Analytic Study of the Effects of Goal Setting on Task Performance: 1966–1984." *Organizational Behavior and Human Decision Processes*, 39 (1987): 52–83.

Merriam, S., and P. M. Cunningham, eds. *Handbook of Adult and Continuing Education*. San Francisco, CA: Jossey-Bass, 1989.

Merriam, S., and R. S. Caffarella. *Learning in Adulthood*. San Francisco, CA: Jossey-Bass, 1991.

Merrill, D. W., and R. H. Reid. *Personal Styles and Effective Performance.* Radnor, PA: Chilton Book Company, 1981.

Miceli, M. P. "Whistle Blowing Research and the Insider: Lessons to Learn and Yet to Be Learned." *Journal of Management Inquiry*, Vol. 13, No. 4 (2004): 364–366.

Miceli, M. P., and J. P. Near. "The Relationship Among Beliefs, Organizational Position, and Whistle Blowing Status: A Discriminate Analysis." *Academy of Management Journal*, Vol. 27, No. 4 (1984): 687–705.

Miceli, M. P., J. P. Near, and C. R. Schweek. "Who Blows the Whistle and Why?" *Industrial and Labor Relations Review*, Vol. 45, No. 1 (1991): 113–130.

Miceli, M. P., M. P. Dozier, and J. Near. "Blowing the Whistle on Data-Fudging: A Controlled Field Experiment." *Journal of Applied Social Psychology*, Vol. 21 (1991): 301–325.

Miles, P. H. *Macro Organizational Behavior.* Santa Monica, CA: Goodyear Publishing Company, Inc., 1980.

Mindy, R. W., J. R. Gordon, A. Sharplan, and S. R. Premeaux. *Management and Organizational Behavior.* Boston: Allyn & Bacon, 1990.

Mojen, H., and S. Tallman. "Control and Performance in International Joint Ventures." *Organization Science*, 8, No. 3 (May–June 1997): 257–274.

Montagu, A. M. F. *Man and Aggression.* New York: Oxford University Press, 1968.

Morrisey, G. L. *Management by Objectives and Results for Business and Industry.* Reading, MA: Addison-Wesley, 1991.

Mowday, R. I. "Equity Theory Predictions of Behavior on Organizations." *Motivation and Work Behavior*, edited by Stears, R. M., and L. W. Porter, 4th ed. New York: McGraw Hill, 1987.

Moyers, B. *Healing and the Mind.* New York: Bantam Doubleday Dell Publishing Group, 1993.

Murphy, E. F., W. A. Snow, P. Carson, and D. Zigarmi. "Values, Sex Differences and Psychological Androgeny." *International Journal of Value-Based Management*, 10, No. 1 (1997): 69–99.

Murphy, K. J. *Effective Listening: Hearing What People Say and Making It Work For You.* New York: Bantam Books, 1987.

Myers, I. B., and P. B. Myers. *Gifts Differing: Understanding Personality Types.* Palo Alto, CA: CPP Books, 1980.

Nadler, D. A. *Feedback and Organization Development: Using Data-Based Methods*. Reading, MA: Addison-Wesley, 1977.

Naisbitt, J., and P. Aburdene. *Re-inventing the Corporation*. New York: Warner Books, 1985.

Napoleon, H. *Think and Grow Rich*. New York: Fawcett Crest Books, 1960.

Near, J. P., and M. P. Micali. "Whistle Blowing: Myth and Reality." *Journal of Management*, Vol. 22, No. 3 (1996): 507–526.

Nelson, B. *1001 Ways to Reward Employees*. New York: Workman Publishing, 1994.

Nelson, T. O., J. Dunlosky, A. Graf, and L. Narens. "Utilization of Meta-Cognitive Judgments in the Allocation of Study During Multi-Trial Learning." *Psychological Sciences*, 5 (1994): 207–213.

Neuman, G.A., and J. Wright. "Team Effectiveness: Beyond Skills and Cognitive Ability." *Journal of Applied Psychology*, 84, No. 3 (1999): 376–389.

Nichol, R. G. *The Lost Art of Listening*. New York: Guilford Press, 1995.

Nissen, M. J., and P. Bullmer. "Attention Requirements of Learning: Evidence From Performance Measures." *Cognitive Psychology*, 19 (1987): 1–32.

O'Connor, M. J. *The Professional Trainer and Consultant's Reference Encyclopedia to the TICS Model*. Coral Gables, FL: Life Associates, Inc., 1986.

Oncken, W., Jr. *Managing Management Time: Who's Got the Monkey?* Englewood Cliffs, NJ: Prentice Hall, 1984.

Orstein, R. *The Roots of Self: Unraveling the Mystery of Who We Are*. San Francisco, CA: Harper, 1993.

Ornstein, R., and D. Sobel. *Healthy Pleasures*. Reading, MA: Addison-Wesley Publishing, 1989.

Osborn, R. N., and J. Hagedoorn. "Institutionalization and Evolutionary Dynamics of Interorganizational Alliances and Networks." *Academy of Management Journal*, 1997, Vol. 40, No. 2: 261–278.

Osgood, C.E., G.J. Suci, and P.H. Tannenbaum. *The Measurement of Meaning, Ninth Edition*. Urban, IL: University of Illinois Press, 1975.

Osteen, J. *Your Best Life Now: 7 Steps to Living at Your Full Potential*. New York, NY: Warner Faith.

Palmore, E. "Predicting Longevity: A Follow-up Controlling for Age." *The Gerontologist*, 9 (1969): 247–259.

Paskevich, D. M., L. R. Brawley, K. D. Dorsch, and W. N. Widmeyer. "Relationship Between Collective Efficacy and Team Cohesion: Conceptual and Measurement Issues." *Group Dynamics: Theory, Research and Practice*, 1999, Vol. 3, No. 3: 210–222.

Penrose, R. *The Emperor's New Mind: Concerning Computers, Minds, and the Law of Physics*. Oxford, England: Oxford University Press, 1989.

Peters, T. J. *Liberation Management: Necessary Disorganization for the Nanosecond Nineties*. New York: Alfred A. Knopf, 1992.

Peters, T. J., and R. H. Waterman. *In Search of Excellence: Lessons from America's Best Run Companies*. New York: Harper and Row, 1982.

Piaget, J. *Science of Education and the Psychology of the Child*. New York: Viking, 1970.

———. *Six Psychological Studies*. New York: Vintage Books, 1968.

Porras, J., S. Emery, and M. Thompson. *Success Built to Last: Creating a Life that Matters*. Upper Saddle River, NJ: Wharton School Publishing, 2006.

Porter, L. W., and E. E. Lawler. *Managerial Attitudes and Performance*. Homewood, IL: Richard D. Irwin Publishers, 1968.

Pratt, D. D. "Andragogy as a Relational Construct." *Adult Education Quarterly*, 38, No. 3 (Spring 1988): 160–181.

Raiche, D. "Making the Darkness Conscious: J.R.R. Tolkien's *The Lord of the Rings*." *Parabola* (Fall 2004): 95–101.

Random House Dictionary of the English Language. New York: Random House, 1987.

Raths, L. E., M. Harmin, and S. B. Simon. *Values and Teaching: Working with Values in the Classroom*. Columbus, OH: Charles E. Merrill Publishing Co., 1966.

Reber, R. A., and J. A. Wallin. "The Effects of Training, Goal Setting and Knowledge of Results on Safe Behavior: A Component Analysis." *Academy of Management Journal*, 27 (1984): 544–560.

Reddin, W. J. *Managerial Effectiveness*. New York: McGraw-Hill Book Company, 1970.

Reeve, J. *Understanding Motivation and Emotion*. Orlando, FL: Harcourt College Publishers, 2004.

Reilly, R. R., J. W. Smither, and N. L. Vasilopoulus. "A Longitudinal Study of Upward Feedback." *Personnel Psychology: A Journal of Applied Research*, 49, No. 3 (Autumn 1996): 599–612.

Reynierse, J. H., D. Ackerman, A. Fink, and J. B. Harker. "The Effects of Personality and Management Role on Perceived Values in Business Settings." *International Journal of Value-Based Management*, 13, No. 1 (2000): 1–13.

Ries, A., and J. Trout. *Positioning: The Battle for Your Mind*. New York: Warner Books, Inc., 1981.

Ring, S. P. and A. H. Van De Ven. "Structuring Cooperative Relationships Between Organizations." *Strategic Management Journal*, 1992, Vol. 13: 483–498.

Rioux, S. M., and L. A. Penner. "The Causes of Organizational Citizenship Behavior: A Motivational Analysis." *Journal of Applied Psychology*, Vol. 86, No. 6 (2001): 1306–1314.

Robbins, A. *Awaking the Giant Within*. New York: Fireside Book, Simon and Schuster, 1991.

Robinson, C. *Themes for Listening and Speaking*. New York: Oxford University Press, 1986.

Rokeach, M. *Beliefs, Attitudes and Values: A Theory of Organization and Change*. San Francisco, CA: Jossey-Bass, 1972.

———. *The Nature of Human Values*. New York: The Free Press, Macmillan Co., 1973.

———. *Understanding Human Values: Individual and Societal*. New York: The Free Press, Macmillan Co., 1979.

Rotter, J. B. *Social Learning and Clinical Psychology*. Englewood Cliffs, NJ: Prentice Hall, 1954.

Rotter, J. B., J. F. Chance, and E. J. Phares. *Applications of Social Learning Theory of Personality*. New York: Holt Rinehart and Winston, 1972.

Rubin, T. I. *Compassion and Self-Hate*. New York: Ballantine, 1976.

Runions, T., and E. Smyth. "Mentorship for the Gifted and Talented." *Canadian Education Association Newsletter*, November–December (1985).

Ryan, A.M., M.J. Schmit, and R. Johnson. "Attitudes and Effectiveness: Examining Relations at an Organizational Level." *Personnel Psychology*, 49, No. 2 (Summer 1996): 853–882.

Ryan, R. M. "Control and Information in the Interpersonal Sphere: An Extension of Cognitive Evaluation Theory." *Journal of Personality and Social Psychology*, 43 (1982): 450–460.

Sales, S. M., and J. House. "Job Dissatisfaction as a Possible Risk Factor in Coronary Heart Disease." *Journal of Chronic Disease*, 23 (1973): 861–873.

Salomon, G. "Television Is Easy and Print Is Tough: The Differential Investment of Mental Effort in Learning as a Function of Perceptions and Attributions." *Journal of Educational Psychology*, 76 (1984): 647–658.

Schappe, S. P. "Bridging the Gap Between Procedural Knowledge and Positive Employee Attitudes." *Group and Organization Management*, Vol. 21, No. 3 (1996): 337–364.

Scharf, P. *Readings in Moral Education*. Minneapolis, MN: Winston Press, 1978.

Schein, E.H. *Organizational Culture and Leadership, Second Edition*. San Francisco, CA: Jossey-Bass Publishers, 1992.

Schmit, M. J., and S. P. Allscheid. "Employee Attitudes and Customer Satisfaction: Making Theoretical and Empirical Connections." *Personnel Psychology: A Journal of Applied Research*, 48, No. 3 (Autumn 1995): 521–536.

Schneider, B. "Service Quality and Profits: Can You Have Your Cake and Eat It Too?" *Human Resource Planning*, 14, No. 2 (1991): 151–157.

Seashore, C. N., E. W. Seashore, and G. W. Weinberg. *What Did You Say? The Art of Giving and Receiving Feedback*. Columbia, MD: Bingham Books, 1997.

Segal, J. A. "Mirror-Image Mentoring." *HR Magazine*, 45 (2000): 157–166.

Seligman, M. E. *Learned Optimism: How to Change Your Mind and Your Life*. New York: Pocket Books, 1990.

Senge, P. *The Fifth Discipline: The Art and Practice of the Learning Organization*. New York: Doubleday Dell Publishing Group, 1990.

Shafir, R. Z. *The Zen of Listening: Mindful Communication in the Age of Distraction*. Chicago, IL: Quest Books, 2000.

Sheehy, G. *New Passages: Mapping Your Life Across Time*. New York: Random House, 1995.

————. *Passages: Predictable Crisis of Adult Life*. New York: E.P. Dutton & Co., 1975.

Sheldrake, R. *A New Science of Life*. Los Angeles, CA: Jeremy Tarcher, 1981.

Sheldrake, R., and D. Bohm. "Morphogenetic Fields and the Implicate Order." *ReVision*, 5 (Fall: 1982).

Shepparel, B. H., R. J. Lewicki, and J. W. Minton. *Organizational Justice: The Search for Fairness*. New York: Lexington Books, 1992.

Siegel, B. *Love, Medicine, and Miracles*. New York: Harper and Row, 1986.

Simons, T., and Q. Roberson. "Why Managers Should Care About Fairness: The Effects of Aggregate Justice Perceptions on Organizational Outcomes." *Journal of Applied Psychology*, Vol. 88, No. 3 (2003): 432–443.

Skinner, B. F. *Beyond Freedom and Dignity*. New York: Alfred A. Knopf, 1971.

————. *Contingencies of Reinforcement*. New York: Appleton-Century-Crofts, 1968.

————. *Science and Human Behavior*. New York: Macmillan, 1953.

Smither, J.W., M. London, and R.R. Reilly. "Does Performance Improve Following Multisource Feedback? A Theoretical Model, Meta-Analysis, and Review of Empirical Findings." *Personnel Psychology*, 58, No. 1 (2005): 33–66.

Sprouse, M., ed. *Sabotage in the American Workplace: Anecdotes of Dissatisfaction, Mischief, and Revenge*. San Francisco, CA: Pressure Drop Press, 1992.

Staw, B. M. *Intrinsic and Extrinsic Motivation*. Morristown, NJ: General Learning Press, 1976.

Steinberg, E. R. "Cognition and Learner Control: A Literature Review, 1977–1988." *Journal of Computer-Based Instruction*, 16 (1989): 117–121.

————. "Review of Student Control in Computer-Assisted Instruction." *Journal of Computer-Based Instruction*, 3 (1977): 84–90.

Stoner, J., and D. Zigarmi. *From Vision to Reality.* Escondidio, CA: The Ken Blanchard Companies, 1993.

Strauss, W., and N. Howe. *The Fourth Turning: An American Prophecy.* New York: Broadway Books, 1997.

————. *Generations: History of American Future 1584 to 2069.* New York: William Morrow, 1991.

Sundstrom, E., K.P. DeMeuse, and D. Futrell. "Work Teams: Applications and Effectiveness." *American Psychologist*, 45, No. 2 (February 1990): 120–133.

Tannebaum, S. I., J. E. Mathieu, E. Salas, and J. A. Cannon-Bowers. "Meeting trainees' expectations: The influence of training fulfillment on the development of commitment, self-efficacy and motivation." *Journal of Applied Psychology*, 76 (1991): 759–769.

Tellegen, A., D. T. Hykken, T. J. Bouchard Jr., K. J. Wilcox, N. L. Segal, and S. Rich. "Personality Similarity in Twins Reared Apart and Together." *Journal of Personality and Social Psychology*, 54 (1988): 1031–1039.

Tepper, B. J., R. J. Eisenback, S. L. Kirby, and P. W. Potter. "Test of a Justice-Based Model of Subordinates' Resistance to Downward Influence Attempts." *Group and Organization Management*, Vol. 86, No. 4 (1998): 789–796.

Terborg, J. R. "Validation and extension of an individual differences model of work performance." *Organizational Behavior and Human Performance*, 18 (1977): 188–216.

Terpstra, D. E., and E. J. Rozell. "The Relationship of Goal Setting to Organizational Profitability." *Group and Organizational Management*, 19, No. 3 (1994): 285–294.

Tett, R. P., D. N. Jackson, and M. Rothstein. "Personality Measures as Predictors of Job Performance: A Meta-Analytical Review." *Personnel Psychology: A Journal of Applied Research*, 44, No. 4 (Winter 1991): 703–742.

Tett, R.P., and J.P. Meyer. "Job Satisfaction, Organizational Commitment, Turnover Intention, and Turnover: Path Analysis Based on Meta-Analytic Findings." *Personnel Psychology*, 46, No. 1 (Spring 1993): 259–293.

Thibaut, J., and L. Walker. *Procedural Justice: A Psychological Analysis.* Hillsdale, NJ: Lawrence Erlbaum Associates, 1975.

Thomas, K. *Intrinsic Motivation at Work.* San Francisco, CA: Berret-Koehler Publishers, Inc., 2000.

Thompson, J.D. *Organizations in Action: Social Science Bases of Administrative Theory.* New York: McGraw-Hill Companies, 1967.

Thorndike, E. L. *Educational Psychology: The Psychology of Learning.*Vol. 2. New York: Teachers College Press, 1913.

Tomas, B. *Walt Disney: An American Original.* New York: Hyperion, 1994.

Tornow, J.W., and J.W. Wiley. "Service Quality and Management Practices: A Look at Employee Attitudes, Customer Satisfaction, and Bottom-Line Consequences." *Human Resource Planning,* 14, No. 2 (1991): 105–115.

Tough, A. *Intentional Changes: A Fresh Approach to Helping People Change.* Chicago, IL: Follet, 1982.

Treacy, M., and F. Wiersema. *The Discipline of Market Leaders: Choose Your Customers, Narrow Your Focus, Dominate Your Market.* Reading, MA: Addison-Wesley, 1995.

Tremblay, M., B. Sire, and A. Pelchat. "A Study of the Determinants and of the Impact of Flexibility on Employee Benefit Satisfaction." *Human Relations,* Vol. 51 (1998): 667–688.

Tremblay, M., B. Sire, and D.B. Balkin. "The Role of Organizational Justice in Pay and Employee Benefit Satisfaction, and Its Effect on Work Attitudes." *Group and Organization Management,* 25, No. 3 (September 2000): 269–290.

Tuckman, B. W. "Developmental Sequence in Small Group." *Psychological Bulletin,* 63 (1965): 384–399

Tulgan, B. *Managing Generation X: How to Bring Out the Best in Young Talent.* Santa Monica, CA: Merritt Publishing, 1995.

Tyagi, P. K. "Inequities in Organizations, Salesperson Motivations and Job Satisfaction." *International Journal of Research in Marketing,* 7 (Dec. 1990): 135–148.

Tyler, T. R. and A. Caine. "The Influence of Outcomes and Procedures on Satisfaction with Formal Leaders." *Journal of Personality and Social Psychology,* Vol. 41, (1981): 642–655.

Tyler, T. R., R. K. Rasinski, and N. Spodik. "The Influence of Voice on Satisfaction with Leaders: Exploring the Meaning of Process Control." *Journal of Personality and Social Psychology*, Vol. 48 (1985): 72–81.

Van de Von, A. H., and A. L. Delbecq. "A task contingent model of work-unit structure." *Administrative Science Quarterly*, 19 (1974): 183–197.

Van Velsor, E., S. Taylor, and J. Leslie. "Self-Rater, Self-Awareness and Leader Effectiveness." Paper presented at the 100th Annual Convention of the American Psychological Association. Washington, D.C., 1992.

Varendonck, J. *The Psychology of Day Dreams*. London, England: George Allen and Unwin, Ltd., 1921.

Vilere, M. F., and S. I. Hartman. "The Key to Motivation Is in the Process: An Examination of the Practical Implications of Expectancy Theory." *Leadership and Organizational Development Journal*, 11, No. 4 (1990): 1–111.

Vroom, V. H. *Work and Motivation*. New York: John Wiley and Sons, Inc., 1964.

Vroom, V. H., and A. G. Jago. *The New Leadership: Managing Participation in Organizations*. Englewood Cliffs, NJ: Prentice Hall, 1988.

Vroom, V. H., and P. Yetton. *Leadership and Decision Making*. Pittsburgh, PA: University of Pittsburgh Press, 1973.

Waclawski, J., "Using Organizational Survey Results to Improve Organizational Performance." *Managing Service Quality*, 6, No. 4 (1996): 53–64.

Wageman, R., "Critical Success Factors for Creating Superb Self-Managing Teams." *Organizational Dynamics*, Vol. 26, Summer (1997): 49–61.

Walker, A. G., and J. W. Smither. "A Five-Year Study of Upward Feedback: What Managers Do With Their Results Matters." *Personnel Psychology: A Journal of Applied Research*, 52, No. 2 (Summer 1999): 393–424.

Walton, M. *Deming Management at Work*. New York: G.P. Putnam's Sons, 1990.

Warren, R. *The Purpose-Driven Life: What On Earth Are We Here For?* Grand Rapids, MI: Zondervan, 2002.

Watson, J. B. *Behaviorism*. New York: W.W. Norton, 1924.

Weber, J. "Managerial Value Orientations: A Typology and Assessment." *International Journal of Value Based Management*, 3, No. 2 (1990): 37–54.

Weinberg, R. S., L. Bruya, and A. Jackson. "Expectations and Performance: An Empirical Test of Bandura's Self-Efficacy Theory." *Journal of Sport Psychology*, 7 (1979): 320–321.

Wheatley, M. J. *Leadership and the New Science: Learning About Organization from an Orderly Universe*. San Francisco, CA: Berrett-Koehler Publishers, 1992.

White, R. M. "Motivation Reconsidered: The Concept of Competence." *Psychological Review*, 66 (1959): 297–333.

Wilbur, J. "Does Mentoring Breed Success?" *Training and Development Journal*, November (1987): 38–41.

Williams, M. D. "A Comprehensive Review of Learner Control: The Role of Learner Characteristics." Simonson, M.R., ed. *Proceedings of the Annual Conference of the Association for Educational Communications and Technology* (1993): 1083–1114.

Wind, Y., and C. Crook. *The Power of Impossible Thinking: Transform the Business of Your Life and the Life of Your Business*. Upper Saddle River, NJ: Wharton School Publishing, 2005.

Winston, S. *Getting Organized*. New York: Warner Books Edition, 1978.

Winter, D., and G. P. Latham. "The Effect of Learning Versus Outcome Goals on Simple Versus a Complex Task." *Group and Organizational Management*, 21, No. 2 (June 1996): 236–250.

Witt, L.A. "Enhancing Organizational Congruence: A Solution to Organizational Politics." *Journal of Applied Psychology*, Vol. 83, (August 1998): 666–674.

Wood, R. E., A. J. Mento, and E. A. Locke. "Task Complexity as a Moderator of Goal Effects: A Meta-Analysis." *Journal of Applied Psychology*, 72, No. 3 (1987): 416–425.

Zaleznik, A. "Managers and Leaders: Are They Different?" *Harvard Business Review*, May–June (1977): 5–16.

Zey, M. G. *The Mentor Connection*. New York: McGraw Hill, 1984.

———. "Mentor Programs: Making the Right Moves." *Personnel Journal* 64, No. 2 (1985): 53–57.

Zigarmi, D., C. Edeburn, and K. Blanchard. *Getting to Know the LBAII: Research Validity and Reliability of the Self and Other Forms, Fourth Edition*. Escondido, CA: Blanchard Training and Development, 1993.

Zigarmi, D., D. Lyles, and S. Fowler. "Context: The Rosetta Stone of Leadership." *Leader to Leader*, Vol. 38 (Fall 2005): 37–44.

Zigarmi, D., K. Blanchard, M. O'Connor, and C. Edeburn. *The Leader Within: Learning Enough About Yourself to Lead Others*. Upper Saddle River, NJ: Prentice Hall, 2004.

Zukov, G. *The Dancing WuLi Masters: An Overview of the New Physics*. New York: William Morrow Company, Inc., 1979.

INDEX

CONTEXTUAL LEADERSHIP™

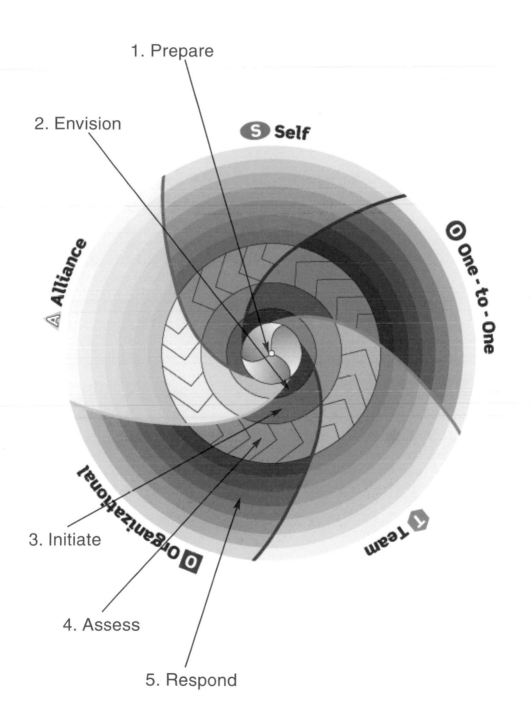

1. Prepare

2. Envision

3. Initiate

4. Assess

5. Respond

S Self

O One - to - One

T Team

O Organizational

A Alliance